DESIGN FOR A BRAIN

DESIGN FOR A BRAIN

The origin of adaptive behaviour

W. ROSS ASHBY

M.A., M.D., D.P.M.

Director, Burden Neurological Institute;
Late Director of Research, Barnwood House, Gloucester

□

SECOND EDITION
REVISED

NEW YORK
JOHN WILEY & SONS, Inc.
LONDON: CHAPMAN & HALL, LIMITED

1960

First Published   *1952*
Reprinted (with corrections)   *1954*
Second Edition (revised)   *1960*

CATALOGUE NO 493/4

Printed in Great Britain by Butler & Tanner Ltd , Frome and London

Preface

THE book is not a treatise on all cerebral mechanisms but a proposed solution of a specific problem: the origin of the nervous system's unique ability to produce adaptive behaviour. The work has as basis the fact that the nervous system behaves adaptively and the hypothesis that it is essentially mechanistic; it proceeds on the assumption that these two *data* are not irreconcilable. It attempts to deduce from the observed facts what sort of a mechanism it must be that behaves so differently from any machine made so far. Other proposed solutions have usually left open the question whether some different theory might not fit the facts equally well: I have attempted to deduce what is necessary, what properties the nervous system *must* have if it is to behave at once mechanistically and adaptively.

For the deduction to be rigorous, an adequately developed logic of mechanism is essential. Until recently, discussions of mechanism were carried on almost entirely in terms of some particular embodiment—the mechanical, the electronic, the neuronic, and so on. Those days are past. There now exists a well developed logic of pure mechanism, rigorous as geometry, and likely to play the same fundamental part, in our understanding of the complex systems of biology, that geometry does in astronomy. Only by the development of this basic logic has the work in this book been made possible.

The conclusions reached are summarised at the end of Chapter 18, but they are likely to be unintelligible or misleading if taken by themselves; for they are intended only to make prominent the key points along a road that the reader has already traversed. They may, however, be useful as he proceeds, by helping him to distinguish the major features from the minor.

Having experienced the confusion that tends to arise whenever we try to relate cerebral mechanisms to observed behaviour, I made it my aim to accept nothing that could not be stated in mathematical form, for only in this language can one be sure, during one's progress, that one is not unconsciously changing the

v

meaning of terms, or adding assumptions, or otherwise drifting towards confusion. The aim proved achievable. The concepts of organisation, behaviour, change of behaviour, part, whole, dynamic system, co-ordination, etc.—notoriously elusive but essential—were successfully given·rigorous definition and welded into a coherent whole. But the rigour and coherence depended on the mathematical form, which is not read with ease by everybody. As the basic thesis, however, rests on essentially common-sense reasoning, I have been able to divide the account into two parts. The main account (Chapters 1–18) is non-mathematical and is complete in itself. The Appendix (Chapters 19–22) contains the mathematical matter.

Since the reader will probably need cross-reference frequently, the chapters have been divided into sections These are indicated thus S 4/5, which means Chapter 4's fifth section. Each figure and table is numbered within its own section. Figure 4/5/2 is the second figure in S. 4/5. Section-numbers are given at the top of every page, so finding a section or a figure should be as simple and direct as finding a page.

It is a pleasure to be able to express my indebtedness to the Governors of Barnwood House and to Dr. G W. T. H. Fleming for their generous support during the prosecution of the work, and to Professor F. L. Golla and Dr. W. Grey Walter for much helpful criticism.

Preface to the Second Edition

AT the time when this book was first written, information theory was just beginning to be known. Since then its contribution to our understanding of the logic of mechanism has been so great that a separate treatment of these aspects has been given in my *Introduction to Cybernetics* * (which will be referred to in this book as *I. to C.*). Its outlook and methods are fundamental to the present work.

The overlap is small. *I. to C.* is concerned with first principles, as they concern the topics of mechanism, communication, and regulation; but it is concerned with the principles and does not appreciably develop their applications. It considers mechanisms as if they go in small discrete steps, a supposition that makes their logical properties very easy to understand. *Design for a Brain*, while based on the same principles, mentions them only so far as is necessary for their application to the particular problem of the origin of adaptive behaviour. It considers mechanisms that change continuously (i.e. as the steps shrink to zero), for this supposition makes their practical properties more evident. It has been written to be complete in itself, but the reader may find *I. to C.* helpful in regard to the foundations.

In the eight years that have elapsed between the preparations of the two editions, our understanding of brain-like mechanisms has improved immeasurably. For this reason the book has been re-arranged, and the latter two-thirds completely re-written. The new version, I am satisfied, presents the material in an altogether clearer, simpler, and more cogent form than the earlier

The change of lay-out has unfortunately made a retention of the previous section-numberings impossible, so there is no correspondence between the numberings in the two editions. I would have avoided this source of confusion if I could, but felt that the claims of clarity and simplicity must be given precedence over all else.

* Chapman & Hall, London : John Wiley & Sons, New York ; 3rd imp. 1958 Also translations in Czech, French, Polish, Russian and Spanish.

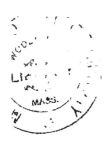

Contents

CONTENTS

CHAPTER 1

The Problem

1/1. How does the brain produce adaptive behaviour ? In attempting to answer the question, scientists have discovered two sets of facts and have had some difficulty in reconciling them. On the one hand the physiologists have shown in a variety of ways how closely the brain resembles a machine: in its dependence on chemical reactions, in its dependence on the integrity of anatomical paths, and in the precision and determinateness with which its component parts act on one another. On the other hand, the psychologists and biologists have confirmed with full objectivity the layman's conviction that the living organism behaves typically in a purposeful and adaptive way. These two characteristics of the brain's behaviour have proved difficult to reconcile, and some workers have gone so far as to declare them incompatible.

Such a point of view will not be taken here. I hope to show that a system can be both mechanistic in nature and yet produce behaviour that is adaptive. I hope to show that the essential difference between the brain and any machine yet made is that the brain makes extensive use of a method hitherto little used in machines. I hope to show that by the use of this method a machine's behaviour may be made as adaptive as we please, and that the method may be capable of explaining even the adaptiveness of Man.

But first we must examine more closely the nature of the problem, and this will be commenced in this chapter. The succeeding chapters will develop more accurate concepts, and when we can state the problem with precision we shall not be far from its solution.

Behaviour, reflex and learned

1/2. The activities of the nervous system may be divided more or less distinctly into two types. The dichotomy is probably an

1

over-simplification, but it will be sufficient until we have developed a more elaborate technique.

The first type is reflex behaviour. It is inborn, it is genetically determined in detail, it is a product, in the vertebrates, chiefly of centres in the spinal cord and in the base of the brain, and it is not appreciably modified by individual experience. The second type is learned behaviour. It is not inborn, it is not genetically determined in detail (more fully discussed in S. 1/9), it is a product chiefly of the cerebral cortex, and it is modified markedly by the organism's individual experiences.

1/3. With the first or reflex type of behaviour we shall not be concerned. We assume that each reflex is produced by some neural mechanism whose physico-chemical nature results inevitably in the characteristic form of behaviour, that this mechanism is developed under the control of the gene-pattern and is inborn, and that the pattern of behaviour produced by the mechanism is usually adapted to the animal's environment because natural selection has long since eliminated all non-adapted variations. For example, the complex activity of 'coughing' is assumed to be due to a special mechanism in the nervous system, inborn and developed by the action of the gene-pattern, and adapted and perfected by the fact that an animal who is less able to clear its trachea of obstruction has a smaller chance of survival.

Although the mechanisms underlying these reflex activities are often difficult to study physiologically, and although few are known in all their details, yet it is widely held among physiologists that no difficulty of principle is involved   Such behaviour and such mechanisms will not therefore be considered further.

1/4. It is with the second type of behaviour that we are concerned: the behaviour that is not inborn but learned. Examples of such reactions exist in abundance, and any small selection must seem paltry   Yet I must say what I mean, if only to give the critic a definite target for attack. Several examples will therefore be given.

A dog selected at random for an experiment with a conditioned response can be made at will to react to the sound of a bell either with or without salivation. Further, once trained to react in one way it may, with little difficulty, be trained to react later in

2

the opposite way. The salivary response to the sound of a bell cannot, therefore, be due to a mechanism of fixed properties.

A rat selected at random for an experiment in maze-running can be taught to run either to right or left by the use of an appropriately shaped maze. Further, once trained to turn to one side it can be trained later to turn to the other.

Perhaps the most striking evidence that animals, after training, can produce behaviour which cannot possibly have been inborn is provided by the circus. A seal balances a ball on its nose for minutes at a time; one bear rides a bicycle, and another walks on roller skates It would be ridiculous to suppose that these reactions are due to mechanisms both inborn and specially perfected for these tricks.

Man himself provides, of course, the most abundant variety of learned reactions· but only one example will be given here. If one is looking down a compound microscope and finds that the object is not central but to the right, one brings the object to the centre by pushing the slide still farther to the right. The relation between muscular action and consequent visual change is the reverse of the usual. The student's initial bewilderment and clumsiness demonstrate that there is no neural mechanism inborn and ready for the reversed relation. But after a few days' practice co-ordination develops.

These examples, and all the facts of which they are representative, show that the nervous system is able to develop ways of behaving which are not inborn and are not specified in detail by the gene-pattern.

1/5. Learned behaviour has many characteristics, but we shall be concerned chiefly with one: when animals and children learn, not only does their behaviour change, but it changes usually for the better. The full meaning of ' better ' will be discussed in Chapter 5, but in the simpler cases the improvement is obvious enough. ' The burned child dreads the fire ': after the experience the child's behaviour towards the fire is not only changed, but is changed to a behaviour which gives a *lessened* chance of its being burned again. We would at once recognise as abnormal any child who used its newly acquired knowledge so as to get to the flames more quickly.

To demonstrate that learning usually changes behaviour from a less to a more beneficial, i.e. survival-promoting, form would need a discussion far exceeding the space available. But in this introduction no exhaustive survey is needed. I require only sufficient illustration to make the meaning clear. For this purpose the previous examples will be examined seriatim.

When a conditioned reflex is established by the giving of food or acid, the amount of salivation changes from less to more. And the change benefits the animal either by providing normal lubrication for chewing or by providing water to dilute and flush away the irritant. When a rat in a maze has changed its behaviour so that it goes directly to the food at the other end, the new behaviour is better than the old because it leads more quickly to the animal's hunger being satisfied. The circus animals' behaviour changes from some random form to one determined by the trainer, who applied punishments and rewards. The animals' later behaviour is such as has decreased the punishments or increased the rewards. In Man, the proposition that behaviour usually changes for the better with learning would need extensive discussion. But in the example of the finger movements and the compound microscope, the later movements, which bring the desired object directly to the centre of the field, are clearly better than the earlier movements, which were ineffective for the microscopist's purpose.

Our problem may now be stated in preliminary form: what cerebral changes occur during the learning process, and why does the behaviour usually change for the better ? What type of mechanistic process could show the same self-advancement ?

1/6.   The nervous system is well provided with means for action. Glucose, oxygen, and other metabolites are brought to it by the blood so that free energy is available abundantly. The nerve cells composing the system are not only themselves exquisitely sensitive, but are provided, at the sense organs, with devices of even higher sensitivity. Each nerve cell, by its ramifications, enables a single impulse to become many impulses, each of which is as active as the single impulse from which it originated. The ramifications are followed by repeated stages of further ramification, so that however small a change at any point we can put hardly any bound to the size of the change or response that may follow as the effect spreads   And by their control of the muscles, the nerve cells can rouse to activity engines of high mechanical power. The nervous system, then, possesses almost unlimited potentialities for action   But do these potentialities solve our problem ? It seems not. We are concerned primarily with the question why, during learning, behaviour changes for the better: and this question is not answered by the fact that a given behaviour can change to one of lesser or greater activity. The examples given in S. 1/5, when examined for the energy changes before and after learning, show that the question of the quantity of activity is usually irrelevant.

But the evidence against regarding mere activity as sufficient for a solution is even stronger: often an increase in the amount of activity is not so much irrelevant as positively harmful. If a dynamic system is allowed to proceed to vigorous action without special precautions, the activity will usually lead to the destruction of the system itself. A motor car with its tank full of petrol may be set into motion, but if it is released with no driver its activity, far from being beneficial, will probably cause the motor car to destroy itself more quickly than if it had remained inactive. The theme is discussed more thoroughly in S. 20/10; here it may be noted that activity, if inco-ordinated, tends merely to the system's destruction. How then is the brain to achieve success if its potentialities for action are partly potentialities for self-destruction?

The relation of part to part

1/7. Our basic fact is that after the learning process the behaviour is usually better adapted than before. We ask, therefore, what property must be possessed by the neurons so that the manifestation by the neuron of this property shall result in the whole organism's behaviour being improved.

A first suggestion is that if the nerve-cells are all healthy and normal as little biological units, then the whole will appear healthy and normal This suggestion, however, must be rejected as inadequate. For the improvement in the organism's behaviour is often an improvement in relation to entities which have no counterpart in the life of a neuron. Thus when a dog, given food in an experiment on conditioned responses, learns to salivate, the behaviour improves because the saliva provides a lubricant for chewing. But in the neuron's existence, since all its food arrives in solution, neither ' chewing ' nor ' lubricant ' can have any direct relevance or meaning. Again, a maze-rat that has learned successfully has learned to produce a particular pattern of movement; yet the learning has involved neurons which are firmly supported in a close mesh of glial fibres and never move in their lives

Finally, consider an engine-driver who has just seen a signal and whose hand is on the throttle. If the light is red, the excitation from the retina must be transmitted through the nervous system so that the cells in the motor cortex send impulses down to those muscles whose activity makes the throttle *close*. If the light is green, the excitation from the retina must be transmitted through the nervous system so that the cells in the motor cortex make the throttle open. And the transmission is to be handled, and the safety of the train guaranteed, by neurons which can form no conception of 'red', 'green', 'train', 'signal', or 'accident'! Yet the system works.

Clearly, 'normality' at the neuronic level is inadequate to ensure normality in the behaviour of the whole organism, for the two forms of normality stand in no definite relationship.

1/8. In the case of the engine-driver, it may be that there is a simple mechanism such that a red light activates a chain of nerve-cells leading to the muscles which close the throttle while a green light activates another chain of nerve-cells leading to the muscles which make it open. In this way the effect of the colour of the signal would be transmitted through the nervous system in the appropriate way.

The simplicity of the arrangement is due to the fact that we are supposing that the two reactions are using two independent mechanisms. This separation may well occur in the simpler reactions, but it is insufficient to explain the events of the more complex reactions. In most cases the 'correct' and the 'incorrect' neural activities are alike composed of excitations, of inhibitions, and of other processes each of which is physiological in itself, but whose correctness is determined *not by the process itself but by the relations which it bears to other processes*.

This dependence of the 'correctness' of what is happening at one point in the nervous system on what is happening at other points would be shown if the engine-driver were to move over to the other side of the cab. For if previously a flexion of the elbow

6

had closed the throttle, the same action will now open it; and what was the correct pairing of red and green to push and pull must now be reversed. So the local action in the nervous system can no longer be regarded as 'correct' or 'incorrect' in any absolute sense, and the first simple solution breaks down.

Another example is given by the activity of chewing in so far as it involves the tongue and teeth in movements which must be related so that the teeth do not bite the tongue. No movement of the tongue can by itself be regarded as wholly wrong, for a movement which may be wrong when the teeth are just meeting may be right when they are parting and food is to be driven on to their line. Consequently the activities in the neurons which control the movement of the tongue cannot be described as either 'correct' or 'incorrect': only when these activities are related to those of the neurons which control the jaw movements can a correctness be determined; and this property now belongs, not to either separately, but only to the activity of the two in combination.

These considerations reveal the main peculiarity of the problem. When the nervous system learns, its behaviour changes for the better. When we consider its various parts, however, we find that the value of one part's behaviour cannot be judged until the behaviour of the other parts is known; and the values of *their* behaviours cannot be known until the first part's behaviour is known. All the valuations are thus *conditional*, each depending on the others. Thus there is no criterion for 'better' that can be given absolutely, i.e. unconditionally. But a neuron must do something. How then do the activities of the neurons become co-ordinated so that the behaviour of the whole becomes better, even though no absolute criterion exists to guide the individual neuron ?

Exactly the same problem faces the designer of an artificial brain, who wants his mechanical brain to become adaptive in its behaviour. How can he specify the 'correct' properties for each part if the correctness depends not on the behaviour of each part but on its relations to the other parts ? His problem is to get the parts properly co-ordinated. The brain does this automatically. What sort of a machine can be *self*-co-ordinating ?

This is our problem. It will be stated with more precision in S. 1/17. But before this statement is reached, some minor topics must be discussed.

The genetic control of cerebral function

1/9. In rejecting the genetic control of the details of cerebral function (in adaptation, S. 1/4) we must be careful not to reject too much. The gene-pattern certainly plays *some* part in the development of adaptive behaviour, for the various species, differing essentially only in their gene-patterns, show characteristic differences in their powers of developing it; the insects, for instance, typically show little power while Man shows a great deal.

One difficulty in accounting for a new-born baby's capacity for developing adaptations is that the gene-pattern that makes the baby what it is has about 50,000 genes available for control of the form, while the baby's brain has about 10,000,000,000 neurons to be controlled (and the number of terminals may be 10 to 100 times as great). Clearly the set of genes cannot determine the details of the set of neurons. Evidently the gene-pattern determines a relatively small number of factors, and then these factors work actively to develop co-ordination in a much larger number of neurons.

This formulation of how the gene-pattern comes into the picture will perhaps suffice for the moment; it will be resumed in S 18/6. (*I. to C.*, S. 14/6, also discusses the topic.)

Restrictions on the concepts to be used

1/10. Throughout the book I shall adhere to certain basic assumptions and to certain principles of method.

I shall hold the biologist's point of view. To him, the most fundamental facts are that the earth is over 2,000,000,000 years old and that natural selection has been winnowing the living organisms incessantly. As a result they are today highly specialised in the arts of survival, and among these arts has been the development of a brain. Throughout this book the brain will be treated simply as an organ that has been developed in evolution as *a specialised means to survival*.

1/11. Conformably with this point of view, the nervous system, and living matter in general, will be assumed to be essentially similar to all other matter. So no use of any 'vital' property or tendency will be made, and no *Deus ex machina* will be invoked.

The sole reason admitted for the behaviour of any part will be of the form that its own state and the condition of its immediate surroundings led, in accordance with the usual laws of matter, to the observed behaviour.

1/12. The ' operational ' method will be followed; so no psychological concept will be used unless it can be shown in objective form in non-living systems; and when used it will be considered to refer solely to its objective form. Related is the restriction that every concept used must be capable of objective demonstration. In the study of Man this restriction raises formidable difficulties extending from the practical to the metaphysical. But as most of the discussion will be concerned with the observed behaviour of animals and machines, the peculiar difficulties will seldom arise.

1/13. No teleological explanation for behaviour will be used. It will be assumed throughout that a machine or an animal behaved in a certain way at a certain moment because its physical and chemical nature at that moment allowed it no other action. Never will we use the explanation that the action is performed because it will later be advantageous to the animal. Any such explanation would, of course, involve a circular argument; for our purpose is to explain the origin of behaviour which appears to be teleologically directed.

1/14. It will be further assumed (except where the contrary is stated explicitly) that the fuctioning units of the nervous system, and of the environment, behave in a determinate way. By this I mean that each part, if in a particular state internally and affected by particular conditions externally, will behave in one way only. (This is the determinacy shown, for instance, by the relays and other parts of a telephone exchange.) It should be noticed that we are not assuming that the *ultimate* units are determinate, for these are atoms, which are known to behave in an essentially indeterminate way; what we shall assume is that the *significant* unit is determinate. The significant unit (e.g. the relay, the current of several milliamperes, the neuron) is usually of a size much larger than the atomic so that only the average property of many atoms is significant. These averages are often determinate

9

in their behaviour, and it is to these averages that our assumption applies

The question whether the nervous system is composed of parts that are determinate or stochastic has not yet been answered. In this book we shall suppose that they are determinate. That the brain is capable of behaving in a strikingly determinate way has been demonstrated chiefly by feats of memory. Some of the demonstrations depend on hypnosis, and are not quite sufficiently clear in interpretation for quotation here. Skinner, however, has produced some striking evidence by animal experiment that the nervous system, if the surrounding conditions can be restored accurately, may behave in a strictly reproducible way. By differential reinforcement with food, Skinner trained twenty young pigeons to peck at a translucent key when it was illuminated with a complex visual pattern. They were then transferred to the usual living quarters where they were used for no further experiments but served simply as breeders. Small groups were tested from time to time for retention of the habit.

> ' The bird was fed in the dimly-lighted experimental apparatus in the absence of the key for several days, during which emotional responses to the apparatus disappeared. On the day of the test the bird was placed in the darkened box. The translucent key was present but not lighted. No responses were made. When the pattern was projected upon the key, all four birds responded quickly and extensively. . . . This bird struck the key within two seconds after presentation of a visual pattern that it had not seen for four years, and at the precise spot upon which differential reinforcement had previously been based.'

The assumption that the parts are determinate is thus not un-reasonable. But we need not pre-judge the issue; the book is an attempt to follow the assumption of determinacy wherever it leads. When it leads to obvious error will be time to question its validity.

1/15. To be consistent with the assumptions already made, we must suppose (and the author accepts) that a real solution of our problem will enable an artificial system to be made that will be able, like the living brain, to develop adaptation in its behaviour. Thus the work, if successful, will contain (at least by implication) a specification for building an artificial brain that will be similarly self-co-ordinating.

The knowledge that the proposed solution must be put to this test will impose some discipline on the concepts used. In particular, this requirement will help to prevent the solution from being a mere verbalistic ' explanation ', for in the background will be the demand that we build a machine to *do* these things.

Consciousness

1/16. The previous sections have demanded that we shall make no use of the subjective elements of experience; and I can anticipate by saying that in fact the book makes no such use. At times its rigid adherence to the objective point of view may jar on the reader and may expose me to the accusation that I am ignoring an essential factor. A few words in explanation may save misunderstanding.

Throughout the book, consciousness and its related subjective elements are not used for the simple reason that at no point have I found their introduction necessary. This is not surprising, for the book deals with only one of the properties of the brain, and with a property—learning—that has long been recognised to have no necessary dependence on consciousness. Here is an example to illustrate their independence. If a cyclist wishes to turn to the left, his first action must be to turn the front wheel to the *right* (otherwise he will fall outwards by centrifugal force). Every practised cyclist makes this movement every time he turns, yet many cyclists, even after they have made the movement hundreds of times, are quite unconscious of making it. The direct intervention of consciousness is evidently not necessary for adaptive learning.

Such an observation, showing that consciousness is sometimes not necessary, gives us no right to deduce that consciousness does not exist. The truth is quite otherwise, for the fact of the existence of consciousness is prior to all other facts. If I perceive —am aware of—a chair, I may later be persuaded, by other evidence, that the appearance was produced only by a trick of lighting; I may be persuaded that it occurred in a dream, or even that it was an hallucination; but there is no evidence in existence that could persuade me that my awareness itself was mistaken—that I had not really been aware at all. This knowledge of personal awareness, therefore, is prior to all other forms of knowledge.

11

If consciousness is the most fundamental fact of all, why is it not used in this book ? The answer, in my opinion, is that Science deals, and can deal, only with what one man can *demonstrate* to another. Vivid though consciousness may be to its possessor, there is as yet no method known by which he can demonstrate his experience to another. And until such a method, or its equivalent, is found, the facts of consciousness cannot be used in scientific method.

The problem

1/17. It is now time to state the problem. Later, when more exact concepts have been developed, it will be possible to state the problem more precisely (S. 5/14).

It will be convenient, throughout the discussion, to have some well-known, practical problem to act as type-problem, so that general statements can always be referred to it. I select the following. When a kitten first approaches a fire its reactions are unpredictable and usually inappropriate. It may walk almost into the fire, or it may spit at it, or may dab at it with a paw, or try to sniff at it, or crouch and ' stalk ' it. Later, however, when adult, its reactions are different. It approaches the fire and seats itself at a place where the heat is moderate. If the fire burns low, it moves nearer. If a hot coal falls out, it jumps away. Its behaviour towards the fire is now ' adaptive '. I might have taken as type-problem some experiment published by a psychological laboratory, but the present example has several advantages   It is well known; it is representative of a wide class of important phenomena; and it is not likely to be called in question by the discovery of some small technical flaw

We take as basic the assumptions that the organism is mechanistic in nature, that it is composed of parts, that the behaviour of the whole is the outcome of the compounded actions of the parts, that organisms change their behaviour by learning, and that they change it so that the later behaviour is better adapted to their environment than the earlier. Our problem is, first, **to identify the nature of the change which shows as learning,** and secondly, **to find why such changes should tend to cause better adaptation for the whole organism.**

CHAPTER 2

Dynamic Systems

2/1. In the previous chapter we have repeatedly used the concepts of a system, of parts in a whole, of the system's behaviour, and of its changes of behaviour.   These concepts are fundamental and must be properly defined   Accurate definition at this stage is of the highest importance, for any vagueness here will infect all the subsequent discussion; and as we shall have to enter the realm where the physical and the psychological meet, a realm where the experience of centuries has found innumerable possibilities of confusion, we shall have to proceed with unusual caution.

That some caution is necessary can be readily shown.   We have, for instance, repeatedly used the concept of a ' change of behaviour ', as when the kitten stopped dabbing at the red-hot coal and avoided it.   Yet behaviour is itself a sequence of changes (e.g. as the paw moves from point to point).   Can we distinguish clearly those changes that constitute behaviour from those changes that are from behaviour to behaviour ?   It is questions such as these which emphasize the necessity for clarity and a secure foundation.   (The subject has been considered more extensively in *I. to C.*, Part I; the shorter version given here should be sufficient for our purpose in this book.)

We start by assuming that we have before us some dynamic system, i.e. something that may change with time.   We wish to study it.   It will be referred to as the ' machine ', but the word must be understood in the widest possible sense, for no restriction is implied at the moment other than that it should be objective

2/2.   As we shall be more concerned in this chapter with principles than with practice, we shall be concerned chiefly with constructing a method for the study of this unknown machine. When the method is constructed, it must satisfy the demands implied by the axioms of S. 1/10–15.

(1) The method must be precisely defined, and in operational form;

13

(2) it must be applicable equally readily (at least in principle) to all material 'machines', whether animate or inanimate,

(3) its procedure for obtaining information from the ' machine ' must be wholly objective (i.e. accessible or demonstrable to all observers);

(4) it must obtain its information solely from the ' machine ' itself, no other source being permitted.

The actual form developed may appear to the practical worker to be clumsy and inferior to methods already in use; it probably is. But it is not intended to compete with the many specialised methods already in use. Such methods are usually adapted to a particular class of dynamic systems: one method is specially suited to electronic circuits, another to rats in mazes, another to solutions of reacting chemicals, another to automatic pilots, another to heart-lung preparations. The method proposed here must have the peculiarity that it is applicable to all, it must, so to speak, specialise in generality.

Variable and system

2/3. In *I to C.*, Chapter 2, is shown how the basic theory can be founded on the concept of unanalysed states, as a mother might distinguish, and react adequately to, three expressions on her baby's face, without analysing them into so much opening of the mouth, so much wrinkling of the nose, etc. In this book, however, we shall be chiefly concerned with the relations between parts, so we will assume that the observer proceeds to record the behaviour of the machine's individual parts. To do this he identifies any number of suitable variables. A **variable** is *a measurable quantity which at every instant has a definite numerical value.* A ' grandfather ' clock, for instance, might provide the following variables: —the angular deviation of the pendulum from the vertical; the angular velocity with which the pendulum is moving; the angular position of a particular cog-wheel; the height of a driving weight; the reading of the minute-hand on the scale; and the length of the pendulum. If there is any doubt whether a particular quantity may be admitted as a ' variable ' I shall use the criterion whether it can be represented by a pointer on a dial

All the quantities used in physics, chemistry, biology, physiology, and objective psychology, are variables in the defined sense.

Thus, the position of a limb can be specified numerically by co-ordinates of position, and movement of the limb can move a pointer on a dial. Temperature at a point can be specified numerically and can be recorded on a dial. Pressure, angle, electric potential, volume, velocity, torque, power, mass, viscosity, humidity, surface tension, osmotic pressure, specific gravity, and time itself, to mention only a few, can all be specified numerically and recorded on dials. Eddington's statement on the subject is explicit · ' The whole subject matter of exact science consists of pointer readings and similar indications.' ' Whatever quantity we say we are " observing ", the actual procedure nearly always ends in reading the position of some kind of indicator on a graduated scale or its equivalent.'

Whether the restriction to dial-readings is justifiable with living subjects will be discussed in the next chapter.

One minor point should be noticed as it will be needed later. The absence of an entity can always be converted to a reading on a scale simply by considering the entity to be present but in zero degree. Thus, ' still air ' can be treated as a wind blowing at 0 m.p h ; ' darkness ' can be treated as an illumination of 0 foot-candles ; and the giving of a drug can be represented by indicating that its concentration in the tissues has risen from its usual value of 0 per cent.

2/4. It will be appreciated that *every real ' machine ' embodies no less than an infinite number of variables,* all but a few of which must of necessity be ignored. Thus if we were studying the swing of a pendulum in relation to its length we would be interested in its angular deviation at various times, but we would often ignore the chemical composition of the bob, the reflecting power of its surface, the electric conductivity of the suspending string, the specific gravity of the bob, its shape, the age of the alloy, its degree of bacterial contamination, and so on. The list of what might be ignored could be extended indefinitely. Faced with this infinite number of variables, the experimenter must, and of course does, select a definite number for examination—in other words, he defines an abstracted system. Thus, an experimenter once drew up Table 2/4/1. He thereby selected his variables, of time and three others, ready for testing. This experiment being finished, he later drew up other tables which included new

Time (mins.)	Distance of secondary coil (cm.)	Part of skin stimulated	Secretion of saliva during 30 secs (drops)
. . .	. .		

TABLE 2/4/1

variables or omitted old. These new combinations were new systems.

2/5. Because any real ' machine ' has an infinity of variables, from which different observers (with different aims) may reasonably make an infinity of different selections, there must first be given an observer (or experimenter); a **system** is then defined as *any set of variables* that he selects from those available on the real ' machine '. It is thus a list, nominated by the observer, and is quite different in nature from the real ' machine '. Throughout the book, ' the system ' will always refer to this abstraction, not to the real material ' machine '.

Among the variables recorded will almost always be ' time ', so one might think that this variable should be included in the list that specifies the system. Nevertheless, time comes into the theory in a way fundamentally different from that of all the others. (The difference is shown most clearly in the canonical equations of S. 19/9.) Experience has shown that a more convenient classification is to let the set of variables be divided into ' system ' and ' time '. Time is thus not to be included in the variables of the system. In Table 2/4/1 for instance, ' the system ' is *defined* to be the three variables on the right.

2/6. The **state** of a system at a given instant is the set of numerical values which its variables have at that instant.

Thus, the six-variable system of S. 2/3 might at some instant have the state: $-4°$, 0·3 radians/sec., 128°, 52 cm., 42·8 minutes, 88·4 cm.

Two states are equal if and only if the two numerical values in each pair are equal, all pairs showing equality.

The operational method

2/7. The variables being decided on, the recording apparatus is now assumed to be connected and the experimenter ready to start observing. We must now make clear what is assumed about his powers of control over the system.

Throughout the book we shall consider only the case in which he has access to all states of the system. It is postulated that the experimenter can control any variable he pleases: that he can make any variable take any arbitrary value at any arbitrary time. The postulate specifies nothing about the methods: it demands only that certain end-results are to be available. In most cases the means to be used are obvious enough. Take the example of S. 2/3: an arbitrary angular deviation of the pendulum can be enforced at any time by direct manipulation; an arbitrary angular momentum can be enforced at any time by an appropriate impulse; the cog can be disconnected and shifted, the driving-weight wound up, the hand moved, and the pendulum-bob lowered.

By repeating the control from instant to instant, the experimenter can force a variable to take any prescribed series of values. The postulate, therefore, implies that any variable can be forced to follow a prescribed course.

Some systems cannot be forced, for instance the astronomical, the meteorological, and those biological systems that are accessible to observation but not to experiment. Yet no change is necessary in principle: the experimenter simply waits until the desired set of values occurs during the natural changes of the system, and he counts that instant as if it were the instant at which the system were started. Thus, though he cannot create a thunderstorm, he can observe how swallows react to one simply by waiting till one occurs 'spontaneously'.

It will also be assumed (except where explicitly mentioned) that he has similarly complete control over those variables that are not in the system yet which have an effect on it. In the experiment of Table 2/4/1 for instance, Pavlov had control not only of the variables mentioned but also of the many variables that might have affected the system's behaviour, such as the lights that might have flashed, the odours that might have been applied, and the noises that might have come from outside.

The assumption that the control is complete is made because, as will be seen later (and as has been shown in *I. to C.*), it makes possible a theory that is clear, simple, and coherent. The theories that arise when we consider the more realistic state of affairs in which not all states are accessible, or not all variables controllable, are tangled and complicated, and not suitable as a *basis*. These complicated variations can all be derived from the basic theory by the addition of complications. For the moment we shall postpone them.

2/8. The **primary operation** that wins new knowledge from the ' machine ' is as follows:—The experimenter uses his power of control to determine (select, enforce) a particular state in the system. He also determines (selects, enforces) the values of the surrounding conditions of the system. He then allows one unit of time to elapse and he observes to what state the system goes as it moves under the drive of its own dynamic nature. He observes, in other words, a **transition,** from a particular state, under particular conditions.

Usually the experimenter wants to know the transitions from many states under many conditions. Then he often saves time by allowing the transitions to occur in chains; having found that *A* is followed by *B*, he simply observes what comes next, and thus discovers the transition from *B*, and so on.

This description may make the definition sound arbitrary and unnatural; in fact, it describes only what every experimenter does when investigating an unknown dynamic system. Here are some examples.

In chemical dynamics the variables are often the concentrations of substances. Selected concentrations are brought together, and from a definite moment are allowed to interact while the temperature is held constant. The experimenter records the changes which the concentrations undergo with time.

In a mechanical experiment the variables might be the positions and momenta of certain bodies. At a definite instant the bodies, started with selected velocities from selected positions, are allowed to interact. The experimenter records the changes which the velocities and positions undergo with time.

In studies of the conduction of heat, the variables are the temperatures at various places in the heated body. A prescribed distribution of temperatures is enforced, and, while the tempera-

tures of some places are held constant, the variations of the
other temperatures are observed after the initial moment.

In physiology, the variables might be the rate of a rabbit's
heart-beat, the intensity of faradisation applied to the vagus
nerve, and the concentration of adrenaline in the circulating
blood. The intensity of faradisation will be continuously under
the experimenter's control. Not improbably it will be kept first
at zero and then increased. From a given instant the changes
in the variables will be recorded.

In experimental psychology, the variables might be ' the number
of mistakes made by a rat on a trial in a maze ' and ' the amount
of cerebral cortex which has been removed surgically '. The
second variable is permanently under the experimenter's control.
The experimenter starts the experiment and observes how the
first variable changes with time while the second variable is held
constant, or caused to change in some prescribed manner.

2/9. The detailed statement just given about what the experimenter can do and observe is necessary because we must (as later
chapters will show) be quite clear about *the sources of the experimenter's knowledge.*

Ordinarily, when an experimenter examines a machine he makes
full use of knowledge ' borrowed ' from past experience. If he
sees two cogs enmeshed he knows that their two rotations will not
be independent, even though he does not see them actually rotate.
This knowledge comes from previous experiences in which the
mutual relations of similar pairs have been tested and observed
directly. Such borrowed knowledge is, of course, extremely useful, and every skilled experimenter brings a great store of it to
every experiment. Nevertheless it must be excluded from any
fundamental method, if only because it is not wholly reliable: the
unexpected sometimes happens; and the only way to be certain
of the relation between parts in a new machine is to test the
relation directly.

2/10. While a single primary operation may seem to yield little
information, the power of the method lies in the fact that the
experimenter can repeat it with variations, and can relate the
different responses to the different variations. Thus, after one
primary operation the next may be varied in any of three ways:

the system may be changed by the inclusion of new variables
or by the omission of old; the initial state may be changed;
or the surrounding states may be changed. By applying these
variations systematically, in different patterns and groupings, the
different responses may be interrelated to yield relations.

By further orderly variations, these relations may be further
interrelated to yield secondary, or hyper-, relations; and so on.
In this way the 'machine' may be made to yield more and more
complex information about its inner organisation.

What is fundamental about this method is that the transition
is a purely objective and demonstrable fact. By basing all our
later concepts on the properties of transitions we can be sure that
the more complex concepts involve no component other than the
objective and demonstrable. All our concepts will eventually be
defined in terms of this method. For example, ' environment ' is
so defined in S. 3/8, ' adaptation ' in S. 5/3, and ' stimulus ' in
S. 6/5. If any have been omitted it is by oversight; for I hold
that this procedure is sufficient for their objective definition.

Phase-space and Field

2/11. Often the experimenter, while controlling the external
conditions, allows the system to pass from state to state without
interrupting its flow, so that if he started it at state A and it went
to B, he allows it then to proceed from B to C, from C to D,
and so on.

A line of behaviour is specified by *a succession of states and the
time-intervals between them.* The first state in a line of behaviour
will be called the **initial** state. Two lines of behaviour are equal
if all the corresponding pairs of states are equal, and if all the
corresponding pairs of time-intervals are equal.

2/12. There are several ways in which a line of behaviour may
be recorded.

The graphical method is exemplified by Figure 2/12/1. The
four variables form, by definition, the system that is being
examined. The four simultaneous values at any instant define
a state. And the succession of states at their particular intervals
constitute and specify the line of behaviour. The four traces
specify one line of behaviour.

Sometimes a line of behaviour can be specified in terms of elementary mathematical functions. Such a simplicity is convenient when it occurs, but is rarer in practice than an acquaintance with elementary mathematics would suggest. With biological material it is rare.

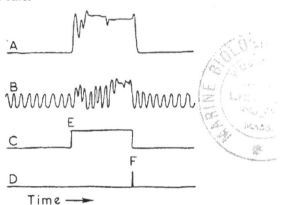

Time ⟶

FIGURE 2/12/1 : Events during an experiment on a conditioned reflex in a sheep. Attached to the left foreleg is an electrode by which a shock can be administered. Line *A* records the position of the left forefoot. Line *B* records the sheep's respiratory movements. Line *C* records by a rise (*E*) the application of the conditional stimulus : the sound of a buzzer. Line *D* records by a vertical stroke (*F*) the application of the electric shock. (After Liddell *et al.*)

Another form is the tabular, of which an example is Table 2/12/1. Each column defines one state; the whole table defines one line of behaviour (other tables may contain more than one line of behaviour). The state at 0 hours is the initial state.

		Time (hours)			
		0	1	3	6
	w	7·35	7·26	7·28	7·29
Variable	x	156·7	154·6	154·1	151·5
	y	110·3	116·7	118·3	118·5
	z	22·2	15·3	15·0	14·6

TABLE 2/12/1 : Blood changes after a dose of ammonium chloride. w = serum pH ; x = serum total base ; y = serum chloride ; z = serum bicarbonate ; (the last three in m. eq. per l.).

21

The tabular form has one outstanding advantage: it contains the facts and nothing more. Mathematical forms are apt to suggest too much: continuity that has not been demonstrated, fictitious values between the moments of observation, and an accuracy that may not be present. Unless specially mentioned, all lines of behaviour will be assumed to be recorded primarily in tabular form.

2/13. The behaviour of a system can also be represented in **phase-space.** By its use simple proofs may be given of many statements difficult to prove in the tabular form.

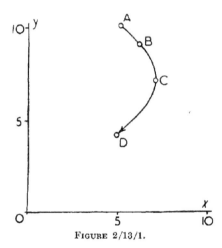

FIGURE 2/13/1.

If a system is composed of two variables, a particular state will be specified by two numbers. By ordinary graphic methods, the two variables can be represented by axes; the two numbers will then define a point in the plane. Thus the state in which variable x has the value 5 and variable y the value 10 will be represented by the point A in Figure 2/13/1. The **representative point** of a state is *the point whose co-ordinates are respectively equal to the values of the variables.* By S. 2/5 'time' is not to be one of the axes.

Suppose next that a system of two variables gave the line of behaviour shown in Table 2/13/1. The successive states will be graphed, by the method, at positions B, C, and D (Figure 2/13/1). So the system's behaviour corresponds to a movement of the representative point along the line in the phase-space.

By comparing the Table and the Figure, certain exact correspondences can be found. Every state of the system corresponds

Time	x	y
0	5	10
1	6	9
2	7	7
3	5	4

TABLE 2/13/1.

uniquely to a point in the plane, and every point in the plane (or in some portion of it) to some possible state of the system. Further, every line of behaviour of the system corresponds uniquely to a line in the plane. If the system has three variables, the graph must be in three dimensions, but each state still corresponds to a point, and each line of behaviour to a line in the phase-space. If the number of variables exceeds three, this method of graphing is no longer physically possible, but the correspondence is maintained exactly no matter how numerous the variables.

2/14. A system's **field*** is *the phase-space containing all the lines of behaviour found by releasing the system from all possible initial states in a* particular *set of surrounding conditions.*

In practice, of course, the experimenter would test only a representative sample of the initial states. Some of them will probably be tested repeatedly, for the experimenter will usually want to make sure that the system is giving reproducible lines of behaviour. Thus in one experiment, in which dogs had been severely bled and then placed on a standard diet, their body-weight x and the concentration y of haemoglobin in their blood were recorded at weekly intervals. This two-variable system, tested from four initial states by thirty-six primary operations, gave the field shown in Figure 2/14/1. Other examples occur frequently later.

It will be noticed that a field is defined, in accordance with

---

* Some name is necessary for such a representation as Figure 2/13/1, especially as the concept must be used incessantly throughout the book. I hope that a better word than 'field' will be found, but I have not found one yet.

S. 2/9, by reference exclusively to the observed values of the variables and to the results of primary operations on them. It is therefore a wholly objective property of the system.

The concept of 'field' will be used extensively. It defines the characteristic behaviour of the system, replacing the vague concept of what a system 'does' or how it 'behaves' (often describable only in words) by the precise construct of a 'field'. Further

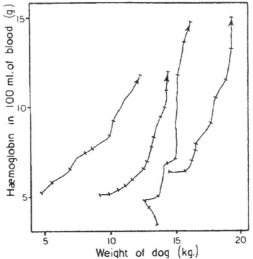

FIGURE 2/14/1 : Arrow-heads show the direction of movement of the representative point ; cross-lines show the positions of the representative point at weekly intervals.

it presents *all* a system's behaviours (under constant conditions) frozen into one unchanging entity that can be thought of as a unit. Such entities can readily be compared and contrasted, and so we can readily compare behaviour with behaviour, on a basis that is as complete and rigorous as we care to make it.

The reader may at first find the method unusual. Those who are familiar with the phase-space of mechanics will have no difficulty, but other readers may find it helpful if at first, whenever the word 'field' occurs, they substitute for it some phrase like 'typical way of behaving'.

The Natural System

2/15. In S. 2/5 a system was defined as any arbitrarily selected set of variables. The right to arbitrary selection cannot be waived, but the time has now come to recognise that both Science and common sense insist that if a system is to be studied with profit its variables must have some naturalness of association. But what is ' natural ' ? The problem has inevitably arisen after the restriction of S. 2/9, where we repudiated all borrowed knowledge. If we restrict our attention to the variables, we find that as every real ' machine ' provides an infinity of variables, and as from them we can form another infinity of combinations, we need some test to distinguish the natural system from the arbitrary.

One criterion will occur to the practical experimenter at once. He knows that if an active and relevant variable is left unobserved or uncontrolled the system's behaviour will become capricious, not capable of being reproduced at will. This concept may readily be made more precise. We simply state formally the century-old idea that a ' machine ' is something that, if its internal state is known, and its surrounding conditions, then its behaviour follows necessarily. That is to say, a particular surrounding condition (or input, i.e. those variables that affect it) and a particular state determine *uniquely* what transition will occur.

So the formal definition goes as follows. Take some particular set of external conditions (or input-value) C and some particular state S ; observe the transition that is induced by its own internal drive and laws ; suppose it goes to state S_i. Notice whether, whenever C and S occur again, the transition is also always to S_i ; if so, record that the transitions that follow C and S are *invariant*. Next, vary C (or S, or both) to get another pair— C_1 and S_1 say ; see similarly whether the transitions that follow C_1 and S_1 are also invariant. Proceed similarly till all possible pairs have been tested. If the outcome at every pair was ' invariant ' then the system is, by definition, a **machine with input**. (This definition accords with that given in *I. to C.*)

In the world of biology, the concept of the machine with input often occurs in the specially simple case in which all the events (in one field) occur in only one set of conditions (i.e. C has the same value for all the lines of behaviour). The field then comes from a system that is isolated. Thus, an experimenter may subject a Protozoon to a drug at a certain concentration; he then observes, without further experimental interference, the whole line of behaviour (which may be long and complex) that follows. This case occurs with sufficient frequency in biological systems and in this book to deserve a special name; it will be referred to here as a **state-determined** system.

Line	Variable	Time (seconds)			
		0	0·1	0·2	0·3
1	x	0	0·2	0·4	0·6
	y	2·0	2·1	2·3	2·6
2	x	− 0·2	− 0·1	0	0·1
	y	2·4	2·2	2·0	1·8

TABLE 2/15/1.

As illustration of the definition, consider Table 2/15/1, which shows two lines of behaviour from a system that is *not* state-determined. On the first line of behaviour the state $x = 0$, $y = 2·0$ was followed after 0·1 seconds by the state $x = 0·2$,

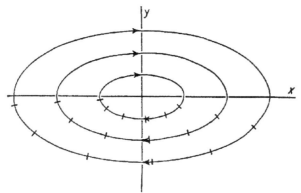

FIGURE 2/15/1 : Field of a simple pendulum 40 cm. long swinging in a vertical plane when g is 981 cm./sec.^{2}. x is the angle of deviation from the vertical and y the angular velocity of movement. Cross-strokes mark the position of the representative point at each one-tenth second. The clockwise direction should be noticed.

$y = 2 \cdot 1$. On line 2 the state $x = 0$, $y = 2 \cdot 0$ occurred again; but after 0·1 seconds the state became $x = 0 \cdot 1$, $y = 1 \cdot 8$ and not $x = 0 \cdot 2$, $y = 2 \cdot 1$. As the two states that follow the state $x = 0$, $y = 2 \cdot 0$ are not equal, the system is not state-determined.

A well-known example of a state-determined system is given by the simple pendulum swinging in a vertical plane. It is known that the two variables—(x) angle of deviation of the string from vertical, (y) angular velocity (or momentum) of the bob—are such that, all else being kept constant, their two values at a given instant are sufficient to determine the subsequent changes of the two variables (Figure 2/15/1).

The field of a state-determined system has a characteristic property: through no point does more than one line of behaviour run. This fact may be contrasted with that of a system that is not state-determined. Figure 2/15/2 shows such a field (the system is described in S. 19/13). The system's regularity would be established if we found that the system, started at A, always went to A', and, started at B, always went to B'. But such a system is not state-determined; for to say that the representative point is leaving C is insufficient to define its

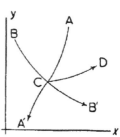

FIGURE 2/15/2 : The field of the system shown in Figure 19/13/1.

future line of behaviour, which may go to A' or B'. Even if the lines from A and B always ran to A' and B', the regularity in no way restricts what would happen if the system were *started* at C: it might go to D. If the system were state-determined, the lines CA', CB', and CD would coincide.

2/16. We can now return to the question of what we mean when we say that a system's variables have a 'natural' association. What we need is not a verbal explanation but a definition, which must have these properties:

    (1) it must be in the form of a test, separating all systems into two classes;

    (2) its application must be wholly objective;

    (3) its result must agree with common sense in typical and undisputed cases.

The third property makes clear that we cannot expect a proposed definition to be established by a few lines of verbal argument: it must be treated as a working hypothesis and used; only experience can show whether it is faulty or sound. (Nevertheless, in *I. to C.*, S. 13/5, I have given reasons suggesting that the property of being state-determined must inevitably be of fundamental interest to every organism that, like the human scientist, wants to achieve mastery over its surroundings.)

Because of its importance, science searches persistently for the state-determined. As a working guide, the scientist has for some centuries followed the hypothesis that, given a set of variables, he can always find a larger set that (1) includes the given variables, and (2) is state-determined. Much research work consists of trying to identify such a larger set, for when the set is too small, important variables will be left out of account, and the behaviour of the set will be capricious. The assumption that such a larger set exists is implicit in almost all science, but, being fundamental, it is seldom mentioned explicitly. Temple, though, refers to '. . . the fundamental assumption of macrophysics that a complete knowledge of the present state of a system furnishes sufficient data to determine definitely its state at any future time or its response to any external influence '. Laplace made the same assumption about the whole universe when he stated that, given its state at one instant, its future progress should be calculable. The definition given above makes this assumption precise and gives it in a form ready for use in the later chapters.

The assumption is now known to be false at the atomic level. We, however, will seldom discuss events at this level; and as the assumption has proved substantially true over great ranges of macroscopic science, we shall use it extensively.

Strategy for the complex system

2/17. The discussion of this chapter may have seemed confined to a somewhat arbitrary set of concepts, and the biologist, accustomed to a great range of variety in his material, may be thinking that the concepts and definitions are much too restricted. As this book puts forward a theory of the origin of adaptation, it must show how a theory, developed so narrowly, can be acceptable.

In this connexion we must note that theories are of various

types. At one extreme is Newton's theory of gravitation—at once simple, and precise, and exactly true. When such a combination is possible, Science is indeed lucky! Darwin's theory, on the other hand. is not so simple, is of quite low accuracy numerically, and is true only in a partial sense—that the simple arguments usually used to apply it in practice (e.g. how spraying with D.D.T. will ultimately affect the genetic constitution of the field mouse, by altering its food supply) are gross simplifications of the complex of events that will actually occur.

The theory attempted in this book is of the latter type. The real facts of the brain are so complex and varied that no theory can hope to achieve the simplicity and precision of Newton's; what then must it do? I suggest that it must try to be exact in certain selected cases, these cases being selected because there we *can* be exact. With these exact cases known, we can then face the multitudinous cases that do not quite correspond, using the rule that if we are satisfied that there is some continuity in the systems' properties, then insofar as each is near some exact case, so will its properties be near to those shown by the exact case.

This scientific strategy is by no means as inferior as it may sound; in fact it is used widely in many sciences of good repute. Thus the perfect gas, the massless spring, the completely reflecting mirror, the leakless condenser are all used freely in the theories of physics. These idealised cases have no real existence, but they are none the less important because they are both simple and exact, and are therefore key points in the general theoretical structure.

In the same spirit this book will attend closely to certain idealised cases, important because they can be exactly defined and because they are manageably simple. Maybe it will be found eventually that not a single mechanism in the brain corresponds *exactly* to the types described here; nevertheless the work will not be wasted if a thorough knowledge of these idealised forms enables us to understand the workings of many mechanisms that resemble them only as approximations.

CHAPTER 3

The Organism as Machine

3/1. In accordance with S 1/11 we shall assume at once that the living organism in its nature and processes is not essentially different from other matter. The truth of the assumption will not be discussed. The chapter will therefore deal only with the technique of applying this assumption to the complexities of biological systems.

The specification of behaviour

3/2. If the method laid down in the previous chapter is to be followed, we must first determine to what extent the behaviour of an organism is capable of being specified by *variables*, remembering that our ultimate test is whether the representation can be by dial readings (S. 2/3).

There can be little doubt that any single quantity observable in the living organism can be treated at least in principle as a variable. All bodily movements can be specified by co-ordinates. All joint movements can be specified by angles. Muscle tensions can be specified by their pull in dynes. Muscle movements can be specified by co-ordinates based on the bony structure or on some fixed external point, and can therefore be recorded numerically. A gland can be specified in its activity by its rate of secretion. Pulse-rate, blood-pressure, temperature, rate of blood-flow, tension of smooth muscle, and a host of other variables can be similarly recorded.

In the nervous system our attempts to observe, measure, and record have met great technical difficulties. Nevertheless, much has been achieved. The action potential, one of the essential events in the activity of the nervous system, can now be measured and recorded. The excitatory and inhibitory states of the centres are at the moment not directly recordable, but there is no reason to suppose that they will never become so.

3/3. Few would deny that the elementary physico-chemical events in the living organism can be treated as variables. But some may hesitate before accepting that readings on dials (and the complex relations deducible from them) are adequate for the description of *all* significant biological events. As the remainder of the book will assume that they are sufficient, I must show how the various complexities of biological experience can be reduced to this standard form.

A simple case which may be mentioned first occurs when an event is recorded in the form 'strychnine was injected at this moment', or 'a light was switched on', or 'an electric shock was administered'. Such a statement treats only the positive event as having existence and ignores the other state as a nullity. It can readily be converted to a numerical form suitable for our purpose by using the device mentioned in S. 2/3. Such events would then be recorded by assuming, in the first case, that the animal always had strychnine in its tissues but that at first the quantity present was 0 mg. per g. tissue; in the second case, that the light was always on, but that at first it shone with a brightness of 0 candlepower; and in the last case, that an electric potential was applied throughout but that at first it had a value of 0 volts. Such a method of description cannot be wrong in these cases for it defines exactly the same set of objective facts. Its advantage from our point of view is that it provides a method which can be used uniformly over a wide range of phenomena: the variable is always present, merely varying in value.

But this device does not remove all difficulties. It sometimes happens in physiology and psychology that a variable seems to have no numerical counter-part. Thus in one experiment two cards, one black and one brown, were shown alternately to an animal as stimuli. One variable would thus be 'colour' and it would have two values. The simplest way to specify colour numerically is to give the wave-length of its light; but this method cannot be used here, for 'black' means 'no light', and 'brown' does not occur in the spectrum. Another example would occur if an electric heater were regularly used and if its switch indicated only the degrees 'high', 'medium', and 'low'. Another example is given on many types of electric apparatus by a pilot light which, as a variable, takes only the two values 'lit' and 'unlit'. More complex examples occur frequently in psychological experiments.

Table 2/1/1, for instance, contains a variable 'part of skin stimulated' which, in Pavlov's Table, takes only two values: 'usual
place' and 'new place'. Even more complicated variables are
common in Pavlov's experiments. Many a Table contains a
variable 'stimulus' which takes such values as 'bubbling water',
'metronome', 'flashing light'. A similar difficulty occurs when
an experimenter tests an animal's response to injections of toxins,
so that there will be a variable 'type of toxin' which may take
the two values 'Diphtheria type Gravis' and 'Diphtheria type
Medius'. And finally the change may involve an extensive
re-organisation of the whole experimental situation. Such would
occur if the experimenter, wanting to test the effect of the general
surroundings, tried the effect of the variable 'situation of the
experiment' by giving it alternately the two values 'in the
animal house' and 'in the open air'. Can such variables be
represented by number?

In some of the examples, the variables might possibly be specified numerically by a more or less elaborate specification of their
physical nature. Thus 'part of skin stimulated' might be
specified by reference to some system of co-ordinates marked on
the skin; and the three intensities of the electric heater might be
specified by the three values of the watts consumed. But this
method is hardly possible in the remainder of the cases; nor is it
necessary. For numbers can be used cardinally as well as
ordinally, that is, they may be used as mere labels without any
reference to their natural order. Such are the numberings of the
divisions of an army, and of the subscribers on a telephone system;
for the subscriber whose number is, say, 4051 has no particular
relation to the subscriber whose number is 4052: the number
identifies him but does not relate him.

It may be shown (S. 21/6) that if a variable takes a few values
which stand in no simple relation to one another, then each value
may be allotted an arbitrary number; and provided that the
numbers are used systematically throughout the experiment, and
that their use is confined to the experiment, then no confusion
can arise. Thus the variable 'situation of the experiment'
might be allotted the arbitrary value of '1' if the experiment
occurs in the animal house, and '2' if it occurs in the open air.

Although 'situation of the experiment' involves a great number
of physical variables, the aggregate may justifiably be treated as

a single variable provided the arrangement of the experiment is such that the many variables are used throughout as one aggregate which can take either of two forms. If, however, the aggregate were split in the experiment, as would happen if we recorded four classes of results·

(1) in the animal house in summer
(2) in the animal house in winter
(3) in the open air in summer
(4) in the open air in winter

then we must either allow the variable ' condition of experiment ' to take four values, or we could consider the experiment as subject to two variables. ' site of experiment ' and ' season of year ', each of which takes two values.   According to this method, what is important is not the material structure of the technical devices but the experiment's logical structure.

3/4. But is the method yet adequate ? Can all the living organisms' more subtle qualities be numericised in this way ?   On this subject there has been much dispute, but we can avoid a part of the controversy; for here we are concerned only with certain qualities defined.

First, we shall be dealing not with qualities but with behaviour: we shall be dealing, not with what an organism feels or thinks, but with what it does.   The omission of all subjective aspects (S. 1/16) removes from the discussion the most subtle of the qualities, while the restriction to overt behaviour makes the specification by variable usually easy.   Secondly, when the non-mathematical reader thinks that there are some complex quantities that cannot be adequately represented by number, he is apt to think of their representation by a single variable.   The use of many variables, however, enables systems of considerable complexity to be treated.   Thus a complex system like ' the weather over England ', which cannot be treated adequately by a single variable, can, by the use of many variables, be treated as adequately as we please.

3/5. To illustrate the method for specifying the behaviour of a system by variables, two examples will be given.   They are of little intrinsic interest; more important is the fact that they demonstrate that the method is exact and that it can be extended to any extent without loss of precision.

The first example is from a physiological experiment. A dog was subjected to a steady loss of blood at the rate of one per cent of its body weight per minute. Recorded are the three variables:

(x) rate of blood-flow through the inferior vena cava,
(y) ,, ,, ,, ,, ,, muscles of a leg,
(z) ,, ,, ,, ,, ,, gut.

The changes of the variables with time are shown in Figure 3/5/1. It will be seen that the changes of the variables show a characteristic pattern, for the blood-flow through leg and gut falls more than that through the inferior vena cava, and this difference is characteristic of the body's reaction to haemorrhage. The use

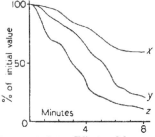 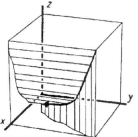

FIGURE 3/5/1 : Effects of haemorrhage on the rate of blood-flow
through : x, the inferior vena cava;
y, the muscles of a leg ; and z, the
gut. (From Rein.)

FIGURE 3/5/2 : Phase-space and
line of behaviour of the data
shown in Figure 3/5/1.

of more than one variable has enabled the *pattern* of the reaction to be displayed.

The changes specify a line of behaviour, shown in Figure 3/5/2. Had the line of behaviour pointed in a different direction, the change would have corresponded to a change in the pattern of the body's reaction to haemorrhage.

The second example uses certain angles measured from a cinematographic record of the activities of a man. His body moved forward but was vertical throughout. The four variables are:

(w) angle between the right thigh and the vertical
(x) ,, ,, ,, left ,, ,, ,, ,,

(*y*) angle between the right thigh and the right tibia
(*z*) ,,   ,,   ,, left   ,,   ,,   ,, left   ,,

In *w* and *x* the angle is counted positively when the knee comes forward: in *y* and *z* the angles are measured behind the knee. The line of behaviour is specified in Table 3/5/1. The reader can easily identify this well-known activity.

		Time (seconds)								
		0	0·1	0·2	0·3	0·4	0·5	0·6	0·7	0·8
Variable	*w*	45	10	— 10	— 20	— 35	0	60	70	45
	x	— 35	0	60	70	45	10	— 10	— 20	— 35
	y	170	180	180	160	120	80	60	100	170
	z	120	80	60	100	170	180	180	160	120

TABLE 3/5/1.

3/6. In a physiological experiment the nervous system is usually considered to be state-determined. That it can be made state-determined is assumed by every physiologist before the work starts, for he assumes that it is subject to the fundamental assumption of S. 2/15: that if every detail within it could be determined, its subsequent behaviour would also be determined. Many of the specialised techniques such as anaesthesia, spinal transection, root section, and the immobilisation of body and head in clamps are used to ensure proper isolation of the system—a necessary condition for it to be state-determined (S. 2/15). So unless there are special reasons to the contrary, the nervous system in a physiological experiment can usually be assumed to be state-determined.

3/7. Similarly it is usually agreed that an animal undergoing experiments on its conditioned reflexes is a physico-chemical system such that if we knew every detail we could predict its behaviour. Pavlov's insistence on complete isolation was intended to ensure that this was so. So unless there are special reasons to the contrary, the animal in an experiment with conditioned reflexes can usually be assumed to be state-determined.

3/8. These two examples, however, are mentioned only as introduction; rather we shall be concerned with the nature of the free-living organism within a natural environment.

Given an organism, its **environment** is defined as *those variables whose changes affect the organism, and those variables which are changed by the organism's behaviour.* It is thus defined in a purely functional, not a material, sense. It will be treated uniformly with our treatment of all variables: we assume it is representable by dials, is explorable (by the experimenter) by primary operations, and is intrinsically state-determined.

Organism and environment

3/9. The theme of the chapter can now be stated: the free-living organism and its environment, taken together, may be represented with sufficient accuracy by a set of variables that forms a state-determined system.

The concepts developed in the previous sections now enable us to treat both organism and environment by identical methods, for the same primary assumptions are made about each.

3/10. As example, that the organism and its environment form a single state-determined system, consider (in so far as the activities of balancing are concerned) a bicycle and its rider in normal progression.

First, the forward movement may be eliminated as irrelevant, for we could study the properties of this dynamic system equally well if the wheels were on some backward-moving band. The variables can be identified by considering what happens. Suppose the rider pulls his right hand backwards: it will change the angular position of the front wheel (taking the line of the frame as reference). The changed angle of the front wheel will start the two points, at which the wheels make contact with the ground, moving to the right. (The physical reasons for this movement are irrelevant: the fact that the relation is determined is sufficient.) The rider's centre of gravity being at first unmoved, the line vertically downwards from his centre of gravity will strike the ground more and more to the left of the line joining the two points As a result he will start to fall to the left This fall will excite nerve-endings in the organs of balance in the ear, impulses

36

will pass to the nervous system, and will be switched through it, if he is a trained rider, by such a route that they, or the effects set up by them, will excite to activity those muscles which push the *right* hand forwards.

We can now specify the variables which must compose the system if it is to be state-determined. We must include · the angular position of the handlebar, the velocity of lateral movement of the two points of contact between wheels and road, the distance laterally between the line joining these points and the point vertically below the rider's centre of gravity, and the angular deviation of the rider from the vertical. These four variables are defined by S. 3/8 to be the ' environment ' of the rider. (Whether the fourth variable is allotted to ' rider ' or to ' environment ' is optional (S. 3/12). To make the system state-determined, there must be added the variables of the nervous system, of the relevant muscles, and of the bone and joint positions.

As a second example, consider a butterfly and a bird in the air, the bird chasing the butterfly, and the butterfly evading the bird. Both use the air around them. Every movement of the bird stimulates the butterfly's eyes and this stimulation, acting through the butterfly's nervous system, will cause changes in the butter-fly's wing movements. These movements act on the enveloping air and cause changes in the butterfly's position. A change of position immediately changes the excitations in the bird's eye, and this leads through its nervous system to changed movements of the bird's wings. These act on the air and change the bird's position. So the processes go on. The bird has as environment the air and the butterfly, while the butterfly has the air and the bird. The whole may reasonably be assumed to be state-determined

3/11. The organism affects the environment, and the environment affects the organism: such a system is said to have ' feedback ' (S. 4/14).

The examples of the previous section provide illustration. The muscles in the rider's arm move the handlebars, causing changes in the environment; and changes in these variables will, through the rider's sensory receptors, cause changes in his brain and muscles. When bird and butterfly manoeuvre in the air, each manoeuvre of one causes reactive changes to occur in the other.

The same feature is shown by the example of S. 1/17—the

type problem of the kitten and the fire. The various stimuli
from the fire, working through the nervous system, evoke some
reaction from the kitten's muscles; equally the kitten's movements, by altering the position of its body in relation to the fire,
will cause changes to occur in the pattern of stimuli which falls
on the kitten's sense-organs. The receptors therefore affect the
muscles (by effects transmitted through the nervous system), and
the muscles affect the receptors (by effects transmitted through
the environment). The action is two-way and the system possesses
feedback.

The observation is not new:

> ' In most cases the change which induces a reaction is brought
> about by the organism's own movements. These cause a
> change in the relation of the organism to the environment:
> to these changes the organism reacts   The whole behaviour
> of free-moving organisms is based on the principle that it
> is the movements of the organism that have brought about
> stimulation.'
>
> (Jennings.)

> ' The good player of a quick ball game, the surgeon con-
> ducting an operation, the physician arriving at a clinical
> decision—in each case there is the flow from signals inter-
> preted to action carried out, back to further signals and on
> again to more action, up to the culminating point of the
> achievement of the task '.
>
> (Bartlett.)

> ' Organism and environment form a whole and must be
> viewed as such.'
>
> (Starling.)

It is necessary to point to the existence of feedback in the
relation between the free-living organism and its environment
because most physiological experiments are deliberately arranged
to avoid feedback. Thus, in an experiment with spinal reflexes,
a stimulus is applied and the resulting movement recorded; but
the movement is not allowed to influence the nature or duration
of the stimulus. The action between stimulus and movement is
therefore one-way. A similar absence of feedback is enforced
in the Pavlovian experiments with conditioned reflexes: the
stimulus may evoke salivation, but the salivation has no effect
on the nature or duration of the stimulus.

Such an absence of feedback is, of course, useful or even essential in the analytic study of the behaviour of a mechanism, whether animate or inanimate. But its usefulness in the laboratory should not obscure the fact that the free-living animal is not subject to these constraints.

Sometimes systems which seem at first sight to be one-way prove on closer examination to have feedback. Walking on a smooth pavement, for instance, seems to involve so little reference to the structures outside the body that the nervous system might seem to be producing its actions without reference to their effects. *Tabes dorsalis*, however, prevents incoming sensory impulses from reaching the brain while leaving the outgoing motor impulses unaffected. If walking were due simply to the outgoing motor impulses, the disease would cause no disturbance to walking. In fact, it upsets the action severely, and demonstrates that the incoming sensory impulses are really playing an essential, though hidden, part in the normal action.

Another example showing the influence of feedback occurs when we try to place a point accurately (e.g. by trying to pass a wire through a small hole in a board) when we cannot see by how much we are in error (e.g. when we have to pass the wire through from the far side, towards us). The difficulty we encounter is precisely due to the fact that while we can affect the movements of the wire, its movements and its relations to the hole can no longer be communicated back to us.

Sometimes the feedback can be demonstrated only with difficulty. Thus, Lloyd Morgan raised some ducklings in an incubator.

> 'The ducklings thoroughly enjoyed a dip. Each morning, at nine o'clock, a large black tray was placed in their pen, and on it a flat tin containing water To this they eagerly ran, drinking and washing in it. On the sixth morning the tray and tin were given them in the usual way, but without any water. They ran to it, scooped at the bottom and made all the motions of the beak as if drinking. They squatted in it, dipping their heads, and waggling their tails as usual. For some ten minutes they continued to wash in non-existent water . . .'

Their behaviour might suggest that the stimuli of tray and tin were compelling the production of certain activities and that the results of these activities were having no back-effect. But further experiment showed that some effect was occurring·

> 'The next day the experiment was repeated with the dry tin.

39

Again they ran to it, shovelling along the bottom with their beaks, and squatting down in it. But they soon gave up. On the third morning they waddled up to the dry tin, and departed '

Their behaviour at first suggested that there was no feedback But on the third day their change of behaviour showed that, in fact, the change in the bath had had some effect on them.

The importance of feedback lies in the fact that systems which possess it have certain properties (S. 4/16) which cannot be shown by systems lacking it. *Systems with feedback cannot adequately be treated as if they were of one-way action*, for the feedback introduces properties which can be explained only by reference to the particular feedback used. (On the other hand a one-way system can, without error, be treated as if it contained feedback: we assume that one of the two actions is present but at zero degree (S. 2/3). In other words, systems without feedback are a subclass of the class of systems with feedback.)

3/12. As the organism and its environment are to be treated as a single system, the dividing line between ' organism ' and ' environment ' becomes partly conceptual, and to that extent arbitrary. Anatomically and physically, of course, there is usually a unique and obvious distinction between the two parts of the system; but if we view the system functionally, ignoring purely anatomical facts as irrelevant, the division of the system into ' organism ' and ' environment ' becomes vague. Thus, if a mechanic with an artificial arm is trying to repair an engine, then the arm may be regarded either as part of the organism that is struggling with the engine, or as part of the machinery with which the man is struggling.

Once this flexibility of division is admitted. almost no bounds can be put to its application. The chisel in a sculptor's hand can be regarded either as a part of the complex biophysical mechanism that is shaping the marble, or it can be regarded as a part of the material which the nervous system is attempting to control. The bones in the sculptor's arm can similarly be regarded either as part of the organism or as part of the ' environment ' of the nervous system. Variables within the body may justifiably be regarded as the ' environment ' of some other part. A child has to learn not only how to grasp a piece of bread, but how to chew without biting his own tongue; functionally both bread and tongue are part of the environment of the cerebral cortex. But the environments with which the cortex has to deal are sometimes even deeper in the body than the tongue: the child has to learn how to play without exhausting itself utterly, and how to talk without getting out of breath.

These remarks are not intended to confuse, but to show that later arguments (in Chapters 15 and 16) are not unreasonable. There it is intended to treat one group of neurons in the brain as the environment of another group. These divisions, though arbitrary, are justifiable because we shall always treat the system as a whole, dividing it into parts in this unusual way merely for verbal convenience in description.

It should be noticed that from now on 'the system' means not the nervous system but the whole complex of the organism and its environment. Thus, if it should be shown that 'the system' has some property, it must not be assumed that this property is attributed to the nervous system: it belongs to the whole; and detailed examination may be necessary to ascertain the contributions of the separate parts.

3/13. In some cases the dynamic nature of the interaction between organism and environment can be made intuitively more obvious by using the device, common in physics, of regarding the animal as the centre of reference. In locomotion the animal would then be thought of as pulling the world past itself. Provided we are concerned only with the relation between these two, and are not considering their relations to any third and independent body, the device will not lead to error. It was used in the 'rider and bicycle' example.

By the use of animal-centred co-ordinates we can see that the animal has much more control over its environment than might at first seem possible. Thus, while a frog cannot change air into water, a frog on the bank of a stream can, with one small jump, change its world from one ruled by the laws of mechanics to one ruled by the laws of hydrodynamics.

Essential variables

3/14. The biologist must view the brain, not as being the seat of the 'mind', nor as something that 'thinks', but, like every other organ in the body, as a specialised means to survival (S. 1/10). We shall use the concept of ' survival ' repeatedly; but before we can use it, we must, by S. 2/10, transform it to our standard form and say what it means in terms of primary operations.

Physico-chemical systems may undergo the most extensive transformations without showing any change obviously equivalent to death, for matter and energy are indestructible. Yet the distinction between a live horse and a dead one is obvious enough Further, there can be no doubt about the objectivity of the difference, for they fetch quite different prices in the market. The distinction must be capable of objective definition.

It is suggested that the definition may be obtained in the following way. That an animal should remain ' alive ', certain variables must remain without certain ' physiological ' limits. What these variables are, and what the limits, are fixed when the species is fixed. In practice one does not experiment on animals in general, one experiments on one of a particular species. In each species the many physiological variables differ widely in their relevance to survival. Thus, if a man's hair is shortened from 4 inches to 1 inch, the change is trivial; if his systolic blood-pressure drops from 120 mm. of mercury to 30, the change will quickly be fatal.

Every species has a number of variables which are closely related to survival and which are closely linked dynamically so that marked changes in any one leads sooner or later to marked changes in the others. Thus, if we find in a rat that the pulse-rate has dropped to zero, we can predict that the respiration rate will soon become zero, that the body temperature will soon fall to room temperature, and that the number of bacteria in the tissues will soon rise from almost zero to a very high number. These important and closely linked variables will be referred to as the **essential** variables of the animal.

How are we to discover them, considering that we may not use borrowed knowledge but must find them by the methods of Chapter 2 ? There is no difficulty. Given a species, we observe what follows when members of the species are started from a variety of initial states We shall find that large initial changes in some variables are followed in the system by merely transient deviations, while large initial changes in others are followed by deviations that become ever greater till the ' machine ' changes

42

to something very different from what it was originally.   The
results of these primary operations will thus distinguish, quite
objectively, the essential variables from the others.

3/15.   The essential variables are not uniform in the closeness or
urgency of their relations to lethality.   There are such variables
as the amount of oxygen in the blood, and the structural integrity
of the medulla oblongata, whose passage beyond the normal limits
is followed by death almost at once.   There are others, such as
the integrity of a leg-bone, and the amount of infection in the
peritoneal cavity, whose passage beyond the limit must be regarded
as serious though not necessarily fatal.   Then there are variables,
such as those of severe pressure or heat at some place on the skin,
whose passage beyond normal limits is not immediately dangerous,
but is so often correlated with some approaching threat that *is*
serious that the organism avoids such situations (which we call
' painful ') as if they were potentially lethal.   All that we require
is the ability to arrange the animal's variables in an approximate
order of importance   Inexactness of the order is not serious, for
nowhere will we use a particular order as a basis for particular
deductions.

   We can now define ' survival ' objectively and in terms of a
field: it occurs when a line of behaviour takes no essential variable
outside given limits.

CHAPTER 4

Stability

4/1. THE words 'stability', 'steady state', and 'equilibrium' are used by a variety of authors with a variety of meanings, though there is always the same underlying theme. As we shall be much concerned with stability and its properties, an exact definition must be provided.

The subject may be opened by a presentation of the three standard elementary examples. A cube resting with one face on a horizontal surface typifies 'stable' equilibrium; a sphere resting on a horizontal surface typifies 'neutral' equilibrium; and a cone balanced on its point typifies 'unstable' equilibrium. With neutral and unstable equilibria we shall have little concern, but the concept of 'stable equilibrium' will be used repeatedly.

These three dynamic systems are restricted in their behaviour by the fact that each system contains a fixed quantity of energy, so that any subsequent movement must conform to this invariance. We, however, shall be considering systems which are abundantly supplied with free energy so that no such limitation is imposed. Here are two examples.

The first is the Watt's governor. A steam-engine rotates a pair of weights which, as they are rotated faster, separate more widely by centrifugal action; their separation controls mechanically the position of the throttle; and the position of the throttle controls the flow of steam to the engine. The connexions are arranged so that an increase in the speed of the engine causes a decrease in the flow of steam. The result is that if any transient disturbance slows or accelerates the engine, the governor brings the speed back to the usual value. By this return the system demonstrates its stability.

The second example is the thermostat, of which many types exist. All, however, work on the same principle: a chilling of the main object causes a change which in its turn causes the heating to become more intense or more effective; and vice versa.

44

The result is that if any transient disturbance cools or overheats the main object, the thermostat brings its temperature back to the usual value. By this return the system demonstrates its stability.

4/2. An important feature of stability is that it does not refer to a material body or ' machine ' but only to some aspect of it. This statement may be proved most simply by an example showing that a single material body can be in two different equilibrial conditions at the same time. Consider a square card balanced exactly on one edge; to displacements at right angles to this edge the card is unstable; to displacements exactly parallel to this edge it is, theoretically at least, stable.

The example supports the thesis that we do not, in general, study physical bodies but only entities carefully abstracted from them. The matter will become clearer when we conform to the requirements of S. 2/10 and define stability in terms of the results of primary operations. This may be done as follows.

4/3. Consider a corrugated surface, laid horizontally, with a ball rolling from a ridge down towards a trough. A photograph taken in the middle of its roll would look like Figure 4/3/1. We might think of the ball as being unstable because it has rolled away from the ridge, until we realise that we can also think of it as stable because it is rolling towards the trough. The duality shows we are approaching the concept in the wrong way. The situation can be made clearer if we remove the ball and consider only the surface. The top of the ridge, as

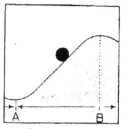

FIGURE 4/3/1.

it would affect the roll of a ball, is now recognised as a position of unstable equilibrium, and the bottom of the trough as a position of stability. We now see that, if friction is sufficiently marked for us to be able to neglect momentum, the system composed of the single variable ' distance of the ball laterally ' is state-determined, and has a definite, permanent field, which is sketched in the Figure.

From *B* the lines of behaviour diverge, but to *A* they converge.

We conclude tentatively that the concept of 'stability' belongs not to a material body but to a field. It is shown by a field if the lines of behaviour converge. (An exact definition is given in S. 4/8.)

4/4. The points A and B are such that the ball, if released on either of them, and mathematically perfect, will stay there. Given a field, a **state of equilibrium** is one from which the representative point does not move. When the primary operation is applied, the transition from that state can be described as 'to itself'.   •

(Notice that this definition, while saying what happens *at* the equilibrial state, does not restrict how the lines of behaviour may run around it. They may converge in to it, or diverge from it, or behave in other ways.)

Although the variables do not change value when the system is at a state of equilibrium, this invariance does not imply that the 'machine' is inactive. Thus, a motionless Watt's governor is compatible with the engine working at a non-zero rate. (The matter has been treated more fully in *I. to C.*, S. 11/15.)

4/5. To illustrate that the concept of stability belongs to a field, let us examine the fields of the previous examples.

The cube resting on one face yields a state-determined system which has two variables:

(x) the angle at which the face makes with the horizontal, and
(y) the rate at which this angle changes

(This system allows for the momentum of the cube.) If the cube does not bounce when the face meets the table, the field is similar to that sketched in Figure 4/5/1. The stability of the cube when resting on a face corresponds in the field to the convergence of the lines of behaviour to the centre.

The square card balanced on its edge can be represented approximately by two variables which measure displacements at right angles (x) and parallel (y) to the lower edge. The field will resemble that sketched in Figure 4/5/2. Displacement from the origin 0 to A is followed by a return of the representative point to 0, and this return corresponds to the stability. Displacement from 0 to B is followed by a departure from the region under

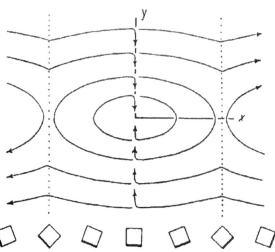

Figure 4/5/1 : Field of the two-variable system described in the text.
Below is shown the cube as it would appear in elevation when its main
face, shown by a heavier line, is tilted through the angle *x*.

consideration, and this departure corresponds to the instability.
The uncertainty of the movements near *O* corresponds to the
uncertainty in the behaviour of the card when released from the
vertical position.

The Watt's governor has a more complicated field, but an
approximation may be obtained without
difficulty.   The system may be specified
to an approximation sufficient for our
purpose by three variables:

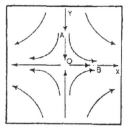

(*x*) the speed of the engine and
governor (r.p.m.),

(*y*) the distance between the weights,
or the position of the throttle,
and

(*z*) the velocity of flow of the steam.

Figure 4/5/2.

(*y* represents either of two quantities because they are rigidly
connected). If, now, a disturbance suddenly accelerates the
engine, increasing *x*, the increase in *x* will increase *y*; this increase
in *y* will be followed by a decrease of *z*, and then by a decrease of
x. As the changes occur not in jumps but continuously, the line

of behaviour must resemble that sketched in Figure 4/5/3. The other lines of the field could be added by considering what would happen after other disturbances (lines starting from points other than *A*). Although having different initial states, all the lines would converge towards *O*.

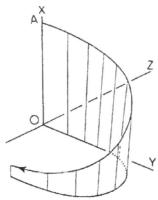

FIGURE 4/5/3 : One line of behaviour in the field of the Watt's governor. For clarity, the resting state of the system has been used as origin. The system has been displaced to *A* and then released.

4/6. In some of our examples, for instance that of the cube, the lines of behaviour terminate in a point at which all movement ceases. In other examples the movement does not wholly cease; many a thermostat settles down, when close to its resting state, to a regular small oscillation. We shall seldom be interested in the details of what happens at the exact centre.

4/7. More important is the underlying theme that in all cases the stable system is characterised by the fact that after a displacement we can assign some *bound* to the subsequent movement of the representative point, whereas in the unstable system such limitation is either impossible or depends on facts outside the subject of discussion. Thus, if a thermostat is set at 37° C. and displaced to 40°, we can predict that in the future it will not go outside specified limits, which might be, in one apparatus, 36° and 40°. On the other hand, if the thermostat has been assembled with a component reversed so that it is unstable (S. 4/14) and if it is displaced to 40°, then we can give no limits to its subsequent temperatures; unless we introduce such new topics as the melting-point of its solder.

4/8. These considerations bring us to the definitions. Given the field of a state-determined system and a region in the field, the region is **stable** if the lines of behaviour from all points in the region stay within the region.

Thus, in Figure 4/3/1 make a mark on either side of *A* to define a region. All representative points within are led to *A*, and none can leave the region; so the region is stable. On the other hand, no such region can be marked around B (unless restricted to the single point of B itself).

The definition makes clear that change of either the field or the region may change the result of the test. We cannot, in general, say of a given system that it is stable (or unstable) unconditionally. The field of Figure 4/5/1 showed this, and so does that of Figure 4/5/2. (In the latter, the regions restricted to any part of the y-axis with the origin are stable; all others are unstable.)

The examples above have been selected to test the definition severely. Often the fields are simpler. In the field of the cube, for instance, it is possible to draw many boundaries, all oval, such that the regions inside them are stable. The field of the Watt's governor is also of this type.

A *field* will be said to be stable if the whole region it fills is stable; the *system* that provided the field can then be called stable.

4/9. Sometimes the conditions are even simpler. The system may have only one state of equilibrium and the lines of behaviour may all either converge in to it or all diverge from it. In such a case the indication of which way the lines go may be given sufficiently by the simple, unqualified, statement that 'it is stable' (or not). A system can be described adequately by such an unqualified statement (without reference to the region) only when its field, i.e. its behaviour, is suitably simple.

4/10. If a line of behaviour is re-entrant to itself, the system undergoes a recurrent cycle. If the cycle is wholly contained in a given region, and the lines of behaviour lead *into* the cycle, the cycle is stable.

Such a cycle is commonly shown by thermostats which, after correcting any gross displacement, settle down to a steady oscillation. In such a case the field will show, not convergence to a point but convergence to a cycle, such as is shown exaggerated in Figure 4/10/1.

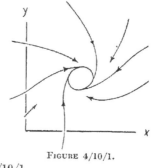

FIGURE 4/10/1.

4/11. This definition of stability conforms to the requirement of S. 2/10; for the observed behaviour of the system determines the field, and the field determines the stability.

The diagram of immediate effects

4/12. The description given in S. 4/1 of the working of the Watt's governor showed that it is arranged in a functional circuit: the chain of cause and effect is re-entrant. Thus if we represent ' A has a direct effect on B ' or ' A directly disturbs B ' by the symbol $A \longrightarrow B$, then the construction of the Watt's governor may be represented by the diagram:

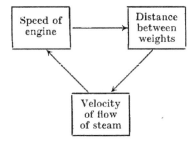

(The number of variables named here is partly optional.)

I now want to make clear that this type of diagram, if accurately defined, can be derived *wholly from the results of primary operations*. No metaphysical or borrowed knowledge is necessary for its construction. To show how this is done, take an actual Watt's governor as example:

Each pair of variables is taken in turn. Suppose the relation between ' speed of engine ' and ' distance between weights ' is first investigated. The experimenter would fix the variable ' velocity of flow of steam ' and all other extraneous variables that might interfere to confuse the direct relation between speed of engine and distance between weights. Then he would try various speeds of the engine, and would observe how these changes affected the behaviour of ' distance between the weights '. He would find that changes in the speed of the engine were regularly followed by changes in the distance between the weights. Thus the transition of the variable ' distance between weights ' (one distance changing to another) *is* affected by the value of the speed of the

50

engine. He need know nothing of the nature of the ultimate physical linkages, but he would observe the fact. Then, still keeping 'velocity of flow of steam' constant, he would try various distances between the weights, and would observe the effect of such changes on the speed of the engine; he would find them to be without effect. He would thus have established that there is an arrow from left to right but not from right to left in

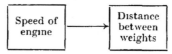

This procedure could then be applied to the two variables 'distance between weights' and 'velocity of flow of steam', while the other variable 'speed of engine' was kept constant. And finally the relations between the third pair could be established.

The method is clearly general. To find the immediate effects in a system with variables A, B, C, D . . . take one pair, A and B say, hold all other variables C, D . . . constant; note B's behaviour when A starts at A_1; and also its behaviour when A starts at A_2. If these behaviours of B are the same, then there is no immediate effect from A to B. But if the B's behaviours are unequal, and regularly depend on what value A starts from, then there *is* an immediate effect, which we may symbolise by $A \rightarrow B$.

By interchanging A and B in the process we can then test for $B \rightarrow A$. And by using other pairs in turn we can determine all the immediate effects. The process consists purely of primary operations, and therefore uses no borrowed knowledge (the process is further considered in S. 12/3). We shall frequently use this **diagram of immediate effects.**

4/13. It should be noticed that this arrow, though it sometimes corresponds to an actual material channel (a rod, a wire, a nerve fibre, etc.), has fundamentally nothing to do with material connexions but is *a representation of a relation between the behaviours at A and B.* Strictly speaking, it refers to A and B only, and not to anything between them.

That it is the functional, behavioural, relation between A and B that is decisive (in deciding whether we may hypothesise a channel of communication between them) was shown clearly on that day in 1888 when Heinrich Hertz gave his famous demonstration. He had two pieces of apparatus (*A* and *B*, say) that manifestly were not connected in any material way; yet whenever at any arbitrarily selected moment he closed a switch in *A* a spark jumped in *B*, i.e. *B*'s behaviour depended at any moment on the position of *A*'s switch. Here was a flat contradiction: materially the two systems were *not* connected, yet functionally their behaviours *were* connected. All scientists accepted that the *behavioural* evidence was final—that some linkage was demonstrated.

Feedback

4/14. A gas thermostat also shows a functional circuit or feedback; for it is controlled by a capsule which by its swelling moves a lever which controls the flow of gas to the heating flame, so the diagram of immediate effects would be:

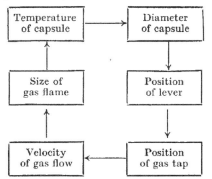

The reader should verify that each arrow represents a physical action which can be demonstrated if all variables other than the pair are kept constant.

Another example is provided by ' reaction ' in a radio receiver. We can represent the action by two variables linked in two ways:

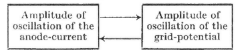

The lower arrow represents the grid-potential's effect within the valve on the anode-current. The upper arrow represents some arrangement of the circuit by which fluctuation in the anode current affects the grid-potential. The effect represented by the lower arrow is determined by the valve-designer, that of the upper by the circuit-designer.

Such systems whose variables affect one another in one or more circuits possess what the radio-engineer calls 'feedback', they are also sometimes described as 'servo-mechanisms'. They are at least as old as the Watt's governor and may be older. But only during the last decade has it been realised that the possession of feedback gives a machine potentialities that are not available to a machine lacking it. The development occurred mainly during the last war, stimulated by the demand for automatic methods of control of searchlight, anti-aircraft guns, rockets, and torpedoes, and facilitated by the great advances that had occurred in electronics. As a result, a host of new machines appeared which acted with powers of self-adjustment and correction never before achieved. Some of their main properties will be described in S. 4/16.

The nature, degree, and polarity of the feedback usually have a decisive effect on the stability or instability of the system. In the Watt's governor or in the thermostat, for instance, the connexion of a part in reversed position, reversing the polarity of action of one component on the next, may, and probably will, turn the system from stable to unstable. In the reaction circuit of the radio set, the stability or instability is determined by the quantitative relation between the two effects.

Instability in such systems is shown by the development of a 'runaway'. The least disturbance is magnified by its passage round the circuit so that it is incessantly built up into a larger and larger deviation from the central state. The phenomenon is identical with that referred to as a 'vicious circle'.

4/15. The examples shown have only a simple circuit. But more complex systems may have many interlacing circuits. If, for instance, as in S. 8/2, four variables all act on each other, the diagram of immediate effects would be that shown in Figure

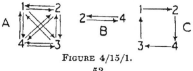

FIGURE 4/15/1.

4/15/1 (*A*). It is easy to verify that such a system contains twenty interlaced circuits, two of which are shown at *B* and *C*.

The further development of the theory of systems with feedback cannot be made without mathematics. But here it is sufficient to note two facts: a system which possesses feedback is usually actively stable or actively unstable; and whether it is stable or unstable depends on the quantitative details of the particular arrangement.

Goal-seeking

4/16. Every stable system has the property that if displaced from a state of equilibrium and released, the subsequent movement is so matched to the initial displacement that the system is brought back to the state of equilibrium. *A variety of disturbances will therefore evoke a variety of matched reactions.* Reference to a simple field such as that of Figure 4/5/1 will establish the point.

This pairing of the line of return to the initial displacement has sometimes been regarded as ' intelligent ' and peculiar to living things. But a simple refutation is given by the ordinary pendulum: if we displace it to the right, it develops a force which tends to move it to the left; and if we displace it to the left, it develops a force which tends to move it to the right. Noticing that the pendulum reacted with forces which though varied in direction always pointed towards the centre, the mediaeval scientist would have said ' the pendulum seeks the centre '. By this phrase he would have recognised that the behaviour of a stable system may be described as ' goal-seeking '. Without introducing any metaphysical implications we may recognise that this type of behaviour does occur in the stable dynamic systems. Thus Figure 4/16/1 shows how, as the control setting of a thermostat

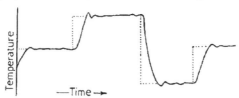

Figure 4/16/1 : Tracing of the temperature (solid line), of a thermostatically controlled bath, and of the control setting (broken line).

was altered, the temperature of the apparatus always followed it, the set temperature being treated as if it were a goal.

Such a movement occurs here in only one dimension (temperature), but other goal-seeking devices may use more. The radar-controlled searchlight, for example, uses the reflected impulses to alter its direction of aim so as to minimise the angle between its direction of aim and the bearing of the source of the reflected impulses. So if the aircraft swerves, the searchlight will follow it actively, just as the temperature followed the setting. Such a system is goal-seeking in two dimensions.

The examples show the common feature that each is ' error-controlled ': each is partly controlled by the deviation of the system's state from the state of equilibrium (which, in these examples, can be moved by an outside operation). The thermostat is affected by the difference between the actual and the set temperatures. The searchlight is affected by the difference between the two directions. Thus, *machines with feedback are not subject to the oft-repeated dictum that machines must act blindly and cannot correct their errors.* Such a statement is true of machines without feedback, but not of machines in general (S. 3/11).

Once it is appreciated that feedback can be used to correct any deviation we like, it is easy to understand that there is no limit to the complexity of goal-seeking behaviour which may occur in machines quite devoid of any ' vital ' factor. Thus, an automatic anti-aircraft gun may be controlled by the radar-pulses reflected back both from the target aeroplane and from its own bursting shells, in such a way that it tends to minimise the distance between shell-burst and plane. Such a system, wholly automatic, cannot be distinguished by its behaviour from a humanly operated gun: both will fire at the target, following it through all manœuvres, continually using the errors to improve the next shot. It will be seen, therefore, that a system with feedback may be both wholly automatic and yet actively and complexly goal-seeking. There is no incompatibility.

4/17. It will have been noticed that stability, as defined, in no way implies fixity or rigidity. It is true that the stable system usually has a state of equilibrium at which it shows no change; but the lack of change is deceptive if it suggests rigidity: if displaced from the state of equilibrium it will show active, perhaps extensive and complex, movements. The stable system is restricted only in that it does not show the unrestricted divergencies of instability.

Stability and the whole

4/18. An important feature of a system's stability (or instability) is that *it is a property of the whole system and can be assigned to no part of it.* The statement may be illustrated by a consideration of the first diagram of S. 4/14 as it is related to the practical construction of the thermostat. In order to ensure the stability of the final assembly, the designer must consider:

(1) The effect of the temperature on the diameter of the capsule, i.e. whether a rise in temperature makes the capsule expand or shrink.
(2) Which way an expansion of the capsule moves the lever.
(3) Which way a movement of the lever moves the gas-tap.
(4) Whether a given movement of the gas-tap makes the velocity of gas-flow increase or decrease.
(5) Whether an increase of gas-flow makes the size of the gas-flame increase or decrease.
(6) How an increase in size of the gas-flame will affect the temperature of the capsule.

Some of the answers are obvious, but they must none the less be included. When the six answers are known, the designer can ensure stability only by arranging the components (chiefly by manipulating (2), (3) and (5)) so that as a whole they form an appropriate combination. Thus five of the effects may be decided, yet the stability will still depend on how the sixth is related to them. *The stability belongs only to the combination; it cannot be related to the parts considered separately.*

In order to emphasise that the stability of a system is independent of any conditions which may hold over the parts which compose the whole, some further examples will be given. (Proofs of the statements will be found in Ss. 20/9 and 21/12.)

(*a*) Two systems may be joined so that they act and interact on one another to form a single system: to know that the two systems when separate were both stable is to know nothing about the stability of the system formed by their junction: it may be stable or unstable.

(*b*) Two systems, both unstable, may join to form a whole which is stable.

(*c*) Two systems may form a stable whole if joined in one way, and may form an unstable whole if joined in another way

(*d*) In a stable system the effect of fixing a variable may be to render the remainder unstable.

Such examples could be multiplied almost indefinitely. They illustrate the rule that the stability (or instability) of a dynamic system depends on the parts and their interrelations as a whole.

4/19. The fact that the stability of a system is a property of the system as a whole is related to the fact that *the presence of stability always implies some co-ordination of the actions between the parts.* In the thermostat the necessity for co-ordination is clear, for if the components were assembled at random there would be only an even chance that the assembly would be stable. But as the system and the feedbacks become more complex, so does the achievement of stability become more difficult and the likelihood of instability greater. Radio engineers know only too well how readily complex systems with feedback become unstable, and how difficult is the discovery of just that combination of parts and linkages which will give stability.

The subject is discussed more fully in S. 20/10: here it is sufficient to note that as the number of variables increases so usually do the effects of variable on variable have to be co-ordinated with more and more care if stability is to be achieved.

CHAPTER 5

Adaptation as Stability

5/1. THE concept of ' adaptation ' has so far been used without definition, this vagueness must be corrected. Not only must the definition be precise, but it must, by S. 2/10, be given in terms that can be reduced wholly to primary operations.

5/2. The suggestion that an animal's behaviour is ' adaptive ' if the animal ' responds correctly to a stimulus ' may be rejected at once. First, it presupposes an action by an experimenter and therefore cannot be applied when the free-living organism and its environment affect each other reciprocally. Secondly, the definition provides no meaning for ' correctly ' unless it means ' conforming to what the experimenter thinks the animal ought to do '. Such a definition is useless.

Homeostasis

5/3. I propose the definition that *a form of behaviour is* **adaptive** *if it maintains the essential variables* (S. 3/14) *within physiological limits*. The full justification of such a definition would involve its comparison with all the known facts—an impossibly large task. Nevertheless it is fundamental in this subject and I must discuss it sufficiently to show how fundamental it is and how wide is its applicability.

First I shall outline the facts underlying Cannon's concept of ' homeostasis '. They are not directly relevant to the problem of learning, for the mechanisms are inborn; but the mechanisms are so clear and well known that they provide an ideal basic illustration. They show that:

(1) Each mechanism is ' adapted ' to its end.
(2) Its end is the maintenance of the values of some essential variables within physiological limits.
(3) Almost all the behaviour of an animal's vegetative system is due to such mechanisms.

5/4. As first example may be quoted the mechanisms which tend to maintain within limits the concentration of glucose in the blood. The concentration should not fall below about 0·06 per cent or the tissues will be starved of their chief source of energy; and the concentration should not rise above about 0.18 per cent or other undesirable effects will occur. If the blood-glucose falls below about 0·07 per cent the adrenal glands secrete adrenaline, which makes the liver turn its stores of glycogen into glucose; this passes into the blood and the fall is opposed. In addition, a falling blood-glucose stimulates the appetite so that food is taken, and this, after digestion, provides glucose. On the other hand, if it rises excessively, the secretion of insulin by the pancreas is increased, causing the liver to remove glucose from the blood. The muscles and skin also remove it; and the kidneys help by excreting glucose into the urine if the concentration in the blood exceeds 0·18 per cent. Here then are five activities all of which have the same final effect. Each one acts so as to *restrict* the fluctuations which might otherwise occur. Each may justly be described as ' adaptive ', for it acts to preserve the animal's life.

The temperature of the interior of the warm-blooded animal's body may be disturbed by exertion, or illness, or by exposure to the weather. If the body temperature becomes raised, the skin flushes and more heat passes from the body to the surrounding air, sweating commences, and the evaporation of the water removes heat from the body; and the metabolism of the body is slowed, so that less heat is generated within it. If the body is chilled, these changes are reversed. Shivering may start, and the extra muscular activity provides heat which warms the body. Adrenaline is secreted, raising the muscular tone and the metabolic rate, which again supplies increased heat to the body. The hairs or feathers are moved by small muscles in the skin so that they stand more erect, enclosing more air in the interstices and thus conserving the body's heat. In extreme cold the human being, when almost unconscious, reflexly takes a posture of extreme flexion with the arms pressed firmly against the chest and the legs fully drawn up against the abdomen. The posture is clearly one which exposes to the air a minimum of surface. In all these ways, the body acts so as to maintain its temperature within limits.

The amount of carbon dioxide in the blood is important in its effect on the blood's alkalinity. If the amount rises, the rate and depth of respiration are increased, and carbon dioxide is exhaled at an increased rate. If the amount falls, the reaction is reversed. By this means the alkalinity of the blood is kept within limits.

The retina works best at a certain intensity of illumination. In bright light the nervous system contracts the pupil, and in dim relaxes it. Thus the amount of light entering the eye is maintained within limits.

If the eye is persistently exposed to bright light, as happens when one goes to the tropics, the pigment-cells in the retina grow forward day by day until they absorb a large portion of the incident light before it reaches the sensitive cells. In this way the illumination on the sensitive cells is kept within limits

If exposed to sunshine, the pigment-bearing cells in the skin increase in number, extent, and pigment-content. By this change the degree of illumination of the deeper layers of the skin is kept within limits.

When dry food is chewed, a copious supply of saliva is poured into the mouth. Saliva lubricates the food and converts it from a harsh and abrasive texture to one which can be chewed without injury. The secretion therefore keeps the frictional stresses below the destructive level.

The volume of the circulating blood may be disturbed by haemorrhage. Immediately after a severe haemorrhage a number of changes occur: the capillaries in limbs and muscles undergo constriction, driving the blood from these vessels to the more essential internal organs; thirst becomes extreme, impelling the subject to obtain extra supplies of fluid; fluid from the tissues passes into the blood-stream and augments its volume; and clotting at the wound helps to stem the haemorrhage. A haemorrhage has a second effect in that, by reducing the number of red corpuscles, it reduces the amount of oxygen which can be carried to the tissues; the reduction, however, itself stimulates the bone-marrow to an increased production of red corpuscles. All these actions tend to keep the variables ' volume of circulating blood ' and ' oxygen supplied to the tissues ' within normal limits.

Every fast-moving animal is liable to injury by collision with hard objects. Animals, however, are provided with reflexes that tend to minimise the chance of collision and of mechanical injury. A mechanical stress causes injury—laceration, dislocation, or fracture—only if the stress exceeds some definite value, depending on the stressed tissue—skin, ligament, or bone. So these reflexes act to keep the mechanical stresses within physiological limits.

Many more examples could be given, but all can be included within the same formula. Some external disturbance tends to drive an essential variable outside its normal limits; but the commencing change itself activates a mechanism that *opposes* the external disturbance. By this mechanism the essential variable is maintained within limits much narrower than would occur if the external disturbance were unopposed. The narrowing is the objective manifestation of the mechanism's adaptation.

5/5. The mechanisms of the previous section act mostly within the body, but it should be noted that some of them have acted partly through the environment. Thus, if the body-temperature is raised, the nervous system lessens the generation of heat within the body and the body-temperature falls, but only because the body is continuously losing heat to its surroundings. Flushing of the skin cools the body only if the surrounding air is cool; and sweating lowers the body-temperature only if the surrounding air is unsaturated. Increasing respiration lowers the carbon dioxide content of the blood, but only if the atmosphere contains less than 5 per cent. In each case the chain of cause and effect passes partly through the environment. The mechanisms that work wholly within the body and those that make extensive use of the environment are thus only the extremes of a continuous series. Thus, a thirsty animal seeks water: if it is a fish it does no more than swallow, while if it is an antelope in the veldt it has to go through an elaborate process of search, of travel, and of finding a suitable way down to the river or pond. The homeostatic mechanisms thus extend from those that work wholly within the animal to those that involve its widest-ranging activities; *the principles are uniform throughout*

Generalised homeostasis

5/6. Just the same criterion for ' adaptation ' may be used in judging the behaviour of the free-living animal in its learned reactions. Take the type-problem of the kitten and the fire. When the kitten first approaches an open fire, it may paw at the fire as if at a mouse, or it may crouch down and start to ' stalk ' the fire, or it may attempt to sniff at the fire, or it may walk unconcernedly on to it. Every one of these actions is liable to lead to the animal's being burned. Equally the kitten, if it is cold, may sit far from the fire and thus stay cold. The kitten's behaviour cannot be called adapted, for the temperature of its skin is not kept within normal limits. The animal, in other words, is not acting homeostatically for skin temperature. Contrast this behaviour with that of the experienced cat: on a cold day it approaches the fire to a distance adjusted so that the skin temperature is neither too hot nor too cold. If the fire burns fiercer, the cat will move away until the skin is again warmed to a moderate degree. If the fire burns low the cat will move nearer. If a red-hot coal drops from the fire the cat takes such action as will keep the skin temperature within normal limits. Without making any enquiry at this stage into what has happened to the kitten's brain, we can at least say that whereas at first the kitten's behaviour was not homeostatic for skin temperature, it has now become so. Such behaviour is ' adapted ': it preserves the life of the animal by keeping the essential variables within limits.

The same thesis can be applied to a great deal, if not all, of the normal human adult's behaviour. In order to demonstrate the wide application of this thesis, and in order to show that even Man's civilised life is not exceptional, some of the surroundings which he has provided for himself will be examined for their known physical and physiological effects. It will be shown that each item acts so as to narrow the range of variation of his essential variables.

The first requirement of a civilised man is a house; and its first effect is to keep the air in which he lives at a more equable temperature. The roof keeps his skin at a more constant dryness. The windows, if open in summer and closed in winter, assist in the maintenance of an even temperature, and so do fires and stoves. The glass in the windows keeps the illumination of the rooms nearer the optimum, and artificial lighting has the same effect. The chimneys keep the amount of irritating smoke in the rooms near the optimum, which is zero.

Many of the other conveniences of civilisation could, with little difficulty, be shown to be similarly variation-limiting An attempt to demonstrate them all would be interminable. But to confirm the argument we will examine a motor-car, part by part, in order to show its homeostatic relation to man.

Travel in a vehicle, as contrasted with travel on foot, keeps several essential variables within narrower limits. The fatigue induced by walking for a long distance implies that some variables, as yet not clearly known, have exceeded limits not transgressed when the subject is carried in a vehicle. The reserves of food in the body will be less depleted, the skin on the soles of the feet will be less chafed, the muscles will have endured less strain, in winter the body will have been less chilled, and in summer it will have been less heated, than would have happened had the subject travelled on foot.

When examined in more detail, many ways are found in which it serves us by maintaining our essential variables within narrower limits. The roof maintains our skin at a constant dryness. The windows protect us from a cold wind, and if open in summer, help to cool us. The carpet on the floor acts similarly in winter, helping to prevent the temperature of the feet from falling below its optimal value. The jolts of the road cause, on the skin and bone of the human frame, stresses which are much lessened by the presence of springs. Similar in action are the shock-absorbers and tyres. A collision would cause an extreme deceleration which leads to very high values for the stress on the skin and bone of the passengers. By the brakes these very high values may be avoided, and in this way the brakes keep the variables ' stress on bone ' within narrower limits. Good headlights keep the luminosity of the road within limits narrower than would occur in their absence.

The thesis that ' adaptation ' means the maintenance of essential variables within physiological limits is thus seen to hold not only over the simpler activities of primitive animals but over the more complex activities of the ' higher ' organisms.

5/7. Before proceeding further, it must be noted that the word ' adaptation ' is commonly used in two senses which refer to different processes.

The distinction may best be illustrated by the inborn homeostatic mechanisms: the reaction to cold by shivering, for instance.

Such a mechanism may undergo two types of ' adaptation '. The first occurred long ago and was the change from a species too primitive to show such a reaction to a species which, by natural selection, had developed the reaction as a characteristic inborn feature. The second type of ' adaptation ' occurs when a member of the species, born with the mechanism, is subjected to cold and changes from not-shivering to shivering. The first change involved the development of the mechanism itself; the second change occurs when the mechanism is stimulated into showing its properties.

In the learning process, the first stage occurs when the animal ' learns ': when it changes from an animal not having an adapted mechanism to one which has such a mechanism. The second stage occurs when the developed mechanism changes from in-activity to activity. In this chapter we are concerned with the characteristics of the developed mechanism. The processes which led to its development are discussed in Chapter 9.

5/8. We can now recognise that ' *adaptive* ' *behaviour is equivalent to the behaviour of a stable system, the region of the stability being the region of the phase-space in which all the essential variables lie within their normal limits.*

The view is not new (though it can now be stated with more precision):

> ' Every phase of activity in a living being must be not only a necessary sequence of some antecedent change in its environment, but must be so adapted to this change as to tend to its neutralisation, and so to the survival of the organism. . . . It must also apply to *all* the relations of living beings. It must therefore be the guiding principle, not only in physiology . . . but also in the other branches of biology which treat of the relations of the living animal to its environment and of the factors determining its survival in the struggle for existence.'
>
> (Starling.)
>
> ' In an open system, such as our bodies represent, compounded of unstable material and subjected continuously to disturbing conditions, constancy is in itself evidence that agencies are acting or ready to act, to maintain this constancy.'
>
> (Cannon.)
>
> ' Every material system can exist as an entity only so long as its internal forces, attraction, cohesion, etc., balance the

external forces acting upon it. This is true for an ordinary stone just as much as for the most complex substances; and its truth should be recognised also for the animal organism. Being a definite circumscribed material system, it can only continue to exist so long as it is in continuous equilibrium with the forces external to it: so soon as this equilibrium is seriously disturbed the organism will cease to exist as the entity it was.'

(Pavlov.)

McDougall never used the concept of ' stability ' explicitly, but when describing the type of behaviour which he considered to be most characteristic of the living organism, he wrote:

' Take a billard ball from the pocket and place it upon the table. It remains at rest, and would continue to remain so for an indefinitely long time, if no forces were applied to it. Push it in any direction, and its movement in that direction persists until its momentum is exhausted, or until it is deflected by the resistance of the cushion and follows a new path mechanically determined. . . . Now contrast with this an instance of behaviour. Take a timid animal such as a guinea-pig from its hole or nest, and put it upon the grass plot. Instead of remaining at rest, it runs back to its hole; push it in any other direction, and, as soon as you withdraw your hand, it turns back towards its hole; place any obstacle in its way, and it seeks to circumvent or surmount it, restlessly persisting until it achieves its end or until its energy is exhausted.'

He could hardly have chosen an example showing more clearly the features of stability.

Survival

5/9. Are there aspects of ' adaptation ' not included within the definition of ' stability ' ? Is ' survival ' to be the sole criterion of adaptation ? Is it to be maintained that the Roman soldier who killed Archimedes in Syracuse was better ' adapted ' in his behaviour than Archimedes ?

The question is not easily answered. It is similar to that of S. 3/4 where it was asked whether all the qualities of the living organism could be represented by number; and the answer must be similar. It is assumed that we are dealing primarily with the simpler rather than with the more complex creatures, though the examples of S. 5/6 have shown that some at least of man's activities may be judged properly by this criterion.

In order to survey rapidly the types of behaviour of the more primitive animals, we may examine the classification of Holmes, who intended his list to be exhaustive but constructed it with no reference to the concept of stability. The reader will be able to judge how far our formulation (S. 5/8) is consistent with his scheme, which is given in Table 5/9/1.

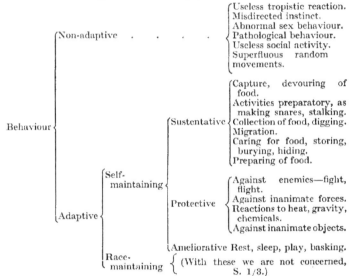

TABLE 5/9/1 : All forms of animal behaviour, classified by Holmes.

For the primitive organism, and excluding behaviour related to racial survival, there seems to be little doubt that the ' adaptiveness ' of behaviour is properly measured by its tendency to promote the organism's survival.

5/10. A most impressive characteristic of living organisms is their mobility, their tendency to change. McDougall expressed this characteristic well in the example of S. 5/8. Yet our formulation transfers the centre of interest to the state of equilibrium, to the fact that the essential variables of the adapted organism change *less* than they would if it were unadapted. Which is important: constancy or change ?

The two aspects are not incompatible, for *the constancy of some variables may involve the vigorous activity of others.* A good thermostat reacts vigorously to a small change of temperature, and the vigorous activity of some of its variables keeps the others within narrow limits. The point of view taken here is that the constancy of the essential variables is fundamentally important, and that the activity of the other variables is important only in so far as it contributes to this end. (The matter is discussed more thoroughly in *I. to C.*, Chapter 10.)

Stability and co-ordination

5/11. So far the discussion has traced the relation between the concepts of 'adaptation' and of 'stability'. It will now be proposed that 'motor co-ordination' also has an essential connexion with stability.

'Motor-co-ordination' is a concept well understood in physiology, where it refers to the ability of the organism to combine the activities of several muscles so that the resulting movement follows accurately its appropriate path. Contrasted to it are the concepts of clumsiness, tremor, ataxia, athetosis. It is suggested that the presence or absence of co-ordination may be decided, in accordance with our methods, by observing whether the movement does, or does not, deviate outside given limits.

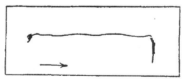

FIGURE 5/11/1.

The formulation seems to be adequate provided that we measure the limb's deviations from some line which is given arbitrarily, usually by a knowledge of the line followed by the normal limb. A first example is given by Figure 5/11/1, which shows the line traced by the point of an expert fencer's foil during a lunge. Any inco-ordination would be shown by a divergence from the intended line.

A second example is given by the record of Figure 5/11/2. The subject, a patient with a tumour in the left cerebellum, was asked to follow the dotted lines with a pen. The left- and right-hand curves were drawn with the respective hands. The tracing shows clearly that the co-ordination is poorer in the left hand. What

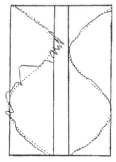

criterion reveals the fact ? The essential distinction is that the deviations of the lines from the dots are larger on the left than on the right.

The degree of motor co-ordination achieved may therefore be measured by the smallness of the deviations from some standard line. Later it will be suggested that there are mechanisms which act to maintain variables within narrow limits. If the identification of this section is accepted, such mechanisms could be regarded as appropriate for the co-ordination of motor activity.

FIGURE 5/11/2 : Record of the attempts of a patient to follow the dotted lines with the left and right hands. (By the courtesy of Dr.W.T. Grant of Los Angeles.)

5/12. So far we have noticed in stable systems only their property of keeping variables within limits. But such systems have other properties of which we shall notice two. They are also shown by animals, and are then sometimes considered to provide evidence that the organism has some power of 'intelligence' not shared by non-living systems. In these two instances the assumption is unnecessary.

The first property is shown by a stable system when the lines of behaviour do not return directly, by a straight line, to the state of equilibrium (e.g. Figure 4/5/3). When this occurs, variables may be observed to move away from their values in the state of equilibrium, only to return to them later. Thus, suppose in Figure 5/12/1 that the field is stable and that at the equilibrial state R x and y have the values X and Y. For clarity, only one line of behaviour is drawn. Let the system be displaced to A and its subsequent behaviour observed. At first, while the representative point moves towards B, y hardly alters; but x, which

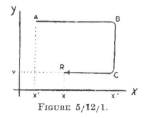

FIGURE 5/12/1.

started at X', moves to X and goes past it to X''. Then x remains almost constant and y changes until the representative point reaches C. Then y stops changing, and x changes towards, and reaches, its resting value X. The system has now reached a state of equilibrium and no further changes occur. This account is just a transcription into words of what the field defines graphically.

Now the shape and features of any field depend ultimately on the real physical and chemical construction of the ' machine ' from which the variables are abstracted. The fact that the line of behaviour does not run straight from A to R must be due to some feature in the ' machine ' such that if the machine is to get from state A to state R, states B and C must be passed through of necessity. Thus, if the machine contained moving parts, their shapes might prohibit the direct route from A to R; or if the system were chemical the prohibition might be thermodynamic. But in either case, if the observer watched the machine work, and thought it alive, he might say: ' How clever! x couldn't get from A to R directly because this bar was in the way, so x went to B, which made y carry x from B to C; and once at C, x could get straight back to R. I believe x shows foresight.'

Both points of view are reasonable. A stable system may be regarded both as blindly obeying the laws of its nature, and also as showing skill in getting back to its state of equilibrium in spite of obstacles.*

5/13. The second property is shown when an organism reacts to a variable with which it is not directly in contact. Suppose, for instance, that the diagram of immediate effects (S. 4/12) is that of Figure 5/13/1; the variables have been divided by the dotted line into ' animal ' on the right and ' environment ' on the left, and the animal is not in direct contact with the variable marked X. The system is assumed to be stable, i.e. to have

---

* I would like to acknowledge that much of what I am describing was arrived at independently by G. Sommerhoff. I met his *Analytical Biology* only when the first edition of *Design for a Brain* was in proof, and I could do no more than add his title to my list of references. Since then it has become apparent that our work was developing in parallel, for there is a deep similarity of outlook and method in the two books. The superficial reader might notice some differences and think we are opposed, but I am sure the distinctions are only on minor matters of definition or emphasis. The reader who wishes to explore these topics further should consult his book as a valuable independent contribution.

arrived at the 'adapted' condition (S. 5/7). If disturbed, its changes will show co-ordination of part with part (S. 5/12), and this co-ordination will hold over the whole system (S. 4/18). It follows that the behaviour of the 'animal'-part will be co-ordinated with the behaviour of X although the 'animal' has no immediate contact with it   (Example in S. 8/7.)

In the higher organisms, and especially in Man, the power to react correctly to something not immediately visible or tangible has been called 'imagination', or 'abstract thinking', or several other names whose precise meaning need not be discussed at the moment.   Here we should notice that the co-ordination of

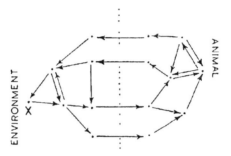

FIGURE 5/13/1

the behaviour of one part with that of another part not in direct contact with it is simply an elementary property of the stable system.

5/14.   Let us now re-state our problem in the new vocabulary. If, for brevity, we omit minor qualifications, we can state it thus: A determinate 'machine' changes from a form that produces chaotic, unadapted behaviour to a form in which the parts are so co-ordinated that the whole is stable, acting to maintain its essential variables within certain limits—how can this happen ? For example, what sort of a thermostat could, if assembled at random, rearrange its own parts to get itself stable for temperature?

It will be noticed that the new statement involves the concept of a machine changing its internal organisation.   So far, nothing has been said of this important concept; so it will be treated in the next chapter.

CHAPTER 6

Parameters

6/1. So far, we have discussed the changes shown by the variables of a state-determined system, and have ignored the fact that all its changes occur on a background, or on a foundation, of constancies. Thus, a particular simple pendulum provides two variables which are known (S. 2/15) to be such that, if we are given a particular state of the system, we can predict correctly its ensuing behaviour ; what has not been stated explicitly is that this is true only if the length of the string remains constant. The background, and these constancies, must now be considered.

Every system is formed by selecting some variables out of the totality of possible variables. ' Forming a system ' means dividing the variables of the universe into two classes: those within the system and those without. These two types of variable are in no way different in their intrinsic physical nature, but they stand in very different relations to the system.

6/2. *Given a system, a variable not included in it is a* **parameter.** The word *variable* will, from now on, be reserved for one within the system.

In general, given a system, the parameters will differ in their closeness of relation to it. Some will have a direct relation to it : change of their value would affect the system to a major degree; such is the parameter ' length of pendulum ' in its relation to the two-variable system of the previous section. Some are less closely related to it, their changes producing only a slight effect on it; such is the parameter ' viscosity of the air ' in relation to the same system. And finally, for completeness, may be mentioned the infinite number of parameters that are without detectable effect on the system; such are the brightness of the light shining on the pendulum, the events in an adjacent room, and the events in the distant nebulae. Those without detectable effect may be ignored; but the relationship of an effective parameter to a system must be clearly understood.

71

Given a system, the effective parameters are usually innumerable, so that a list is bounded only by the imagination of the writer. Thus, parameters whose change might affect the behaviour of the same system of two variables are:

(1) the length of the pendulum (hitherto assumed constant),
(2) the lateral velocity of the air (hitherto assumed to be constant at zero),
(3) the viscosity of the surrounding medium (hitherto assumed constant),
(4) the movement, if any, of the point of support,
(5) the force of gravity,
(6) the magnetic field in which it swings,
(7) the elastic constant of the string of the pendulum,
(8) its electrostatic charge, and the charges on bodies nearby ;
but the list has no end.

Parameter and field

6/3. The effect on a state-determined system of a change of parameter-value will now be shown. Table 6/3/1 shows the

Length (cm.)	Line	Variable	Time						
			0	0·05	0·10	0·15	0·20	0·25	0·30
40	1	x	0		14	20	25	28	29
		y	147	142	129	108	80	48	12
	2	x	14	20	25	28	29	29	27
		y	129	108	80	48	12	— 24	— 58
60	3	x	0	7	14	21	26	31	34
		y	147	144	135	121	101	78	51
	4	x	21	26	31	34	36	36	35
		y	121	101	78	51	23	— 6	— 36

TABLE 6/3/1.

results of twenty-four primary operations applied to the two-variable system mentioned above. x is the angular deviation from the vertical, in degrees, y is the angular velocity, in degrees per second, the time is in seconds.

The first two Lines show that the lines of behaviour following the state $x = 14$, $y = 129$ are equal, so the system, as far as it has been tested, is state-determined. The line of behaviour is shown solid in Figure 6/3/1. In these swings the length of the pendulum was 40 cm. This parameter was then changed to 60 cm. and two further lines of behaviour were observed. On these two, the lines of behaviour following the state $x = 21$, $y = 121$ are equal, so the system is again state-determined. The line of behaviour is shown dotted in the same figure. But the change of parameter-value has caused the line of behaviour from $x = 0$, $y = 147$ to change.

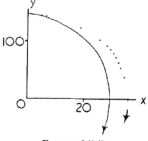

FIGURE 6/3/1.

The relationship which the parameter bears to the two variables is therefore as follows :

(1) So long as the parameter is constant, the system of x and y is state-determined, and has a definite field.

(2) After the parameter changes from one constant value to another, the system of x and y becomes again state-determined, and has a definite field, but this field is not the same as the previous one.

The relation is general. A change in the value of an effective parameter changes the line of behaviour from each state. From this follows at once: *a change in the value of an effective parameter changes the field.*

From this follows the important quantitative relation: a system can, in general, show as many fields as its parameters can show combinations of values.

6/4. The importance of distinguishing between change of a variable and change of a parameter, that is, between change of state and change of field, can hardly be over-estimated. It is this distinction that will enable us to avoid the confusion threatened in S. 2/1 between those changes that *are* behaviour and changes that occur from one behaviour to another. In order to make the distinction clear I will give some examples.

In a working clock, the single variable defined by the reading
of the minute-hand on the face is state-determined as a one-
variable system, for after some observations of its behaviour, we
can predict the line of behaviour which will follow any given state.
If now the regulator (the parameter) is moved to a new position,
so that the clock runs at a different rate, and the system is re-
examined, it will be found to be still state-determined but to have
a different field.

If a healthy person drinks 100 g. of glucose dissolved in water,
the amount of glucose in his blood usually rises and falls as A
in Figure 6/4/1.   The single variable ' blood-glucose ' is not state-

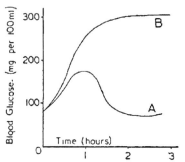

FIGURE 6/4/1 . Changes in blood-glucose after the ingestion of 100 g.
of glucose . (A) in the normal person, (B) in the diabetic.

determined, for a given state (e.g. 120 mg./100 ml.) does not
define the subsequent behaviour, for the blood-glucose may rise or
fall. By adding a second variable, however, such as ' rate of
change of blood-glucose ', which may be positive or negative, we
obtain a two-variable system which is sufficiently state-determined
for illustration   The field of this two-variable system will resemble that of A in Figure 6/4/2.   But if the subject is diabetic,
the curve of the blood-glucose, even if it starts at the same initial
value, rises much higher, as B in Figure 6/4/1.   When the field
of this behaviour is drawn (B, Figure 6/4/2), it is seen to be not the
same as that of the normal subject.   The change of value of the
parameter ' degree of diabetes present ' has thus changed the
field.

Girden and Culler developed a conditioned response in a dog
which was under the influence of curare (a paralysing drug).

When later the animal was not under its influence, the conditioned response could not be elicited. But when the dog was again put under its influence, the conditioned response returned   Thus

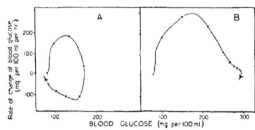

FIGURE 6/4/2. Fields of the two lines of behaviour, A and B from Figure 6/4/1. Cross-strokes mark each quarter-hour.

two characteristic lines of behaviour (two responses to the stimulus) existed, and one line of behaviour was shown when the parameter ' concentration of curare in the tissues ' had a high value, and the other when the parameter had a low value.

Stimuli

6/5. Many stimuli may be represented adequately as a change of parameter-value, so it is convenient here to relate the physiological and psychological concept of a ' stimulus ' to our methods.

In all cases the diagram of immediate effects is

(experimenter) $\rightarrow$ stimulator $\rightarrow$ animal $\rightarrow$ recorders.

In some cases the animal, at some state of equilibrium, is subjected to a sudden change in the value of the stimulator, and the second value is sustained throughout the observation. Thus, the pupillary reaction to light is demonstrated by first accustoming the eye to a low intensity of illumination, and then suddenly raising the illumination to a high level which is maintained while the reaction proceeds. In such cases the stimulator is parameter to the system ' animal and recorders '; and the physiologist's comparison of the previous control-behaviour with the behaviour after stimulation is equivalent, in our method, to a comparison of the two lines of behaviour that, starting from the same initial state, run in the two fields provided by the two values of the stimulator. In this type, the stimulator behaves as a step-function (S. 7/13).

Sometimes a parameter is changed sharply and is immediately returned to its initial value, as when the experimenter applies a a tap on a tendon. The effect of the parameter-change is a brief change of field which, while it lasts, carries the representative point away from its original position. When the parameter is returned to its original value, the original field and state of equilibrium are restored, but the representative point is now away from the state of equilibrium; it therefore moves along a line of behaviour, and the organism 'responds'. (Usually the point returns to the same state of equilibrium: but if there is more than one, it may go to some other state of equilibrium.) Such a stimulus will be called **impulsive.**

It will be necessary later to be more precise about what we mean by 'the' stimulus. Consider, for instance, a dog developing a conditioned reflex to the ringing of an electric bell. What is the stimulus exactly? Is it the closing of the contact switch? The intermittent striking of the hammer on the bell? The vibrations in the air? The vibrations of the ear-drum, of the ossicles, of the basilar membrane? The impulses in the acoustic nerve, in the temporal cortex? If we are to be precise we must recognise that the experimenter controls directly only the contact switch, and that this acts as parameter to the complexly-acting system of electric bell, middle ear, and the rest.

When the 'stimulus' becomes more complex we must generalise. One generalisation increases the number of parameters made to alter, as when a conditioned dog is subjected to combinations of a ticking metronome, a smell of camphor, a touch on the back, and a flashing light. Here we should notice that if the parameters are not all independent but change in groups, like the variables in S. 3/3, we can represent each undivided group by a single value and thus avoid using unnecessarily large numbers of parameters.

Joining dynamic systems

6/6. We can now make clear what is meant, essentially, by the concept of two (or more) systems being 'joined'.

This concept is of the highest importance in biology, in which it occurs frequently and prominently. It occurs whenever we think of one system having an effect on another, or communicating with it, or forcing it, or signalling to it.

(The exact nature of the operation of joining is shown most clearly in the mathematical form (S. 21/9) for there one can see what is essential and what irrelevant   A detailed treatment has been given in *I. to C.*, S. 4/6; here we can discuss it less rigorously.)

To join two systems, *A* and *B* say, so that *A* affects *B*, *A* must affect *B*'s conditions.   In other words, the values of some of *B*'s parameters (perhaps one only) must become functions of (dependent on) the values of *A*'s variables.   Thus, if *B* is a developing egg in an incubator and *A* is the height of the barometer, then *A* could be ' joined ' so as to affect *B* if the temperature (or other suitable parameter) were made sensitive to the pressure.

In this example there is no obvious way of making the development of the egg affect the height of the barometer, so the joining of *B* to *A* can hardly be done.   In most cases, however, joinings are possible in either direction.   If both are made, then feedback has been set up between the two systems.

In very simple cases, the behaviour of the whole formed by joining parts can be traced step by step by logical or mathematical deduction.   Each part can be thought of as having its own phase-space, filled by a field, which field it is will depend on the position of the other part's representative point.   Each representative point now undergoes a transition, guided by its own field, whose form depends on the position of the other.   So step by step, each goes forward guided by the other and also guiding it.   (The process has been traced in detail in *I. to C.*, S. 4/7.)

This picture is too complicated for any imaginative grasp of how two actual systems will behave; the details must be worked out by some other method.   What is important is that the nature of the process is conceptually quite free from vagueness or ambiguity; so it may properly be included in a rigorous theory of dynamic systems.

Parameter and stability

6/7.   We now reach the main point of the chapter.   Because a change of parameter-value changes the field, and because a system's stability depends on its field, *a change of parameter-value will in general change a system's stability in some way.*

A simple example is given by a mixture of hydrogen, nitrogen, and ammonia, which combine or dissociate until the concentrations reach the state of equilibrium. If the mixture was originally derived from pure ammonia, the single variable 'percentage dissociated' forms a one-variable state-determined system. Among its parameters are temperature and pressure. As is well known, changes in these parameters affect the position of the state of equilibrium.

Such a system is simple and responds to the changes of the parameters with only a simple shift of equilibrium. No such limitation applies generally. Change of parameter-value may result in any change which can be produced by the substitution of one field for another: stable systems may become unstable, states of equilibrium may be moved, single states of equilibrium may become multiple, states of equilibrium may become cycles; and so on. Figure 21/8/1 provides an illustration.

Here we need only the relationship, which is reciprocal. in a state-determined system, *a change of stability can only be due to change of value of a parameter*, and *change of value of a parameter causes a change in stability*

Equilibria of part and whole

6/8. In general, as S. 4/18 showed, the relation between the stabilities of the parts and that of the whole may be complex, and may require specialised methods for its treatment. There is, however, one quite simple relationship that will be of the greatest use to us and which can be readily described.

Suppose we join two parts, A with variables u and v, and B with variables w, x and y. If A's variables have values 7 and 2, and B's have values 3, 1 and 5, then the whole is, naturally, a system with the five variables u, v, w, x and y; and in the corresponding state the variables of the whole have the values 7, 2, 3, 1 and 5 respectively.

Suppose now that this state—(7, 2, 3, 1, 5)—of the whole is a state of equilibrium of the whole. This implies that the transition is from that state to itself (S. 4/4). This implies that A, with the values 3, 1, 5 on its parameters, goes from (7, 2) to (7, 2); i.e. does not change. Thus, the whole's being at a state of equilibrium at (7, 2, 3, 1, 5) implies that A, when at (7, 2), with values (3, 1, 5) on its parameters, must be at a state of equilibrium. Similarly B, when its parameters are at (7, 2), must have a state of equilibrium at (3, 1, 5). So, the whole's being at a state of equilibrium implies that each part must be at a state of equilibrium, in the conditions provided (at its parameters) by the other parts.

Conversely, suppose A is in equilibrium at state (7, 2) when its parameters have the values (3, 1, 5); and that B is in equilibrium at state (3, 1, 5) when its parameters are at (7, 2). It follows that the whole will have a state of equilibrium at the state (7, 2, 3, 1, 5), for at this state neither A nor B can change.

To sum up: *That a whole dynamic system should be in equilibrium at a particular state it is necessary and sufficient that each part should be in equilibrium at that state. in the conditions given to it by the other parts.*

6/9.   Suppose now that a whole, made by joining parts, is moving along a line of behaviour. Suppose the line of behaviour meets a state that is one of equilibrium for one part (in the conditions given at that moment by the others) but not equilibrial for the other parts. The part in equilibrium will stop, momentarily; but the other parts, not in equilibrium, will change their states and will thereby change the conditions of the part in equilibrium. Usually the change of conditions (change of parameter-values) will make the state no longer one of equilibrium· so the part that stopped willl now start moving again.

Clearly, at any state of the whole, if a single part is not at equilibrium (even though the remainder are) this part will change, will provide new conditions for the other parts, will thus start them moving again, and will thus prevent that state from being one of equilibrium for the whole   As equilibrium of the whole requires that *all* the parts be in equilibrium, we can say (metaphorically) that every part has a *power of veto* over the states of equilibrium of the whole.

6/10.   The importance of this fact can now be indicated. By this fact each part acts *selectively* towards the set of possible equilibria of the whole. Since Chapter 1 we have been looking for some factor that can be both mechanistic and also selective. The next chapter will show this factor in action.

CHAPTER 7

The Ultrastable System

7/1. WE have now assembled the necessary concepts. They are all defined as relations between primary operations, so they are fully objective and conform to the basic requirements of S. 2/10. We can now reconsider the basic problem of S. 5/14, and can consider what is implied by the fact that the kitten changes from having a cerebral mechanism that produces un-adapted behaviour to having one which produces behaviour that is adapted.

The implications of adaptation

7/2. In accordance with S. 3/11, the kitten and environment are to be considered as interacting; so the diagram of immediate effects will be of the form of Figure 7/2/1. (The diagram resembles

FIGURE 7/2/1.

that of Figure 5/13/1, except that the fine net-work of linkages that actually exists in environ-ment and R has been represented by shading.) The arrows to and from R represent, of course, the sensory and motor channels. The part R belongs to the organism, but is here defined purely func-tionally; at this stage any attempt to identify R with anatomical or histological structures must be made with caution. R is defined as the *system* that acts when the kitten reacts to the fire—the part responsible for the overt behaviour.

It was also given, in S. 5/14, that the kitten has a variety of possible reactions, some wrong, some right. This variety of reactions implies, by S. 6/3, that some parameters, call them S, have a variety of values, i.e. are not fixed throughout. These parameters, since their primary action is to affect the kitten's behaviour (and only mediately that of the environment), evidently have an immediate effect on R but not on the environment.

Thus we get Figure 7/2/2. By S. 6/3, the number of distinct values possible to S must be at least as great as the number of distinct ways of behaving (both adapted and non-adapted) possible to R.

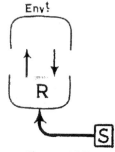

FIGURE 7/2/2.

7/3. The essential variables must now be introduced; what affects them ? Clearly they must be affected by something, for we are not interested in the case of the organism that is immortal because nothing threatens it. Possibilities are that they are affected by the environment, by R, or by both.

The case of most interest is that in which they are immediately affected by the environment only. This case makes the problem for the kitten as harsh, as realistic as possible. This is the case when a hot coal falls from the fire and rolls towards the kitten: the environment threatens to have a direct effect on the essential variables, for if the kitten's brain does nothing the kitten will get burnt. This is the case when the animal in the desert is being dried by the heat, so that if the animal does nothing it will die of thirst.

Immediate effects from R to the essential variables would be appropriate if the kitten's brain could act so as to change it from an organism that must not get burnt to one that benefited by being burnt ! (Such a change of goal may be of importance in the higher functionings of the nervous system, when a *sub*-goal may be established or changed provisionally; but the situation does not occur at the fundamental level that we are considering here, and we shall not consider such possibilities further.)

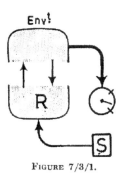

FIGURE 7/3/1.

The diagram of immediate effects now has the form of Figure 7/3/1. The essential variables have been represented collectively by a dial with a pointer, and with two limit-marks, to emphasise that what matters about the essential variables is whether or not the value is within physiological limits.

7/4. Continuing to examine the case that gives the kitten the maximal difficulty, let us consider the case in which the effects that the various states of the environment will have on the essential variables, though definite, is not known to the reacting part R. This is the case of a bird, driven to a strange island and seeing a strange berry, who does not know whether it is poisonous or not. It is the case of the cat in Thorndike's cage, who does not know whether the lever must be pushed to right or left for the door to open. It is the assumption made in S.1/17, where the kitten was confronted with a fire as an example of an organism in a situation where its previous experience gave no reliable indication of how the various states of the environment were paired to the states ' within ' and ' without ' the physiological limits of the essential variables.

To be adapted, the organism, guided by information from the environment, must control its essential variables, forcing them to go within the proper limits, by so manipulating the environment (through its motor control of it) that the environment then acts on them appropriately. Thus the diagram of immediate effects of this process is

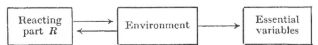

In the case we are considering, the reacting part R is not specially related or adjusted to what is in the environment and how it is joined to the essential variables. Thus the reacting part R can be thought of as an organism trying to control the output of a Black Box (the environment), the contents of which is unknown to it.

It is axiomatic (for *any* Black Box when the range of its inputs is *given*) that the only way in which the nature of its contents can be elicited is by the transmission of actions through it. This means that input-values must be given, output-values observed, and the relationships in the paired values noticed. In the kitten's case, this means that the kitten must *do* various things to the environment and must later act in accordance with how these actions affected the essential variables. In other words, it must proceed by trial and error.

Adaptation by trial and error is sometimes treated in psychological writings as if it were merely one way of adaptation, and an inferior way at that. The argument given above shows that the method of trial and error holds a much more fundamental place in the methods of adaptation. The argument shows, in fact, that when the organism has to adapt (to get its essential variables within physiological limits) by working through an environment that is of the nature of a Black Box, then the process of trial and error is *necessary*, for only such a process can elicit the required information.

The process of trial and error can thus be viewed from two very different points of view. On the one hand it can be regarded as simply an attempt at success; so that when it fails we give zero marks for success. From this point of view it is merely a second-rate way of getting to success. There is, however, the other point of view that gives it an altogether higher status, for the process may be playing the invaluable part of *gathering information*, information that is absolutely necessary if adaptation is to be successfully achieved. It is for this reason that the process *must* enter into the kitten's adaptation.

7/5. As the kitten proceeds by trial and error, its final behaviour will depend on the outcome of the trials, on how the essential variables have been affected. This is equivalent to saying that the essential variables are to have an effect on *which* behaviour the kitten will produce; and this is equivalent to saying that in the diagram of immediate effects there must be a channel *from* the essential variables *to* the parameters S; so it will resemble Figure 7/5/1. The organism that can adapt thus has a motor output to the environment and *two* feedback loops. The first loop was shown in Figure 7/2/1; it consists of the ordinary sensory input from eye, ear, joints, etc., giving the organism non-affective information about the world around it.

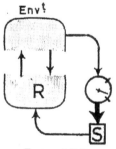

FIGURE 7/5/1.

The second feedback goes through the essential variables (including such correlated variables as the pain receptors, S. 3/15); it carries information about whether the essential variables are or are not driven outside the normal limits, and it acts on the parameters S. The first feedback plays its part *within* each reaction; the second determines which reaction shall occur

7/6. Since the argument here is crucial, let us trace it in detail, using the basic operational concepts of S 2/7–10.

We start with the common observation that the burned kitten dreads the fire. Translated into full operational form, this observation becomes:

(1) with the essential variables *within* their limits, the overt behaviour (of R) is such as is consequent on the parameters having values S_1;

(2) when the essential variables are sent *outside* the limits (i.e if the kitten is burned), the overt behaviour is such as is consequent on their having values S_2.

That the overt behaviour is changed shows that S_2 is not the same as S_1. Thus the two different values at the essential variables have led to *different* values at S; there is therefore *an immediate effect from the essential variables to the parameters S*.

7/7. The same data will now provide us with the necessary information about what happens within the second loop, i.e. how the essential variables affect the parameters.

The basic rule for adaptation by trial and error is —If the trial is unsuccessful, change the way of behaving; when and only when it is successful, retain the way of behaving Now consider the system S and how it must behave. Within this system are the variables that are identical with the parameters to R (a mere change of name), and to this system the essential variables are parameters, i e. come as input. The basic rule is equivalent to the following formulation:

(1) When the essential variables are not all within their normal limits (i.e. when the trial has failed), *no* state of S is to be equilibrial (for the rule here is that S must go to some other state).

(2) When the essential variables *are* all within normal limits then *every* state of S is to be equilibrial (i.e. S is to be in neutral equilibrium).

84

7/8. What has been deduced so far in this Chapter is *necessary*. That is to say, *any* system that has essential variables with given limits, and that adapts by the process of testing various behaviours by how each affects ultimately the essential variables, must have a second feedback formally identical (isomorphic) with that described here. This deduction holds equally for brains living and mechanical.

To be quite clear in this matter, let us consider the alternative. Suppose some new species, or some new mechanical brain, were found to change from the non-adapted to the adapted condition (S. 5/7), doing this consistently even when confronted with quite new situations; and suppose that, in spite of what was said above, investigation showed conclusively that there was no second feedback of the type described—what would we say?

There seem to be only two possibilities. We must either invoke a hitherto unknown channel (in spite of the investigations), as one was invoked after the demonstration by Hertz (S. 4/13); or we must be willing to accept as natural that the system S should go to correct values without being given an appropriate input. This second possibility would be accepted by no one, for the situation would be like asking an examiner to accept as natural a candidate who gives the correct answers without being given the questions! If this possibility is rejected, we are left only with the possibility that the second channel, in some form or other, *must* be there.

The implications of double feedback

7/9. We may now usefully consider the relation between adaptive behaviour and mechanism from the opposite point of view. So far in this chapter we have taken the facts of adaptive behaviour as given and have deduced something of the underlying mechanism. We will now take the mechanism and ask: Given such a mechanism, in whatever material form, will it necessarily show adaptive behaviour? The answer to this question will occupy the remainder of this chapter and the next.

7/10. Let us get the basic assumptions clear for a completely new start, assuming from here to the end of the chapter only what is stated explicitly.

We assume that we have before us some system that has the diagram of immediate effects shown in Figure 7/5/1. Some variable, or several, called ' essential ', is given to act on a system S so that if the variable (or all of them) is within given limits, S is unchanging; but if it is outside the limits, S changes always. (An adequate variety of values is assumed possible to S so that it does not develop, for instance, simple cyclic repetitions.)   A system called ' environment ' interacts with another system R. Environment has some effect on the variable called essential, and S has some effect on R.   Given this, and nothing more, does it follow that the system R will change from acting non-adaptively towards the environment, to acting adaptively towards it?   (At the moment I wish to add no further assumption; in particular I do not wish to restrict the generality by making any assumption that R is composed of parts resembling neurons.)

7/11.   Because the whole consists of two parts coupled—on the one side the environment and reacting part R, and on the other the essential variables and S—we can use the veto-theorem of S. 6/9.   This says that the whole can have as states of equilibrium only such states as allow a state of equilibrium in both the essential variables and S.   Now S is at equilibrium only when the essential variables are within the given limits.   It follows that all the possible equilibria of the whole have the essential variables within the given limits.   So if the whole is started at some state and goes along the corresponding line of behaviour, then if it goes to an equilibrium, *the equilibrium will always be found to be an adapted one.*

Thus we arrive at the solution of the problem posed at the end of Chapter 1; the mechanism has been shown to be necessary by S. 7/8, and sufficient by the present section

7/12.   This solution, however, is severely abstract and leaves unanswered a great number of supplementary questions that are apt to be asked on the topic.   Further, it leaves one with no vivid imaginative or intuitive conception of what is going on when a system (one as complex as a human being, say) goes about its business.   The remainder of the book will therefore be concerned with expanding the solution's many implications and specialisations.

Here, however, a difficulty arises. The attempt to follow, conceptually and imaginatively, the actual events in the whole system, as environment poses problems to the essential variables (by threatening to drive them outside their normal limits), as the values in S determine a particular way of behaving in R, as R behaves in that way, interacting with the environment at every moment, as the outcome falls on the essential variables, as S is (or perhaps is not) changed, as R behaves in a new way—all this is apt to be exceedingly complex and difficult to grasp conceptually if the variables in environment, R, and S all change continuously, i.e. by infinitesimal steps.

Experience has shown that the whole system, and its psychological and physiological implications, are much easier to grasp and understand if we study the particular case in which the variables in environment and R all vary continuously, while those in S vary discretely (i e by finite jumps, occurring at finite intervals) Evidence will be given, in S. 9/4, suggesting that such discrete variables are in fact likely sometimes to be of real importance in the subject; for the time, however, let us regard them as merely selected by us for our easier apprehension.

Step-functions

7/13. Sometimes the behaviour of a variable (or parameter) can be described without reference to the cause of the behaviour· if we say a variable or system is a 'simple harmonic oscillator' the meaning of the phrase is well understood. In this book we shall be more interested in the extent to which a variable displays constancy. Four types may be distinguished, and are illustrated in Figure 7/13/1. (A) The **full-function** has no finite interval of constancy; many common physical variables are of this type: the height of the barometer, for instance. (B) The **part-function** has finite intervals of change and finite intervals of constancy; it will be considered more fully in S. 12/18. (C) The **step-function** has finite intervals of constancy separated by instantaneous jumps. And, to complete the set, we need (D) the **null-function**, which shows no change over the whole period of observation. The four types obviously include all the possibilities, except for mixed forms. The variables of Figure 2/12/1 will be found to be part-, full-, step-, and step-functions respectively.

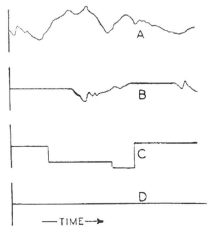

FIGURE 7/13/1 : Types of behaviour of a variable : *A*, the full-function ; *B*, the part-function ; *C*, the step-function ; *D*, the null-function.

In all cases the type-property is assumed to hold only over the period of observation: what might happen at other times is irrelevant.

Sometimes physical entities cannot readily be allotted their type. Thus, a steady musical note may be considered either as unvarying in intensity, and therefore a null-function, or as represented by particles of air which move continuously, and therefore a full-function. In all such cases the confusion is at once removed if one ceases to think of the real physical object with its manifold properties, and selects that variable in which one happens to be interested.

7/14. Step-functions occur abundantly in nature, though the very simplicity of their properties tends to keep them inconspicuous. ' Things in motion sooner catch the eye than what not stirs '. The following examples approximate to the step-function, and show its ubiquity:

> (1) The electric switch has an *electrical resistance* which remains constant except when it changes by a sudden jump.
> (2) The *electrical resistance* of a fuse similarly stays at a low value for a time and then suddenly changes to a very high value.

(3) If a piece of rubber is stretched, the pull it exerts is approximately proportional to its length. The *constant of proportionality* has a definite constant value unless the elastic is stretched so far that it breaks. When this happens the constant of proportionality suddenly becomes zero, i.e. it changes as a step-function.

(4) If strong acid is added in a steady stream to an unbuffered alkaline solution, the pH changes in approximately step-function form.

(5) If alcohol is added slowly with mixing to an aqueous solution of protein, the *amount of protein* precipitated changes in approximately step-function form.

(6) As the pH is changed, the *amount of adsorbed substance* often changes in approximately step-function form.

(7) By quantum principles, many *atomic* and *molecular variables* change in step-function form.

(8) Any variable which acts only in ' all or none ' degree shows this form of behaviour if each degree is sustained over a finite interval.

7/15.   Whether a real variable may or may not be represented by a step-function will usually depend on the method and perhaps instrumentation of observation. Observers and instruments do not, in practice, record values over both very short and very long intervals simultaneously. Thus if the honey-gathering flights of a bee are being studied throughout a day, the observer does not

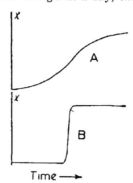

FIGURE 7/15/1 : The same change viewed . (*A*) over one interval of time, (*B*) over an interval twenty times as long.

usually follow the bee's movements into the details of the wing going up and down, neither does he follow the changes that correspond to the bee's being a little older after the day's work. The changes of wing-position are ignored as being too fast, only an average being noticed, and the changes of age are ignored as being too slow, the values being treated as approximately constant. Thus, whether a variable of a real object behaves as a step-function cannot in general be decided until the details of the method of observation is specified

The distinction is illustrated in Figure 7/15/1 in which $x = \tanh t$ has been graphed. If observed from $t = -2$ to $t = +2$, the graph has form A, and is obviously not of step-function form. But if graphed from $t = -100$ to $t = +100$, the result is B, and the curve is approximating to the step-function form.

7/16. As a second example, consider the Post Office type relay. If observed from second to second the conductivity across its contacts varies almost exactly in step-function form. If, however, the conductivity is observed over microseconds, the values change in a much more continuous way, for the contacts can now be seen to accelerate, decelerate, and bounce with a graceful and continuous trajectory. And if the relay is observed over many years and the conductivity plotted, the curve will not be flat but will fall gradually as oxidation and wear affect the contacts.

We have here yet another example of the thesis that specifying a real object does not uniquely specify the system or the behaviour (Ss 2/4 and 6/2). A question such as ' Is the behaviour of the Post Office relay *really* of step-function form ? ' is improperly put, for it asks about a real object what is determined only by the system, which must be specified. (The matter is taken up again in S. 9/10.)

7/17. Behaviour of step-function form is likely to be seen whenever we observe a ' machine ' whose component parts are fast-acting. Thus, if we casually alter the settings of an unknown electronic machine we are not unlikely to observe, from time to time, sudden changes of step-function form, the suddenness being due to the speed with which the machine changes.

A reason can be given most simply by reference to Figure 4/3/1.

Suppose that the curvature of the surface is controlled by a para-meter which makes A rise and B fall. If the ball is resting at A, the parameter's first change will make no difference to the ball's lateral position, for it will continue to rest at A (though with lessened reaction if displaced). As the parameter is changed further, the ball will continue to remain at A until A and B are level. Still the ball will make no movement. But if the para-meter goes on changing and A rises above B, and if gravitation is intense and the ball fast-moving, then the ball will suddenly move to B. And here it will remain, however high A becomes and however low B. So, if the parameter changes steadily, the lateral position of the ball will tend to change in step-function form, approximating more closely as the passage of the ball for a given degree of slope becomes swifter.

The possibility need not be examined further, for no exact deductions will be drawn from it. The section is intended only to show that step-functions occur not uncommonly when the system under observation contains fast-acting components. The subject will be referred to again in S. 9/8.

7/18. In any state-determined system, the behaviour of a variable at any instant depends on the values which the variable and the others have at that instant (S. 2/15). If one of the variables behaves as a step-function the rule still applies: whether the variable remains constant or undergoes a change is determined both by the value of the variable and by the values of the other variables. So, given a state-determined system with a step-mechanism* at a particular value, all the states with the step-mechanism at that value can be divided into two classes: those whose occurrence does and those whose occurrence does not lead to a change in the step-mechanism's value. The former are its **critical states**: should one of them occur, the step-function will change value. The critical state of an electric fuse is the number of amperes which will cause it to blow. The critical state of the ' constant of proportionality ' of an elastic strand is the length at which it breaks.

An example from physiology is provided by the urinary bladder

---

* I am indebted to Dr. J. O. Wisdom for the suggestion that a mechanism showing a step-function as its main characteristic could conveniently be called a ' step-mechanism '

when it has developed an automatic intermittently-emptying action after spinal section. The bladder fills steadily with urine, while at first the spinal centres for micturition remain inactive. When the volume of urine exceeds a certain value the centres become active and urine is passed. When the volume falls below

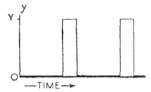

FIGURE 7/18/1 : Diagram of the changes in x, volume of urine in the bladder, and y, activity in the centre for micturition, when automatic action has been established after spinal section.

a certain value, the centre becomes inactive and the bladder refills. A graph of the two variables would resemble Figure 7/18/1. The two-variable system is state-determined, for it has the field of Figure 7/18/2. The variable y is approximately a step-function.

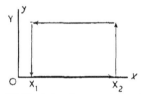

FIGURE 7/18/2 : Field of the changes shown in Figure 7/18/1.

When it is at 0, its critical state is $x = X_2$, $y = 0$, for the occurrence of this state determines a jump from 0 to Y. When it is at Y, its critical state is $x = X_1$, $y = Y$, for the occurrence of this state determines a jump from Y to 0.

7/19. A common, though despised, property of every machine is that it may ' break '. This event is in no sense unnatural, since it must follow the basic laws of physics and chemistry and is therefore predictable from its immediately preceding state. In general, when a machine ' breaks ' the representative point has met some critical state, and the corresponding step-function has changed value.

As is well known, almost any machine or physical system will break if its variables are driven far enough away from their usual values. Thus, machines with moving parts, if driven ever faster, will break mechanically; electrical apparatus, if subjected to ever higher voltages or currents, will break in insulation; machines made too hot will melt—if made too cold they may encounter other sudden changes, such as the condensation which stops a steam-engine from working below 100° C.; in chemical dynamics, increasing concentrations may meet saturation, or may cause precipitation of proteins.

Although there is no rigorous law, there is nevertheless a widespread tendency for systems to show changes of step-function form if their variables are driven far from some usual value. Later (S. 9/7) it will be suggested that the nervous system is not exceptional in this respect.

Systems containing step-mechanisms

7/20. When a state-determined system includes a step-function among its variables, the whole behaviour can undergo a simplification not possible when the variables are all full-functions.

Suppose that we have a system with three variables, A, B, S; that it has been tested and found state-determined; that A and B are full-functions; and that S is a step-mechanism. (Variables A and B, as in S. 21/7, will be referred to as **main** variables.) The phase-space of this system will resemble that of Figure 7/20/1 (a possible field has been sketched in). The phase-space no longer fills all three dimensions, but as S can take only discrete values, here assumed for simplicity to be a pair, the phase-space is restricted to two planes normal to S, each plane corresponding to a

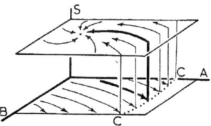

FIGURE 7/20/1 : Field of a state-determined system of three variables, of which S is a step-function. The states from C to C are the critical states of the step-function for lines in the lower plane.

particular value of S. A and B being full-functions, the representative point will move on curves in each plane, describing a line of behaviour such as that drawn more heavily in the Figure. When the line of behaviour meets the row of critical states at $C-C$, S jumps to its other value, and the representative point continues along the heavily marked line in the upper plane. In such a field the movement of the representative point is everywhere state-determined, for the number of lines from any point never exceeds one.

If, still dealing with the same real ' machine ', we ignore S, and repeatedly form the field of the system composed of A and B (S being free to take sometimes one value and sometimes the other), we shall find that we get sometimes a field like I in Figure 7/20/2,

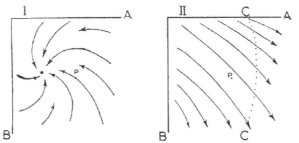

FIGURE 7/20/2 : The two fields of the system composed of A and B. P is in the same position in each field.

and sometimes a field like II, the one or the other appearing according to the value that S happens to have at the time.

The behaviour of the system AB, in its apparent possession of two fields, should be compared with that of the system described in S. 6/3, where the use of two parameter-values also caused the appearance of two fields. But in the earlier case the change of the field was caused by the arbitrary action of the experimenter, who forced the parameter to change value, while in this case the change of the field of AB is caused by the inner mechanisms of the ' machine ' itself.

The property may now be stated in general terms. Suppose, in a state-determined system, that some of the variables are due to step-mechanisms, and that these are ignored while the remainder (the main variables) are observed on many occasions by having their field constructed. Then so long as no step-mechanism changes value during the construction, the main variables will be found to form a state-determined system, and to have a definite field. But *on different occasions different fields may be found.*

7/21. These considerations throw light on an old problem in the theory of mechanisms.

Can a ' machine ' be at once determinate and capable of spontaneous change ? The question would be contradictory if posed by one person, but it exists in fact because, when talking of living organisms, one school maintains that they are strictly determinate while another school maintains that they are capable of spontaneous change. Can the schools be reconciled ?

The presence of step-mechanisms in a state-determined system enables both schools to be right, provided that those who maintain the determination are speaking of the system which comprises *all* the variables, while those who maintain the possibility of spontaneous change are speaking of the main variables only. For the whole system, which includes the step-mechanisms, has one field only, and is completely state-determined (like Figure 7/20/1). But the system of main variables may show as many different forms of behaviour (like Figure 7/20/2, I and II) as the step-mechanisms possess combinations of values. And if the step-mechanisms are not accessible to observation, the change of the main variables from one form of behaviour to another will seem to be spontaneous, for no change or state in the main variables can be assigned as its cause.

7/22. If the system had contained two step-mechanisms, each of two values, there would have been four fields of the main variables. In general, n step-mechanisms, each of two values, will give 2^n fields. A moderate number of step-mechanisms may thus give a very much larger number of fields.

7/23. After this digression on step-functions we can return to the system of S. 7/9, with its corrective feedback, and consider its behaviour.

To bring the concepts into correspondence, we assume that the main variables (the continuous) are in the environment, in R, and in the essential variables. The step-functions will be in S. It follows that their critical states will be distributed over those regions of the main variables' phase-space at which the essential variables are outside their normal limits. Thus if the main variables were as few as two (for graphical purposes), the distribution might be as the dots in I of Figure 7/23/1. The distribution means that the organism is in tolerable physiological conditions if the representative point stays within the undotted region.

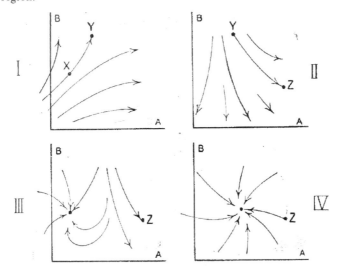

FIGURE 7/23/1 : Changes of field in an ultrastable system. The critical states are dotted.

Suppose now that the first set of values on the step-functions S gives such a field as is shown in I, and that the representative point is at X. The line of behaviour from X is not stable in the region, and the representative point follows the line to the boundary. Here (Y) it meets a critical state and a step-function changes value; a new field, perhaps like II, arises. The representative point is now at Y, and the line from this point is still unstable in regard to the region. The point follows the line of behaviour, meets a critical state at Z, and causes a change of a step-function: a new field (III) arises. The point is at Z, and the field includes a state of stable equilibrium, but from Z the line leads further out of the region. So another critical state is met, another step-function changes value, and a new field (IV) arises. In this field, the line of behaviour from Z is stable with regard to the region, so the representative point moves to the state of equilibrium and stops there.   No further critical states are met, no further step-functions change value, and therefore no further changes of field take place.   From now on, if the field of the main variables is examined, it will be found to be stable.   The organism, if displaced moderately from the state of equilibrium, will return to it, thus demonstrating the various evidences of adaptation noticed in Chapter 5.

7/24.   This field, and this state of equilibrium, will, under constant external conditions, persist indefinitely.   If the system is now subjected to occasional small impulsive disturbances (that simply displace the representative point as in S. 6/5) the whole will as often display its stability; in the same action, the organismal part will display that it now possesses an ' adapted ' mechanism for dealing with the environmental part.

During the description of the previous section, much notice was taken of the trials and failures, and field IV seemed to be only the end of a succession of failures.   We thus tended to lose a sense of proportion; for what is really important to the living and learning organism is the great number of times on which it can display that it has already achieved adaptation; in fact, unless the circumstances allow this number to be fairly large and the number of trial-failures to be fairly small, there is no gain to the organism in having a brain that can learn.

7/25.   It should be noticed that the second feedback makes, for its success, no demands either on the construction of the reacting part R or on the successive values that are taken by S.   Another way of saying this is to say that the mechanism is in no way put out of order if R is initially constructed at random or if the successive values at S occur at random.   (The meaning of ' constructed at random ' is given in S. 13/1.)

Such a construction at random probably occurs to some extent in the nervous system, where the ultimate units (dendrons, pieds terminaux, protein molecules perhaps) occur in numbers far too great for their determination by the gene-pattern in detail (S. 1/9). In the formation of the embryo brain, therefore, some of the final details may be determined by the accidents of local minutiae—

of oxygen or salt concentration perhaps, or local strains. If the reacting part R is initially formed by such a process, then the action of the second feedback is unaffected: it will bring the organism to adaptation.

In the same way, nothing was supposed about the successive values at S (except that they must not be appreciably correlated with the events within the field). Any uncorrelated source will therefore serve for their supply; so they too can be, in the defined sense, random.

The ultrastable system

7/26. In the first edition the system described in this chapter was called 'ultrastable', and S. 8/6 will show why the adjective is defensible. At that time the system was thought to be unique, but further experience (outlined in *I. to C.*, S. 12/8–20) has shown that this form is only one of a large class of related forms, in which it is conspicuous only because it shows certain features, of outstanding biological interest, with unusual clarity. The word may usefully be retained, in accordance with the strategy of S. 2/17, because it represents a well-defined type, useful as a fixed type around which discussion may move without ambiguity, and to which a multitude of approximately similar forms, occurring mostly in the biological world, may be related.

For convenience, its definition will be stated formally. Two systems of continuous variables (that we called 'environment' and 'reacting part') interact, so that a primary feedback (through complex sensory and motor channels) exists between them. Another feedback, working intermittently and at a much slower order of speed, goes from the environment to certain continuous variables which in their turn affect some step-mechanisms, the effect being that the step-mechanisms change value when and only when these variables pass outside given limits. The step-mechanisms affect the reacting part; by acting as parameters to it they determine how it shall react to the environment.

(From this basic type a multitude of variations can be made. Their study is made much easier by a thorough grasp of the properties of the basic form just defined.)

7/27. The basic form has many more properties of interest than have yet been indicated. Their description in words, however, is apt to be tedious and unconvincing. A better demonstration can be given by a machine, built so that we know its nature exactly and on which we can observe just what will happen in various conditions. (We can describe it either as 'a machine to do our thinking for us' or, more respectably, as 'an analogue computer'.) One was built and called the 'Homeostat'. Its construction, and how it behaved, will be described in the next chapter.

CHAPTER 8

The Homeostat

8/1. THE ultrastable system is much richer in interesting properties than might at first be suspected. Some of these properties are of special interest to the physiologist and the psychologist, but they have to be suitably displayed before their physiological and psychological applications can be perceived. For their display, a machine was built according to the definition of the ultrastable system. What it is, and how it behaves, are the subjects of this chapter.*

8/2. The Homeostat (Figure 8/2/1) consists of four units, each of which carries on top a pivoted magnet (Figure 8/2/2, M in Figure 8/2/3). The angular deviations of the four magnets from the central positions provide the four main variables.

Its construction will be described in stages. Each unit emits a D.C. output proportional to the deviation of its magnet from the central position. The output is controlled in the following way. In front of each magnet is a trough of water; electrodes at each end provide a potential gradient. The magnet carries a wire which dips into the water, picks up a potential depending on the position of the magnet, and sends it to the grid of the triode. J provides the anode-potential at 150 V., while H is at 180 V.; so E carries a constant current If the grid-potential allows just this current to pass through the valve, then no current will flow through the output. But if the valve passes more, or less, current than this, the output circuit will carry the difference in one direction or the other. So after E is adjusted, the output is approximately proportional to M's deviation from its central position.†

* It was given the name of ' Homeostat ' for convenience of reference, and the noun seems to be acceptable. The derivatives ' homeostatic ' and ' homeostatically ', however, are unfortunate, for they suggest reference to the machine, whereas priority demands that they be used only as derivatives of Cannon's ' homeostasis '.

† Following the original machine in principle, Mr. Earl J. Kletsky, at the Technische Hogeschool, Delft, Holland, has designed and built a form that replaces the magnet, coils, vane and water by Kirchhoff adding circuits and capacitors.

FIGURE 8/2/1 : The Homeostat. Each unit carries on top a magnet and
coil such as that shown in Figure 8/2/2. Of the controls on the front
panel, those of the upper row control the potentiometers, those of the
middle row the commutators, and those of the lower row the switches S
of Figure 8/2/3.

FIGURE 8/2/2 : Typical magnet (just visible), coil, pivot, vane, and water
potentiometer with electrodes at each end. The coil is quadruple, con-
sisting of A, B, C and D of Figure 8/2/3.

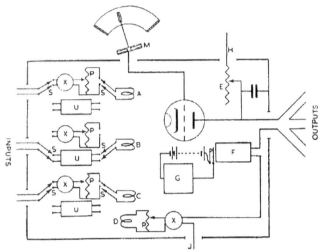

FIGURE 8/2/3 : Wiring diagram of one unit. (The letters are explained in the text.)

Next, the units are joined together so that each sends its output to the other three; and thereby each receives an input from each of the other three.

These inputs act on the unit's magnet through the coils A, B, and C, so that the torque on the magnet is approximately proportional to the algebraic sum of the currents in A, B, and C. (D also affects M as a self-feedback.) But before each input current reaches its coil, it passes through a commutator (X), which determines the polarity of entry to the coil, and through a potentiometer (P), which determines what fraction of the input shall reach the coil.

As soon as the system is switched on, the magnets are moved by the currents from the other units, but these movements change the currents, which modify the movements, and so on. It may be shown (S. 19/11) that if there is sufficient viscosity in the troughs, the four-variable system of the magnet-positions is approximately state-determined. To this system the commutators and potentiometers act as parameters.

When these parameters are given a definite set of values, the magnets show some definite pattern of behaviour; for the parameters determine the field, and thus the lines of behaviour. If the field is stable, the four magnets move to the central position, where they actively resist any attempt to displace them. If displaced, a *co-ordinated* activity brings them back to the centre. Other parameter-settings may, however, give instability; in which case a ' runaway ' occurs and the magnets diverge from the central positions with increasing velocity—till they hit the ends of the troughs.

So far, the system of four variables has been shown to be dynamic, to have Figure 4/15/1 (*A*) as its diagram of immediate effects, and to be state-determined. Its field depends on the thirty-two parameters *X* and *P*. It is not yet ultrastable. But the inputs, instead of being controlled by parameters set by hand, can be sent by the switches *S* through similar components arranged on a uniselector (or ' stepping-switch ') *U*. The values of the components in *U* were deliberately randomised by taking the actual numerical values from Fisher and Yates' Table of Random Numbers. Once built on to the uniselectors, the values of these parameters are determined at any moment by the positions of the uniselectors. Twenty-five positions on each of four uni-selectors (one to each unit) provide 390,625 combinations of parameter-values.

F represents the essential variable of the unit. Its contacts close when and only when the output current exceeds a certain value. When this happens, the coils *G* of the uniselector can be energised, moving the parameters to new values   The power to *G* is also interrupted by a device (not shown) that allows the power to test *F*'s contacts only at intervals of one to ten seconds (the operator can adjust the frequency). Thus, if set at 3-second intervals, at every third second the uniselector will either move to new values (if *F* be receiving a current exceeding the limits) or stay where it is (if *F*'s current be within).

8/3.   That the machine described is ultrastable can be verified by an examination of the correspondences.

There are four main variables—the positions of the four magnets. (There can, of course, be fewer if not all the units are used.) These four represent both the environment and the reacting part *R* of Figure 7/2/1, the allotment of the four to the two subsystems being arbitrary. The relays *F* correspond to the essential variables, and the physiological limits correspond to the currents that flow in F when the needles are deviated to more than about 45 degrees from the central positions. The main variables are continuous, and act and react on one another, giving the primary feedback, which is complex, like A of Figure 4/15/1. The field of the four main variables has only one state of equilibrium (at the centre), which may be stable or unstable. Thus the system is either stable and self-correcting for small impulsive displacements to the needles, or unstable and self-aggravating, running away to the limits of the troughs. Which it will be depends on the quantitative details of the primary feedbacks, which are dependent on the values on the step-mechanisms.

The step-mechanisms of S. 7/12 can be made to correspond to structures on the Homeostat in several ways, which are equivalent. Perhaps the simplest way is to identify them with the twelve values presented by the uniselectors at any given moment (three on each). If the needle of a unit diverges for more than a few seconds outside the limits of $\pm 45°$, the three values of its step-functions will be changed to three new values. These new values have no special relation either to the previous values or to the problem in hand—they are just the values that next follow in Fisher and Yates' table.

It is easily seen that if any one, two, or three of the units are used (as is often done for simplicity) this subsystem will still be ultrastable.

The Homeostat as adapter

8/4. A remarkable property of the nervous system is its ability to adapt itself to surgical alterations of the bodily structure. From the first work of Marina to the recent work of Sperry, such experiments have aroused interest and no little surprise.

Over forty years ago, Marina severed the attachments of the internal and external recti muscles of a monkey's eyeball and re-attached them in crossed position so that a contraction of the external rectus would cause the eyeball to turn not outwards but inwards. When the wound had healed, he was surprised to discover that the two eyeballs still moved together, so that binocular vision was preserved.

More recently Sperry severed the nerves supplying the flexor and extensor muscles in the arm of the spider monkey, and re-joined them in crossed position. After the nerves had regenerated, the animal's arm movements were at first grossly inco-ordinated, but improved until an essentially normal mode of progression was re-established. The two examples are typical of a great number of experiments, and will suffice for the discussion. Let us see what the Homeostat will do under a similar operation.

Figure 8/4/1 shows the Homeostat simplified to two units

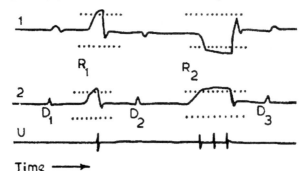

FIGURE 8/4/1 : Two units (1 and 2) interacting. Line 1 represents the side-to-side movements of Unit 1's needle by vertical changes. Similarly line 2 shows the behaviour of Unit 2's needle. The lowest line (U) shows a mark whenever Unit 1's uniselector advanced a step. The dotted lines correspond to critical states. The displacements D were caused by the operator so as to force the system to show its response.

interacting. The diagram of immediate effects was $1 \rightleftarrows 2$; the effect $1 \rightarrow 2$ was hand-controlled, and $2 \rightarrow 1$ was uniselector-controlled. At first the step-mechanism values combined to give stability, shown by the responses to D_1. (The reader should bear in mind, of course, that this trifling return after displacement is *representative* of all the complex returns after displacement considered in Chapter 5: Adaptation as stability.) At R_1, reversal of the commutator by hand rendered the system unstable, a runaway occurred, and the variables transgressed the critical states. The uniselector in Unit 1 changed position and, as it happened, gave at its first trial a stable field. It will be noticed that whereas before R_1 the upstroke of D_1 in 2 caused an *up*-stroke in 1, it caused a *down*stroke in 1 after R_1, showing that the action $2 \rightarrow 1$ had been reversed by the uniselector. This reversal *compensated* for the reversal of $1 \rightarrow 2$ caused at R_1.

At R_2 the whole process was repeated. This time three uni-selector changes were required before stability was restored. A comparison of the effect of D_3 on 1 with that of D_2 shows that compensation has occurred again.

If the two phenomena are to be brought into correspondence, we must notice, as in S. 3/12, that the anatomical criterion for dividing the system into ' animal ' and ' environment ' is not the only possible: a functional criterion is also possible.   Suppose a monkey, to get food from a box, has to pull a lever towards itself; if we sever the flexor and extensor muscles of the arm and re-attach them in crossed position then, so far as the cerebral cortex is concerned, the change is not essentially different from that of dismantling the box and re-assembling it so that the lever has to be pushed instead of pulled.   Spinal cord, peripheral nerves, muscles, bones, lever, and box—all are ' environment ' to the cerebral cortex.   A reversal in the cerebral cortex will compensate for a reversal in its environment whether in spinal cord, muscles, or lever.   It seems reasonable, therefore, to expect that the cerebral cortex will use the same compensatory process whatever the site of reversal.

To apply the principle of ultrastability we must add an assumption that ' binocular vision ' and ' normal progression ' have neural correlates such that deviations from binocular vision or from normal progression cause an excitation sufficient to cause changes of step-function form in those cerebral mechanisms that determine the actions.   (The plausibility of this assumption will be discussed in S. 9/4.)   Ultrastability will then automatically lead to the emergence of behaviour which produces binocular vision or normal progression.

8/5.   A more complex example is shown in Figure 8/5/1.   The machine was arranged so that its diagram of immediate effects was

The effect $3 \rightarrow 1$ was set permanently so that a movement of 3 made 1 move in the opposite direction.   The action $1 \rightarrow 2$ was uniselector-controlled, and $2 \rightarrow 3$ hand-controlled.   When the tracing commenced, the actions $1 \rightarrow 2$ and $2 \rightarrow 3$ were demonstrated by the downward movement, forced by the operator, of 1 at S_1: 2 followed 1 downward (similar movement), and 3

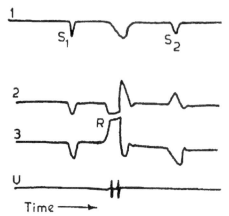

FIGURE 8/5/1 : Three units interacting. At R the effect
of 2 on 3 was reversed in polarity.

followed 2 downward (similar movement). 3 then forced 1 up-
ward, opposed the original movement, and produced stability.

At R, the hand-control ($2 \rightarrow 3$) was reversed, so that 2 now
forced 3 to move in the *opposite* direction to itself. This change
set up a vicious circle and destroyed the stability; but uniselector
changes occurred until the stability was restored. A forced downward movement of 1, at S_2, demonstrated the regained stability.

The tracing, however, deserves closer study. The action $2 \rightarrow 3$
was reversed at R, and the responses of 2 and 3 at S_2 demonstrate
this reversal; for while at S_1 they moved similarly, at S_2 they
moved oppositely. Again, a comparison of the uniselector-
controlled action $1 \rightarrow 2$ before and after R shows that whereas
beforehand 2 moved similarly to 1, afterwards it moved oppositely. The reversal in $2 \rightarrow 3$, caused by the operator, thus
evoked a reversal in $1 \rightarrow 2$ controlled by the uniselector. The
second reversal is compensatory to the first.

The nervous system provides many illustrations of such a series
of events: first the established reaction, then an alteration made
in the environment by the experimenter, and finally a reorganisa-
tion within the nervous system, compensating for the experimental
alteration. The Homeostat can thus show, in elementary form,
this power of self-reorganisation.

8/6. We can now appreciate how different an ultrastable system is from a simple stable system when the conditions allow the difference to show clearly.

The difference can best be shown by an example. The automatic pilot is a device which, amongst other actions, keeps the aeroplane horizontal. It must therefore be connected to the ailerons in such a way that when the plane rolls to the right, its output must act on them so as to roll the plane to the left. If properly joined, the whole system is stable and self-correcting: it can now fly safely through turbulent air, for though it will roll frequently, it will always come back to the level. The Homeostat, if joined in this way, would tend to do the same. (Though not well suited, it would, in principle, if given a gyroscope, be able to correct roll.)

So far they show no difference; but connect the ailerons in reverse and compare them. The automatic pilot would act, after a small disturbance, to *increase* the roll, and would persist in its wrong action to the very end. The Homeostat, however, would persist in its wrong action only until the increasing deviation made the step-mechanisms start changing. On the occurrence of the first suitable new value, the Homeostat would act to stabilise instead of to overthrow; it would return the plane to the horizontal; and it would then be ordinarily self-correcting for disturbances.

There is therefore some justification for the name ' ultrastable '; for if the main variables are assembled so as to make their field unstable, the ultrastable system will change this field till it is stable. The degree of stability shown is therefore of an order higher than that of the system with a single field

8/7. The experiments of Marina and Sperry provide an excellent introduction because they are conceptually so simple. Sometimes a simple experiment on adaptation may need a little thought before we can identify the essential features. Thus Mowrer put a rat into a box with a grilled metal floor. The grill could be electrified so as to give shocks to the rat's paws. Inside the box was a pedal which, if depressed, at once stopped the shocks.

When a rat was put into the box and the electric stimulation started, the rat would produce various undirected activities such as jumping, running, squealing, biting at the grill, and random thrashing about. Sooner or later it would depress the pedal and stop the shocks. After the tenth trial, the application of the shock would usually cause the rat to go straight to the pedal and depress it. These, briefly, are the observed facts.

Consider the internal linkages in this system. We can sufficiently specify what is happening by using six variables, or sets of variables: those shown in the box-diagram below. By con-

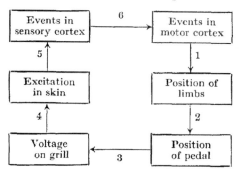

sidering the known actions of part on part in the real system we can construct the diagram of immediate effects. Thus, the excitations in the motor cortex certainly control the rat's bodily movements, and such excitations have no direct effect on any of the other five groups of variables; so we can insert arrow 1, and know that no other arrow leaves that box. (The single arrow, of course, represents a complex channel.) Similarly, the other arrows of the diagram can be inserted. Some of the arrows, e.g. 2 and 4, represent a linkage in which there is not a positive physical action all the time; but here, in accordance with S. 2/3, we regard them as permanently linked though sometimes acting at zero degree.

Having completed the diagram, we notice that it forms a functional circuit. The system is complete and isolated, and may therefore be treated as state-determined. To apply our thesis, we assume that the cerebral part, represented by the boxes around arrow 6, contains step-mechanisms whose critical states will be transgressed if stimuli of more than physiological intensity are sent to the brain.

We now regard the system as ultrastable, and predict what its behaviour must be. It is started, by hypothesis, from an initial state at which the voltage is high. This being so, the excitation at the skin and in the brain will be high. At first the pattern of impulses sent to the muscles does not cause that pedal movement which would lower the voltage on the grill These high excitations in the brain will cause some step-mechanisms to change value, thus causing different patterns of body movement to occur. The step-mechanisms act directly only at stage 6, but changes there will (S. 12/9) affect the field of all six groups of main variables. These changes of field will continue to occur as long as the high excitation in the brain persists. They will cease when, and only when, the linkages at stage 6 transform an excitation of skin receptors into such a bodily movement as will cause, through the pedal, a reduction in the excitation of the skin receptors; for only such linkages can stop further encounters with critical states. The system, that is, will change until there occurs a stable field. The stability will be shown by an increase in the voltage on the grill leading to changes through skin, brain, muscles, and pedal that have the effect of *opposing* the increase in voltage. The stability, in addition, has the property that it keeps the essential variables within physiological limits; for by it the rat is protected from electrical injury, and the nervous system from exhaustion.

It will be noted that although action 3 has no direct connexion, either visually in the real apparatus or functionally in the diagram of immediate effects, with the site of the changes at 6, yet the latter become adapted to the nature of the action at 3. (The subject was discussed in S. 5/13.)

This example shows, therefore, that if the rat and its environment formed an ultrastable system and acted purely automatically, they would go through the same changes as were observed by Mowrer.

Training

8/8. The process of ' training ' will now be shown in its relation to ultrastability.

All training involves some use of ' punishment ' or ' reward ', and we must translate these concepts into our form. ' Punishment ' is simple, for it means that some sensory organs or nerve endings have been stimulated with an intensity high enough to cause step-function changes in the nervous system (S. 7/19 and 9/7). The concept of ' reward ' is more complex. It usually involves the supplying of some substance (e.g. food) or condition (e.g. escape) whose absence would act as 'punishment'. The chief difficulty is that the evidence suggests that the nervous system, especially the mammalian, contains intricate and specialised mechanisms which give the animals properties not to be deduced from basic principles alone. Thus it has been shown that dogs with an oesophageal fistula, deprived of water for some hours, would, when offered water, drink approximately the quantity that would correct the deprivation, and would then stop drinking; they would stop although no water had entered stomach or system. The properties of these mechanisms have not yet been fully elucidated; so training by reward uses mechanisms of unknown properties. Here we shall ignore these complications. We shall assume that the training is by pain, i.e. by some change which threatens to drive the essential variables outside their normal limits; and we shall assume that training by reward is not essentially dissimilar.

It should be noticed that in training-experiments the experimenter often plays a dual role. He first plans the experiment, deciding what rules shall be obeyed during it. Then, when these have been fixed, he takes part in the experiment and obeys these rules. With the first role we are not concerned. In the second, however, it is important to note that the experimenter is now *within* the functional machinery of the experiment. The truth of this statement can be appreciated more readily if his place is taken by an untrained but obedient assistant who carries out the instructions blindly; or better still if his place is taken by an apparatus which carries out the prescribed actions automatically.

When the whole training is arranged to occur automatically the feedback is readily demonstrated if we construct the diagram of immediate effects. Thus, a pike in an aquarium was separated from some minnows by a sheet of glass; every time he dashed at the minnows he struck the glass. The following immediate effects can be clearly distinguished:

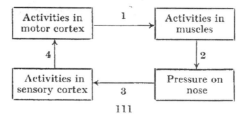

The effect 1 represents the control exerted through spinal cord and motor nerves. Effect 2 is discontinuous but none the less clear: the experiment implies that some activities led to a high pressure on the nose while others led to a zero pressure. Effects 3 and 4 are the simple neuro-physiological results of pressures on the nose.

Although the diagram has some freedom in the selection of variables for naming, the system, regarded as a whole, clearly has feedback.

In other training experiments, the regularity of action 2 (supplied above by the constant physical properties of glass) may be supplied by an assistant who constantly obeys the rules laid down by the experimenter. Grindley, for instance, kept a guinea-pig in a silent room in which a buzzer was sounded from time to time. If and only if its head turned to the right did a tray swing out and present it with a piece of carrot; after a few nibbles the carrot was withdrawn and the process repeated. Feedback is demonstrably present in this system, for the diagram of immediate effects is:

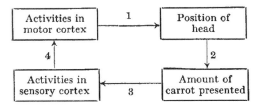

The buzzer, omitted for clarity, comes in as parameter and serve merely to call this dynamic system into functional existence; for only when the buzzer sounds does the linkage 2 exist.

This type of experiment reveals its essential dynamic structure more clearly if contrasted with elementary Pavlovian conditioning. In the experiments of Grindley and Pavlov, both use the sequences '. . . buzzer, animal's response, food . . .' In Grindley's experiment, the value of the variable ' food ' *depended on the animal's response*: if the head turned to the left, ' food ' was ' no carrot ', while if the head turned to the right, ' food ' was ' carrot given '. But in Pavlov's experiments the nature of every stimulus throughout the session was already determined *before the session commenced*. The Pavlovian experiment, therefore, allows no effect from the variable 'animal's behaviour' to 'quantity of food given'; there is no functional circuit and no feedback.

It may be thought that the distinction (which corresponds to that made by Hilgard and Marquis between 'conditioning' and 'instrumental learning') is purely verbal. This is not so, for the description given above shows that the distinction may be made objectively by examining the structure of the experiment.

It will be seen, therefore, that the 'training' situation necessarily implies that the trainer, or some similar device, is an integral part of the whole system, which has feedback:

We shall now suppose this system to be ultrastable, and we shall trace its behaviour on this supposition. The step-mechanisms are, of course, assumed to be confined to the animal; both because the human trainer may be replaced in some experiments by a device as simple as a sheet of glass (in the example of the pike); and because the rules of the training are to be decided in advance (as when we decide to punish a house-dog whenever he jumps into a chair), and therefore to be invariant throughout the process. Suppose then that jumping into a chair always results in the dog's sensory receptors being excessively stimulated. As an ultrastable system, step-function values which lead to jumps into chairs will be followed by stimulations likely to cause them to change value. But on the occurrence of a set of step-function values leading to a remaining on the ground, excessive stimulation will not occur, and the values will remain. (The cessation of punishment when the right action occurs is no less important in training than its administration after the wrong action.)

8/9. The process can be shown on the Homeostat. Figure 8/9/1 provides an example. Three units were joined:

and to this system was joined a 'trainer', actually myself, which acted on the rule that if the Homeostat did not respond to a forced movement of 1 by an *opposite* movement of 2, then the trainer would force 3 over to an extreme position. The diagram of immediate effects is therefore really

Part of the system's feedbacks, it will be noticed, pass through T.

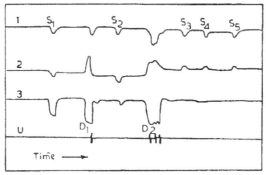

FIGURE 8/9/1 : Three units interacting. The downstrokes at S are forced by the operator. If 2 responds with a downstroke, the trainer drives 3 past its critical surface.

At S_1, 1 was moved and 2 moved similarly. This is the ' forbidden ' response; so at D_1, 3 was forced by the trainer to an extreme position. Step-mechanisms changed value. At S_2, the Homeostat was tested again: again it produced the forbidden response; so at D_2, 3 was again forced to an extreme position. At S_3, the Homeostat was tested again: it moved in the desired way, so no further deviation was forced on 3. And at S_4 and S_5 the Homeostat continued to show the desired reaction.

From S_1 onwards, T's behaviour is determinate at every instant; so the system composed of 1, 2, 3, T, and the uniselectors, is state-determined.

Another property of the whole system should be noticed. When the movement-combination ' 1 and 2 moving similarly ' occurs, T is thereby impelled, under the rules of the experiment, to force 3 outside the region bounded by the critical states. Of any inanimate system which behaved in this way we would say, simply, that the line of behaviour from the state at which 1 and 2 started moving was unstable. So, to say in psychological terms that the 'trainer' has 'punished' the 'animal' is equivalent to saying in our terms that the system has a set of parameter-values that make it unstable.

In general, then, we may identify the behaviour of the animal in 'training' with that of the ultrastable system adapting to another system of fixed characteristics.

8/10. How will the ultrastable system behave if it has to adapt to two environments, which alternate ? Such a situation is not uncommon: the diving bird has to adapt to situations both on land and in the water; British birds have to adapt both to full foliage in the summer and to bare branches in the winter; and the kitten has to adapt both to the mouse that tries to escape into a hole and to the bird that tries to escape by flying upwards.

Such cases are equivalent (by Ss. 6/3 and 7/20) to the case in which there is one environment affected by a parameter with two values. Each value, provided it is sustained long enough for the characteristic behaviours of adaptation to be displayed, gives one form to the environment; and the two forms may, if we please, be thought of as two environments. The question can therefore be investigated by allowing the Homeostat to adapt in the presence of an alternating parameter, each value of which must be sustained long enough so that the change does not interrupt the process of trial and error.

Let the Homeostat be arranged so that it is partly under uniselector-, and partly under hand-, control. Let it be started so that it works as an ultrastable system. Select a commutator switch, and from time to time reverse its polarity This reversal provides the system with the equivalent of two environments which alternate. We can now predict that *it will be selective for fields that give adaptation to both environments.* For consider what field can be terminal: a field that is terminal for only one of the parameter-values will be lost when the parameter next changes; but the first field terminal for both will be retained. Figure 8/10/1 illustrates the process. At R_1, R_2, R_3, and R_4 the hand-controlled commutator H was reversed. At first the change of value caused a change of field, shown at A. But the second

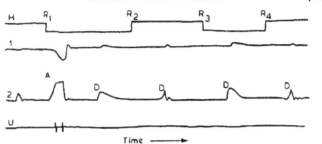

FIGURE 8/10/1 : Record of Homeostat's behaviour when a commutator H was reversed from time to time (at the R's). The first set of uniselector values which gave stability for both commutator positions was terminal.

uniselector position happened to provide a field which gave stability with both values of H. So afterwards, the changes of H no longer caused changes in the step-mechanisms. The responses to the displacements D, forced by the operator, show that the system is stable for both values of H. The slight but distinct difference in the behaviour after D at the two values of H show that the two fields are different.

The ultrastable system is, therefore, selective for step-mechanism values which give stability for both values of an alternating parameter.

8/11. What will happen if the ultrastable system is given an unusual environment ? Before the question is answered we must be clear about what is meant by ' unusual '.

In S. 6/2 it was shown that every dynamic system is acted on by an indefinitely large number of parameters, many of which are taken for granted, for they are always given well-understood ' obvious ' values. Thus, in mechanical systems it is taken for granted, unless specially mentioned, that the bodies carry a zero electrostatic charge; in physiological experiments, that the tissues, unless specially mentioned, contain no unusual drug; in biological experiments, that the animal, unless specially mentioned, is in good health. All these parameters, however, are effective in that, had their values been different, the variables would not have followed the same line of behaviour. Clearly the field of a state-determined system depends not only on those parameters which have been fixed individually and specifically, but on all the great number which have been fixed incidentally.

Now the ultrastable system proceeds to a terminal field which is stable in conjunction with *all* the system's parameter-values (and it is clear that this must be so, for whether the parameters are at their ' usual ' values or not is irrelevant). The ultrastable system will therefore always produce a set of step-mechanism values which is so related to the particular set of parameter-values that, *in conjunction with them*, the system is stable. If the parameters have unusual values, the step-mechanisms will also finish with values that are compensatingly unusual. To the casual observer this adjustment of the step-mechanism values to the parameter-values may be surprising; we, however, can see that it is inevitable.

The fact is demonstrable on the Homeostat. After the machine was completed, some ' unusual ' complications were imposed on it (' unusual ' in the sense that they were not thought of till the machine had been built), and the machine was then tested to see how it would succeed in finding a stable field when affected by the peculiar complications. One such test was made by joining

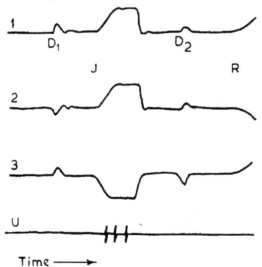

FIGURE 8/11/1 : Three units interacting. At *J*, units 1 and 2 were constrained to move together. New step-mechanism values were found which produced stability. These values give stability in conjunction with the constraint, for when it is removed, at *R*, the system becomes unstable.

the front two magnets by a light glass fibre so that they had to move together. Figure 8/11/1 shows a typical record of the changes. Three units were joined together and were at first stable, as shown by the response when the operator displaced magnet 1 at D_1. At J, the magnets of 1 and 2 were joined so that they could move only together. The result of the constraint in this case was to make the system unstable. But the instability evoked step-mechanism changes, and a new terminal field was found. This was, of course, stable, as was shown by its response to the displacement, made by the operator, at D_2. But it should be noticed that the new set of step-mechanism values was adjusted to, or 'took notice of', the constraint and, in fact, used it in the maintenance of stability; for when, at R, the operator gently lifted the fibre away the system became unstable.

There are other unusual problems, of course, for which the Homeostat's repertoire contains no solution; putting too powerful a magnet at one side to draw the magnets over would set such a 'problem'; so would a shorting of the relay F (Figure 8/2/3) In such a situation the Homeostat, or any ultrastable system, would have no state of equilibrium and would thus fail to adapt So, too, would a living organism, if set a problem for which its total repertoire contained no solution.

Some apparent faults

8/12. It will be apparent that the principle of ultrastability, as demonstrated by the Homeostat, does not seem to represent adequately the great richness of adaptations developed by the higher animals; with some of the inadequacies we shall deal later in the book. There are, however, some 'faults' of the ultrastable system that are found on closer scrutiny actually to support the thesis that the living brain adapts by ultrastability. We will examine them in the next few sections.

8/13. If the relation of S. 7/5 does not hold between the essential variables and the step-mechanisms, that is, if an ultrastable system's critical surfaces are not disposed in proper relation to the limits of the essential variables, the system may seek an inappropriate goal or may fail to take corrective action when the essential variables are dangerously near their limits.

In animals, though we cannot yet say much about their critical states, we can observe failures of adaptation that may well be due to a defect of this type. Thus, though animals usually react defensively to poisons like strychnine—for it has an intensely bitter taste, stimulates the taste buds strongly, and is spat out —they are characteristically defenceless against a tasteless or odourless poison: precisely because it stimulates no nerve-fibre excessively and causes no deviation from the routine of chewing and swallowing.

An even more dramatic example, showing how defenceless is the living organism if pain has not its normal effect of causing behaviour to change, is given by those children who congenitally lack the normal self-protective reflexes. Boyd and Nie have described such a case. a girl, aged 7, who seemed healthy and normal in all respects except that she was quite insensitive to pain. Even before she was a year old her parents noticed that she did not cry when injured. At one year of age her arm was noticed to be crooked: X-rays showed a recent fracture-dislocation. The child had made no complaint, nor did she show any sign of pain when the fragments were re-set without an anaesthetic. Three months later the same injury occurred to her right elbow. At the seaside she crawled on the rocks until her hands and knees were torn and denuded of skin. At home her mother on several occasions smelt burning flesh and found the child leaning unconcernedly against the hot stove.

It seems, then, that if an imperfectly formed ultrastable system is, under certain conditions, defenceless, so may be an imperfectly formed living organism.

8/14. Even if the ultrastable system is suitably arranged—if the critical states are encountered before the essential variables reach their limits—it usually cannot adapt to an environment that behaves with sudden discontinuities. In the earlier examples of the Homeostat's successful adaptations the actions were always arranged to be continuous; but suppose the Homeostat had controlled a relay which was usually unchanging but which, if the Homeostat passed through some arbitrarily selected state, would suddenly release a powerful spring that would drag the magnets away from their ' optimal ' central positions. the Homeostat, if it happened to approach the special state, would take no step to avoid it and would blindly evoke the 'lethal' action. The Homeostat's method for achieving adaptation is thus essentially useless when its environment contains such 'lethal' discontinuities.

The living organism, however, is also apt to fail with just the same type of environment. The pike that collided with the glass plate while chasing minnows failed at first to avoid collision precisely because of the suddenness of the transition from not seeing clear glass to feeling the impact on its nose. This flaw in the living organism's defences has, in fact, long been known and made use of by the hunter. The stalking cat's movements are such as will maintain as long as possible, for the prey, the appearance of a peaceful landscape, to be changed with the utmost possible suddenness into one of mortal threat. In the whole process the suddenness is essential. Consider too the essential features of any successful trap; and the necessity, in poisoning vermin, of ensuring that the first dose is lethal.

If, then, the ultrastable system usually fails when attempting to adapt to an environment with sudden discontinuities, so too does the living organism.

8/15. Another weakness shown by the ultrastable system's method is that success is dependent on the system's using a suitable period of delay between each trial. Thus, the system shown in Figure 7/23/1 must persist in Trial IV long enough for the representative point to get away from the region of the critical states. Both extremes of delay may be fatal: too hurried a change from trial to trial may not allow time for 'success' to declare itself; and too prolonged a testing of a wrong trial may allow serious damage to occur. The optimal duration of a trial is clearly the time taken by information to travel from the step-mechanisms that initiate the trial, through the environment, to the essential variable that shows the outcome. If the ultrastable system requires the duration to be adjusted, so does the living organism; for there can be little doubt that on many occasions living organisms have missed success either by abandoning a trial too quickly, or by persisting too long with a trial that was actually useless. (The topic is referred to again in S. 17/10.)

The same difficulty, then, confronts both ultrastable system and living organism.

8/16. If we grade an ultrastable system's environments according to the difficulty they present, we shall find that at the 'easy' end are those that consist of a few variables, independent of each other, and that at the 'difficult' end are those that contain many variables richly cross-linked to form a complex whole. (The topic is developed from Chapter 11 on.)

The living organism, too, would classify environments in essentially the same way. Not only does common experience show this, but the construction and use of 'intelligence tests' has shown in endless ways that the easy problem is the one whose components are few and independent, while the difficult problem is the one with many components that form a complex whole. So when confronted with environments of various 'difficulties', the ultrastable system and the living organism are likely to fail together.

8/17. The last few sections have shown, in several ways, how several 'inadequacies' of the ultrastable system have made us realise, on closer scrutiny, the inadequacies not of the ultrastable system but of the living brain. Clearly we must beware of condemning a proposed model for not showing a certain property until we are sure that the living organism really shows it.

Since this book was first published, I have often had put to me some objection of the form 'Surely an ultrastable system could not . . .' When one goes into the matter, it is surprising how often the reply proves to be 'No, and a human being couldn't do it either !'

CHAPTER 9

Ultrastability in the Organism

9/1. In the early sections of Chapter 7 we considered the elementary behavioural facts of the kitten adapting, and related them to a mechanistic theoretical construction, the 'ultrastable' system. In the present chapter we will consider some further elementary relations between the real organism and the theoretical construct. We will consider, in particular, what can be said about the simple theoretical system shown in Figure 7/5/1. How does it correspond to the real organism and the real environment? We must go with caution, for experience has shown that a jump to conclusions that are grossly in error is only too easy.

9/2. We must be particularly careful not to take for granted that a diagram of immediate effects—that of Figure 7/5/1 for instance—gives a picture of what is to be *seen* in the nervous system. Just as one real 'machine' can give rise to a variety of systems, so it can give rise to a variety of diagrams of immediate effects, if the experimenter examines the real 'machine' with a variety of different technical methods. An electrical network, for instance, may give very different diagrams of functional connexion if it is explored first with slowly varying potentials and then with potentials oscillating at a high frequency. Sometimes it happens that two techniques may give the same diagram—exploring a metallic network firstly with direct currents and then by the sense of touch, say. When this happens we are delighted, for we have found a simplicity; but we must not expect this to happen always.

Many simple bodies have one diagram that is so obtrusive that one is apt to think of it as *the* specification of how the parts are joined. This is the diagram built up by considering the parts' positions in three-dimensional space, and studying how each part moves when some other part is moved. In this way (using a method just the same as that of S. 4/12) scientist and man in the street alike build up their ideas of how things are connected in the simple material or anatomical sense. So the child learns that when he picks up one end of a rattle the other end comes up too; and so the demonstrator of anatomy shows that if a certain tendon in the forearm is pulled, the thumb moves. These operations specify a diagram of immediate effects, a pattern of connectivity, of great commonness and importance. But we must beware of thinking that it is the only pattern; for there are also systems whose parts or variables have no particular position in space relative to one another, but are related dynamically in some quite different way. Such occurs when a mixture of substrates, enzymes, and other substances occur in a flask, and in which the variables are *concentrations*. Then the 'system' is a set of concentrations, and the diagram of immediate effects shows how the concentrations affect one another. Such a diagram, of course, shows nothing that can be seen in the distribution of matter in space; it is purely functional. Nothing that has been said so far excludes the possibility that the anatomical-looking Figure 7/5/1 may not be of the latter type. We must proceed warily.

9/3. The chief part of Figure 7/5/1 that calls for comment is the feedback from environment, through essential variables and step-mechanisms, to the reacting part R. The channel from environment to essential variables hardly concerns us, for it will depend on the practical details for the particular circumstances in which, at any particular time, the free-living organism finds itself.

The essential variables, being determined by the gene-pattern (S. 3/14), will often have some simple anatomical localisation. Some of them, for instance, are well known to be sited in the medulla oblongata; and others, such as the signals for pain, are known to pass through certain sites in the midbrain and optic thalamus. More accurate identification of these variables demands only detailed study.

Step-mechanisms in the organism

9/4. Quite otherwise is it with the step-mechanisms. We have at present practically no idea of where to look, nor what to look for. In these matters we must be very careful to avoid making assumptions unwittingly, for the possibilities are very wide.

We must beware, for instance, of asking where they are; for this question assumes that they must be somewhere, and then the ' where ' is apt to be interpreted anatomically, or histologically, or in some other way that is not appropriate to the actual variable. Some calculating machines, for instance, carry their records in the form of a train of pulses that circulates around a cyclic path that includes a long column of mercury.   Each pulse behaves as a step-function in that it has only two values: present or absent. It *is* localised by its position in the sequence, but it has *no* localisation in any particular part of the column.   (This is the sort of ' localisation ' that the Fraunhofer lines have as sunlight comes to us: they occupy a definite place in the spectrum but no unique place in three-dimensional space.)

With these warnings in mind, a brief review will now be given of some of the possibilities.   (The list is almost certainly not complete, and at the present time it is probably most important that we should be alert for forms not yet considered.)

9/5.   A possibility early suggested by Young was that a closed circuit of neurons might carry a stream of impulses and be self-maintaining in this excited state.   Unexcited it would stay at rest, excited it would be active maximally; such a system could carry permanently the effects of some event.

Lorente de Nó has provided abundant histological evidence that neurons form not only chains but circuits.   Figure 9/5/1 is taken

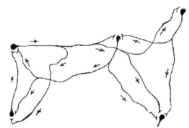

FIGURE 9/5/1 · Neurons and their connexions in the trigeminal
reflex arc   (Semi-diagrammatic , from Lorente de Nó.)

from one of his papers.   Such circuits are so common that he has enunciated a ' Law of Reciprocity of Connexions ': ' if a cell-complex A sends fibres to cell or cell-complex B, then B also sends fibres to A, either direct or by means of one internuncial neuron '.

A simple circuit, if excited, would tend either to sink back to zero excitation, if the amplification-factor was less than unity, or to rise to maximal excitation if it was greater than unity. Such a circuit tends to maintain only two degrees of activity: the inactive and the maximal. Its activity will therefore be of step-function form if the time taken by the chain to build up to maximal excitation can be neglected. Its critical states would be the smallest excitation capable of raising it to full activity, and the smallest inhibition capable of stopping it. McCulloch has referred to such circuits as ' endromes ' and has studied some of their properties.

9/6. Another source of step-functions would be provided if neurons were amoeboid, so that their processes could make or break contact with other cells.

That nerve-cells are amoeboid in tissue-culture has been known since the first observations of Harrison. When nerve-tissue from chick-embryo is grown in clotted plasma, filaments grow outwards at about 0·05 mm. per hour. The filament terminates in an expanded end, about $15 \times 25\mu$ in size, which is actively amoeboid, continually throwing out processes as though exploring the medium around. Levi studied tissue-cultures by micro-dissection, so that individual cells could be stimulated. He found that a nerve-cell, touched with the needle-point, would sometimes throw out processes by amoeboid movement.

The conditions of tissue-culture are somewhat abnormal, and artefacts are common; but this objection cannot be raised against the work of Speidel, who observed nerve-fibres growing into the living tadpole's tail. The ends of the fibres, like those in the tissue-culture, were actively amoeboid. Later he observed the effects of metrazol in the same way: there occurred an active retraction and, later, re-extension. More recently Carey and others have studied the motor end-plate. They found that it, too, is amoeboid, for it contracted to a ball after physical injury.

To react to a stimulus by amoeboid movement is perhaps the most ancient of reactions. So the hypothesis that neurons are amoeboid assumes only that they have never lost their original property. It is possible, therefore, that step-functions are provided in this way.

9/7. Every cell contains many variables that might change in a way approximating to the step-function form, especially if the time of observation is long compared with the average time of cellular events. Monomolecular films, protein solutions, enzyme systems, concentrations of hydrogen and other ions, oxidation-reduction potentials, adsorbed layers, and many other constituents or processes might act as step-mechanisms.

If the cell is sufficiently sensitive to be affected by changes of atomic size, then such changes might be of step-function form, for they could change only by a quantum jump. But this source of step-functions is probably unavailable, for changes of this size may be too indeterminate for the production of the regular and reproducible behaviour considered in this book (S. 1/14).

Round the neuron, and especially round its dendrons and axons, there is a sensitive membrane that might provide step-functions, though the membrane is probably wholly employed in the transmission of the action potential. Nerve 'fibrils' have been described for many years, though the possibility that they are an artefact cannot yet be excluded. If they are real their extreme delicacy of structure suggests that they might behave as step-functions.

The delicacy everywhere evident in the nervous system has often been remarked. This delicacy must surely imply the existence of step-functions; for the property of being 'delicate' can mean little other than 'easily broken', and it was observed in S. 7/19 that the phenomenon of something 'breaking' is the expression of a step-function changing value. Though the argument is largely verbal, it gives some justification for the opinion that step-mechanisms are by no means unlikely in the nervous system.

> 'The idea of a steady, continuous development', said Jacques Loeb, 'is inconsistent with the general physical qualities of protoplasm or colloidal material. The colloidal substances in our protoplasm possess critical points. . . The colloids change their state very easily, and a number of conditions . . . are able to bring about a change in their state. Such material lends itself very readily to a discontinuous series of changes.'

A molecular basis for memory?

9/8. What is *necessary* that any material entity should serve as a step-mechanism in ultrastability? Only that it should be a step-mechanism, that it should be able to be changed by the essential variables, and that it should have an effective action on the reacting part R.

As a dynamic system, the brain is so extremely sensitive, and is such a powerful amplifier, that we can hardly put a limit to the smallness of a physical change that still has a major effect in behaviour. Even a change on a single molecule cannot be dismissed as ineffective, for many events in the nervous system depend critically on how some variable is related to a threshold; and near the threshold a small change may have great consequences.

It is therefore not impossible that molecular events should provide the step-functions. There are plenty of events that might provide such forms: whether a molecule is in the *dextro-* or the *laevo-* state, in the *cis-* or *trans-* state; whether a hydrogen bond does or does not exist; whether a double bond between carbon atoms lies in this plane or that; and so on. Such bases would have the advantage in the living organism of providing the necessary function at a minimal cost in weight and bulk, matters of considerable importance to the free-living organism.

Pauling has discussed these possibilities and has suggested limits that would narrow the field of search. If the molecular entity is too small, thermal agitation will prevent it from showing the constancy which it must have if it is to act as basis for such behaviour as that of Skinner's pigeons (S. 1/14). If too large, it will be unsuitable for the miracle of ' miniaturisation ' that has actually been achieved in the mammalian brain.

9/9. With all these possible forms of step-mechanism in mind, it is difficult for us to say much that is definite about the feedback channels from essential variable through step-mechanisms to the reacting part R of Figure 7/5/1. Clearly there is not the least *necessity* for the channels to consist of anatomical or histological tracts; for if the step-mechanisms were molecular, the channel *to* them might be biochemical or hormonic in nature; while the channel *from* them to R might be extremely short, and of almost any nature, if they were sited *inside* the neurons in which they exerted their action

Evidently much more knowledge will be necessary before we can identify accurately this part of the second-order feedback. What is most important at the present time is that we should avoid unwittingly taking for granted what has yet to be demonstrated.

Are step-mechanisms necessary?

9/10. Since S. 7/12 we have been considering adaptation when the variables affecting the reacting part R of Figure 7/5/1 behave as step-functions. The justification given then was that this case is of central theoretic importance because of its peculiar simplicity and clarity· even if the nervous system contained no step-mechanisms. the student of the subject would still find consideration of this form helpful to get a clear grasp of how a nervous system can adapt. But is there no justification stronger than this? Does the evidence, perhaps, *prove* that the process of adaptation implies the existence of step-mechanisms?

9/11. We have already seen (S. 7/16) that even so typical a mechanism as a Post Office relay cannot be said to *be* (unconditionally) a step-mechanism, for some ways of observing it (e.g. over microseconds or over years) do not show this form; and no particular mode of observation can claim absolute priority. Thus even if some object in a Black Box gave convincing evidence that it was a Post Office relay, the observer still could not claim that the real object was a step-mechanism unconditionally.

9/12. On the other hand, contrasted with a full-function the step-function has a remarkable simplicity of behaviour, and not every real object can be made to show such a simplicity. To say of the object in the Black Box that it *can* be made to show behaviour of step-function type is thus to say something unconditionally true about it.

Again, if a system of three variables is studied and found to produce such a field as that of Figure 7/20/1 (in which three possible dimensions are reduced to two two-dimensional planes), then again the observer can claim that he has demonstrated something special, in the sense that the fully three-dimensional fields (e.g. that of Figure 3/5/2) cannot be reduced to the simple form.

Thus certain behaviours, though they do not permit the deduction that they are due to something that *is* a step-mechanism, may none the less permit the deduction that they are produced by some entity with the special property that its behaviour *can* be reduced to step-function form; and the latter is a meaningful statement, for not all entities produce behaviour that can be so reduced.

9/13. What of the nervous system ? If the variables in S (of Figure 7/5/1) were to vary as full-functions, the observer would see only one very complex system moving by a complex continuous trajectory to an eventual equilibrium. Often, however, he observes that the organism ' makes a trial ', i.e. produces some recognisable form of behaviour and then *persists* in this way of behaving for some appreciable time. Then the trial is abandoned, a new way of behaving occurs, and this too is persisted in for an appreciable time; and so on.

When this happens, the observer may justly claim that the system is showing less than its full complexity; for, through the duration of the trial, the fact that it is persisting as *this* particular form of trial means that some redundancy is occurring. The redundancy is similar to that of the sequence of letters that goes, e.g.

FFFFFLLLLLLLLTTTTTJJJJJJJ

rather than with full variety:

EJYMSNASGCGHLAAPEYPJVRQJ

Within each trial, if it shows a characteristic way of behaving, there will be defined a field; and these fields will follow one another in a discrete succession, as in Figure 7/23/1. When this occurs, if the observer is willing to assume that the changes of field are occurring in a state-determined whole, he may legitimately deduce that the parameters responsible for the changes from field to field are of such a nature, and so joined to the main variables, that they *may be* represented by step-functions (for full-functions could not give the discrete movement from distinct trial to distinct trial). That they *may* be so represented is a meaningful restriction on their nature

If now we couple this deduction with what has been called

Dancoff s principle—that systems made efficient by natural selection will not use variety or channel capacity much in excess of the minimum—then we can deduce that when organisms regularly use the method of trials there is strong presumptive (though not conclusive) evidence that their trials will be controlled by material entities having (relative to the rest of the system) not much more than the minimal variety. There is therefore strong presumptive evidence that the significant variables in S (of Figure 7/5/1) are step-functions, and that the material entities embodying them are of such a nature as will easily show such functional forms.

Levels of feedback

9/14. We can next consider how the formulation of Chapter 7, and Figure 7/5/1, compares with the real organism's organisation in respect of the division of the feedbacks into two clearly distinguishable orders: between organism and environment by the usual sensory and motor channels, and that passing through the essential variables and step-mechanisms to the reacting part R.

Chapter 7 followed the strategy described in S. 2/17: we attempted to get a type-system *perfectly* clear, so that it would act as a suitable reference for many real systems that do not correspond to it exactly. To get a clear case we assumed that the system (organism and environment joined) was subject to just two types of disturbance from outside. Of one type is the impulsive disturbance to the system's main variables; by this their state is displaced to some non-equilibrial position; this happens if a Homeostat's needle is pushed away from the centre, as at D_1 in Figure 8/4/1; or if the fire by the kitten suddenly blazes up. Then the organism, if adapted, demonstrates its adaptation by taking the action appropriate to the new state. A number of such impulsive disturbances, each with an interval for reaction to occur, are necessary if the organism's adaptation is to be tested and demonstrated.

Of the other type is the disturbance in which some parameter to the whole system is changed (from the value it had over the many impulsive disturbances, to some new value). This change stands in quite a different relation to the system from the change implied by the impulse. Whereas the impulse made the system demonstrate its stability, the change at the parameter made the system demonstrate (if possible) its ultrastability. Whereas the system demonstrates, after the impulse, its power of returning to the *state* of equilibrium, it demonstrates, after the change of parameter-value, its power of returning the field (of its main variables) to a stable *form*. The ultrastable system is thus the appropriate form for the organism if the disturbances that come to it from the world around fall into two clearly defined classes:

(1) Frequent (or even continuous) small impulsive disturbances to the main variables

(2) Occasional changes, of step-function form, to its parameters.

The ultrastable system is thus not merely a didactic device; it may, in some cases, actually be the optimal mechanism by which an organism can ensure its survival. *When the disturbances that threaten the organism have, over many generations, had the bi-modal form just described, we may expect to find that the organism will, under natural selection, have developed a form fairly close to the ultrastable, in that it will have developed two readily distinguishable feedbacks.*

9/15. It is not for a moment suggested that all natural stimuli, disturbances, and problems come to kittens in the tidily dichotomous way in which we have brought them to the Homeostat. Neither is it suggested that the real brain can always be viewed as ultrastable, if only we can find the right way of approach. On the contrary, it is only when we scientists are fortunate that we will find that a complex system can be reduced conceptually into manageable subsystems, as the Homeostat is reducible into its continuous part with feedbacks between the needles, and its stepwise varying part around the second feedback If there are many feedback loops, and there is no convenient way of individualising them, then simplicity is not to be had, and there is nothing for it but to treat the system as one whole, of high complexity. (The subject is discussed from Chapter 11 through the remainder of the book)

The control of aim

9/16. The ultrastable systems discussed so far, though developing a variety of fields, have sought a constant goal. The Homeostat sought central positions and the rat sought zero grill-potential.

In this section will be described some methods by which the goal may be varied. Variations in the goal will be important in those cases in which the goal is only a sub-goal, sought temporarily or provisionally for the achievement of some other goal that is permanent (S. 3/15).

If the critical states' distribution in the main-variables' phase-space is altered by any means whatever, the ultrastable system will be altered in the goal it seeks. For the ultrastable system will always develop a field which keeps the representative point within the region of the critical states (S. 7/23). Thus if (Figure 9/16/1) for some reason the critical states moved to surround B

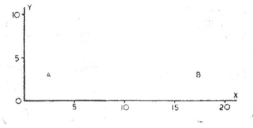

FIGURE 9/16/1.

instead of A, then the terminal field would change from one which kept x between 0 and 5 to one which kept x between 15 and 20.

A related method is illustrated by Figure 9/16/2. An ultra-

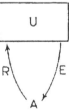

FIGURE 9/16/2.

stable system U interacts with a variable A. E and R represent the immediate effects which U and A have on each other; they may be thought of as U's effectors and receptors. If A should have a marked effect on the ultrastable system, the latter will, of course, develop a field stabilising A; at what value will depend markedly on the action of R. Suppose, for instance, that U has its critical states all at values 0 and 10, so that it always selects a field stabilising all its main variables between these values. If R is such that, if A has some value a, R transmits to U the value $5a - 20$, then it is easy to see that U will develop a field holding A within one unit of the value 5; for if the field makes A go outside the range 4 to 6, it will make U go outside the range 0 to 10, and this will destroy the field. So U becomes '5-seeking'. If the action of R is now changed to transmitting, not $5a - 20$ but $5a + 5$, then U will change fields until it holds A within one unit of 0, and U is now '0-seeking'. So anything that controls the b in $R = 5a + b$ controls the 'goal' sought by U.

As a more practical example, suppose U is mobile and is ultrastable, with its critical states set so that it seeks situations of high illumination; such would occur if its critical states resembled, in Figure 9/16/1, B rather than A. Suppose too that R is a ray of light. If in the path of R we place a red colour-filter, then green light will count as 'no light' and the system will actively seek the red places and avoid the green   If now we merely replace the red filter by a green, the whole aim of its movements will be altered, for it will now seek the green places and avoid the red.

Next, suppose R is a transducer that converts a temperature at A into an illumination which it transmits to U. If R is arranged so that a high temperature at A is converted into a high illumination, then U will become actively goal-seeking for hot places. And if the relation within R is reversed, U will seek for cold places. Clearly, whatever controls R controls U's goal.

There is therefore in general no difficulty in accounting for the fact that a system may seek one goal at one time and another goal at another time.

Sometimes the change, of critical states or of the transducer R. may be under the control of a single parameter. When this happens we must distinguish two complexities. Suppose the parameter can take only two values and the system U is very complicated. Then the system is simple in the sense that it will seek one of only two goals, and is complicated in the sense that the behaviour with which it gets to the goal is complicated. That the behaviour is complicated is no proof, or even suggestion, that the parameter's relations to the system must be complicated; for, as was shown in S. 6/3, the number of fields is equal to the number of values the parameter can take, and has nothing to do with the number of main variables. It is this latter that determines, in general, the complexity of the goal-seeking behaviour.

These considerations may clarify the relations between the change of concentration of a sex-hormone in the blood of a mammal and its consequent sexual goal-seeking behaviour. A simple alternation between 'present' and 'absent', or between two levels with a threshold, would be sufficient to account for any degree of complexity in the two behaviours, for the complexity is not to be related to the hormone-parameter but to the nervous system that is affected by it. Since the mammalian nervous system is extremely complex, and since it is, at almost every point, sensitive to both physical and chemical influences, there seems to be no reason to suppose that the directiveness of the sex-hormones on the brain's behaviour is essentially different from that of any parameter on the system it controls. (That the sex-hormones evoke specifically sexual behaviour is, of course, explicable by the fact that evolution, through natural selection, has constructed specific mechanisms that react to the hormone in the specific way.)

The gene-pattern and ultrastability

9/17. We can now return to the questions of S. 1/9 and ask what part is played by the gene-pattern in the determination of the process of adaptation.

Taking the diagram of immediate effects (Figure 7/5/1) as basis, the question is answerable without difficulty if we take the system part by part and channel by channel.

The environment is, of course, assumed to be given arbitrarily; so is the channel by which the environment affects the essential variables (S. 7/3). The essential variables and their limits are determined by the gene-pattern (S. 3/14); for these are species' characteristics.

In the living organism, the reacting part R has, in effect, three types of 'input': there is the sensory input from the environment, there are the values of its parameters in S, and there are those parameters that were determined genetically during embryonic development. (That all three may be regarded as 'input' has been shown in I. to C., S. 13/11). These three sets of parameters vary on very different time-scales: the genetic parameters, those that make this a dog-brain and that a bird-brain, are in evidence only at one period in a lifetime; the parameters in S, if the adaptation proceeds by clearly marked trials, change only between trial and trial; and the parameters at the sensory input vary more or less continuously   The influence of the gene-pattern can thus be traced in R, giving it certain anatomical tracts, biochemical processes, histological structures, and thus determining whether it shall adapt as a dog does or as a starfish does.

The nature of the parameters in S is wholly under genetic control, for their physical embodiment has probably been selected for suitability by natural selection. (Here the *nature* of the parameters—whether they are reverberating circuits, or molecular configurations, etc —must be clearly distinguished from the *values* that any one parameter may take)

Finally there is the relation between the essential variables and those in S—that the essential variables must force those in S to change when the essential variables are outside their physiological limits, and not to change otherwise (S. 7/7). As this relation is entirely *ad hoc*, it must be determined by the gene-pattern, for there is no other source for its selection.

These are the ways, then, in which the gene-pattern must act as determinant to the living organism's mechanism for adaptation.

9/18. A question that must be answered is whether ultrastability, as described here, can reasonably be supposed to have been developed by natural selection; for the *ad hoc* features of the previous section have no other determinant adequate for their selection and adjustment.

For ultrastability to have been developed by natural selection, it is necessary and sufficient that there should exist a sequence of forms, from the simplest to the most complex, such that each form has better survival-value than that before it.   In other words, ultrastability must not become of value to the organism only when some complex form has all its parts and relations correct simultaneously, for such an event occurs only rarely.

Suppose the original organism had no step-mechanisms; such an organism would have a permanent, invariable set of reactions. If a mutation should lead to the formation of a single step-mechanism whose critical states were such that, when the organism became distressed, it changed value *before* the essential variables transgressed their limits, and if the step-mechanism affected in any way the reaction between the organism and the environment, then such a step-mechanism might increase the organism's chance of survival.   A single mutation causing a single step-mechanism might therefore prove advantageous; and this advantage, though slight, might be sufficient to establish the mutation as a species characteristic. Then a second mutation might continue the process. The change from the original system to the ultrastable can therefore be made by a long series of small changes, each of which improves the chance of survival. The change is thus possible under the action of natural selection

Summary

9/19. The solution of the problem of Chapter 1 is now completed in its essentials. It may be summarised as follows:

In the type-problem of S. 1/17 the disturbances that come to the organism are of two widely different types (the distribution is bi-modal). One type is small, frequent, impulsive, and acts on the main variables. The other is large, infrequent, and induces a change of step-function form on the parameters to the reacting part. Included in the latter type is the major disturbance of embryogenesis, which first sends the organism into the world with a brain sufficiently disorganised to require correction (in this respect, learning and adaptation are related, for the same solution is valid for both)

To such a distribution of disturbances the appropriate regulator (to keep the essential variables within physiological limits) is one whose total feedbacks fall into a correspondingly bi-modal form. There will be feedbacks to give stability against the frequent impulsive disturbances to the main variables, and there will be a slower-acting feedback giving changes of step-function form to give stability against the infrequent disturbances of step-function form.

Such a whole can be regarded simply as one complex regulator that is stable against a complex (bi-modal) set of disturbances. Or it can equivalently be regarded as a first-order regulator (against the small impulsive disturbances) that can reorganise itself to achieve this stability after the disturbance of embryogenesis or after a major change in its conditions has destroyed this stability. When the biologist regards the system in this second way, he says that the organism has ' learned ', and he notices that the learning always tends towards the better way of behaving

9/20. Such is the solution in outline. The reader, however, may well feel that the amount of information given by the solution is small.

To some extent, the generality of the ultrastable system, the degree to which it does *not* specify details, is correct. Adaptation can be shown by systems far wider in extent than the mammalian and cerebral, and any proposed solution would manifestly be wrong if it stated that, say, myelin was necessary, when the Homeostat obviously contains none. Thus the generality, or if you will the vagueness, of the ultrastable system is, from that point of view, as it should be.

However, the attempt to apply this general formulation to the real nervous system soon encounters major difficulties. What these are, and how they are to be treated, will occupy the remainder of the book.

CHAPTER 10

The Recurrent Situation

10/1. With the previous chapter we came to the end of our study of how the organism changes from the unadapted to the adapted condition. But this simple problem and solution is only a first step towards our understanding of the living, and especially of the human, brain. To the simple ultrastable system we must obviously add further complications. Thus the living organism not only becomes adapted, but it does so by a process that shows some evidence of efficiency, in the sense that the adaptation is reached by a path that is not grossly far from the path that would involve the least time, and energy, and risk. Though ' efficiency ' is not yet accurately defined in this context, few would deny that the Homeostat's performance suggests something of inefficiency. But before we rush in to make ' improvements ' we must be clear about what we are assuming.

10/2. Let us return to first principles. ' Success ', or ' adaptation ', means to an organism that, in spite of the world doing its worst, the organism so responded that it survived for the duration necessary for reproduction.

Now ' what the world did ' can be regarded as a single, life-long, and very complex Grand Disturbance (*I. to C.*, Chapter 10), to which the organism produces a single, life-long, and very complex Grand Response; how they are related determines the Grand Outcome—success or failure. In the most general case, the partial disturbances that make up this Grand Disturbance, and the partial responses that make up the organism's Grand Response (*I. to C.*, S. 13/8) may be interrelated to any degree, from zero to complete. (The interrelation is ' complete ' when the Grand Outcome is a function of *all* the partial responses; it would correspond to an extremely complex relation between partial responses and final outcome.)

The case of the complete interrelation, though fundamental

theoretically (because of its complete generality), is of little importance in practice, for its occurrence in the terrestrial world is rare (though it may occur more commonly in models or in processes of adaptation set up in large computers). Were it common, a brain would be useless (*I. to C.*, S. 13/5). In fact, brains have been developed because the terrestrial environment usually confronts the organism with a Grand Disturbance that has a major degree of constraint within its component parts, of which the organism can take advantage. Thus the organism commonly faces a world that repeats itself, that is consistent to some degree in obeying laws, that is not wholly chaotic. The greater the degree of constraint, the more can the adapting organism specialise against the particular forms of environment that do occur. As it specialises so will its efficiency against the particular form of environment increase. If the reader feels the ultrastable system, as described so far, to be extremely low in efficiency, this is because it is as yet quite unspecialised; and the reader is evidently unconsciously pitting it against a set of environments that he has restricted in some way not yet stated explicitly in this book.

10/3. The chapters that follow will consider several constraints of outstanding commonness and will show how the appropriate specialisations exemplify the above propositions in several ways. They will consider certain ways in which the ordinary terrestrial environments fail to show the full range; and we will see how these restrictions indicate ways in which the living organism can specialise so as to take advantage of them.

The recurrent situation

10/4. In this chapter we will consider the case, of great importance in real life, in which the occasional disturbances (class 2 of S. 9/14) are sometimes repetitive, and in which a response, if adaptive on the disturbance's first appearance, is also adaptive when the same disturbance appears for the second, third, and later times.

We must not take for granted that one response will be adaptive to all occurrences of the disturbance, for there are cases in which what is appropriate to a disturbance depends on how many times it has appeared before. An outstanding example is given by the rat facing that environment (a natural one by S. 3/1) in which food will appear on two successive nights at the same place, followed, on the third night, by a lethal mixture of the same food and poison (the method of 'pre-baiting'). Environments such as this are intrinsically complex. Complete adaptation here (under the assumptions made) demands the reaction-pattern: eat, eat, abstain. This reaction-pattern is more complex than the simple reaction-pattern of eating, or of abstaining: for the three parts must be related, and the triple organised holistically.

In this chapter we shall consider the other case, of frequent occurrence, in which what is appropriate to the disturbance is conditional on which disturbance it is, but not on when it occurs in the sequence of disturbances

So far, the ultrastable system (represented, say, by the Homeostat) has been presented (e.g. in the Figures throughout Chapter 8) with changes of parameter-value such that the later value is merely different from the earlier; now we consider the case in which the parameter takes a sequence of values, e.g.

$$P_2 \, P_8 \, P_2 \, P_1 \, P_6 \, P_4 \, P_6 \, P_1 \, P_2 \, \ldots$$

in which repetitions occur at irregular intervals, and in which a response to P_2, say, if adaptive on P_2's first occurrence, is also adaptive to P_2 on its later occurrences.

When this is the case, the opportunity exists for advantage to be taken of the fact that P_2 can be responded to at once on its later occurrences, without the necessity of a second exploratory series of trials and errors.

This case is particularly important because (S. 8/10) it includes the case in which the changes of P-value correspond to changes from one environment to another. Suppose, for instance, that a wild rat learns first to adapt to conditions in a stable (P_2), then to conditions in a nearby barn (P_3), and so on. Having adapted first to the stable and then to the barn, its survival value would obviously be enhanced if it could return to the stable and at once resume the adaptations that it had previously developed there. An organism with such a power can *accumulate* adaptations.

10/5. To see what is necessary, let us see what happens in the Homeostat A little reflection, or an actual test, soon shows that the present model is totally devoid of such power of accumulation. Thus in Figure 8/4/1 the reversal at R_2 restores the external conditions to which it was already adapted at D_1; yet after the events following the first reversal (at R_1), the first adaptation (at D_1) is totally lost; and the Homeostat treats the situation after R_2 as if the situation had occurred for the first time

In general, if the Homeostat is given a problem A, then a problem B, and then A again, it treats A as if it had never encountered A before; the activities during the adaptation to B have totally destroyed the previous adaptation to A. (The psychologist would say that retroactive inhibition was complete, S. 16/12.)

This way of adapting to A on its second presentation cannot be improved upon if the environment is such that there is no implication that the second reaction to A should be the same as the first. The Homeostat's behaviour might then be described as that of a system that ' does not jump to conclusions ' and that ' treats every new situation on its merits '. In a world in which pre-baiting was the rule, the Homeostat would be better than the rat ! When, however, the environment *does* show the constraint assumed in this chapter, the Homeostat fails to take advantage of it. How should it be modified to make this possible ?

10/6. The Homeostat has, in fact, a small resource for dealing with recurrent situations, but the method is of small practical use. In S. 8/10 we saw that the Homeostat's ultimate field is one that is stable to all the situations, so that a change from one to another demands no new trials.

10/7. This method, however, cannot be used extensively in the adaptations of real life, for two reasons. The first is that when the number of values is increased beyond a few, the time taken for a suitable set of step-function values to be found is likely to increase beyond anything ordinarily available, a topic that will be treated more thoroughly in Chapter 11. The second is that the adaptation, even if established, is secure only if the set of parameter-values is closed, i.e. so long as no new value occurs. Should a new value occur, everything goes back into the melting-pot, and adaptation to the new set of values (the old set increased by one new member) has to start from scratch. Common observation shows, of course, that each new adaptation does not destroy all the old; evidently the method of S. 8/10 is of little practical importance.

The accumulator of adaptations

10/8. To see what is necessary, let us take for granted that organisms are usually able to add new adaptations without destroying the old. Let us take this as given, and deduce what modifications it enforces on the formulation of S. 7/5. Suppose, then, that an organism has adapted to a value P_1, has then adapted to P_2 by trial and error as in S. 7/23, and that when P_1 is restored the organism is found to be adapted *at once*, without further trials. What can we deduce ?

(The arguments that culminated in S. 7/8 apply here without alteration, so we can take for granted that the adaptation to each individual value of P takes place through the second feedback, with essential variables controlling step-functions as in S. 7/7. The modification to be made can be found by a direct application of the method of S. 4/12, seeing whether variation at one variable leads to variation at another.)

To follow the argument through, let us define two sub-sets of the step-mechanisms in S that affect R (Figure 7/5/1).

S_1: those step-mechanisms whose change, with P at P_1, would cause a loss of the adaptation to P_1 (i.e. those step-mechanisms that are effective towards R when P is at P_1);

S_2. those step-mechanisms that were permanently changed in value after the trials that led to the adaptation to P_2.

First it follows that *the sets S_1 and S_2 are disjunct*, i.e. have no common member. For if there were such a common member it would (as a member of S_2) be changed in value when P_1 was applied for the second time, and therefore (as a member of S_1) would force the behaviour at P_1 to be changed on P_1's second presentation, contrary to hypothesis. Thus, for the retention of adaptation to P_1, in spite of that to P_2, the step-mechanisms must fall into *separate classes*

(That the step-mechanisms must be split into classes can be made plausible by thinking of the step-mechanisms, in any ultra-stable system, as *carrying information about how the essential variables have behaved in the past*. When P_1 is presented for the second time, for the behaviour to be at once adaptive, information must be available somewhere about how the essential variables behaved in the past (for by hypothesis they are to give none now, and they are the only source). Thus somewhere in the system there must be this information stored; and these stores must *not* be accessible while P_2 is acting, or they will be affected by the events and the stored information over-written. Thus there must be separate stores for P_1 and P_2, and provision for their separate use.)

Next, consider the channel from the essential variables. In condition P_2, the channel from them to the step-mechanisms in S_2 was evidently open, for events at the essential variables (whether within physiological limits or not) affected what happened in S_2 (by the ordinary processes of adaptation). On the other hand, during this time the channel from the essential variables to the step-mechanisms in S_1 was evidently closed, for changes in the essential variables were followed by *no* changes in the step-mechanisms of S_1. Thus the channel from the essential variables to the step-mechanisms S must be divisible into sections, so that some can conduct while the others do not; and the determination of which is to conduct must be, at least partly, under the control of the conditions P, varying as P varies between P_1 and P_2.

Finally, consider the channels from S_1 and S_2 to the reacting part R. When P_1 is applied for the second time, the channel from S_2 to R is evidently closed, for though the parameters in S_2 are changed (before and after P_2), yet no change occurs in R's behaviour (by hypothesis). On the other hand, that from S_1 is evidently open, for it is S_1's values that determine the behaviour under P_1, and it is the adapted form that is made to appear.

10/9. To summarise:—Let it be given that the organism has adapted to P_1 by trial and error, then it adapted similarly to P_2, and that when P_1 was given for the second time the organism was adapted at once, without further trials. From this we may deduce that the step-mechanisms *must* be divisible into non-overlapping sets, that the reactions to P_1 and P_2 must each be due to their particular sets, and that the presentation of the problem (i.e. the value of P) must determine which set is to be brought into functional connexion, the remainder being left in functional isolation.

Thus if the diagram of Figure 7/5/1 is taken as basic, it must be modified so that the step-mechanisms are split into sets, there must be some gating mechanism Γ to determine which set shall be on the feedback circuit, and the gating mechanism Γ must be controlled (usually through R, as this is the organism's structure) by the value of P.

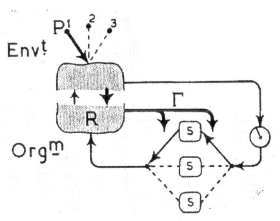

FIGURE 10/9/1.

Figure 10/9/1 presents the diagram of immediate effects, but the Figure is best thought of as a mere mnemonic for the functional relations, lest it suggest some anatomical form too strongly. The parameter P can be set at various values, P_1, P_2, ... The step-mechanisms are divided into sets, and there is a gating mechanism Γ, controlled by P through the environment and the reacting part R, that determines which of the sets shall be effective in the second feedback *via* the essential variables.

10/10. The diagram of Figure 10/9/1 and the behaviour of the gating mechanism may seem somewhat complex, but we must beware of seeing into it more complexity than is necessary. All that is *necessary* is that the step-mechanisms involved in any particular problem P_i be distinct from those involved in the others, that if S_i be affected by the essential variables then S_i shall be the mechanisms that affect R, and that there shall be a correspondence between the problems and the sets of step-mechanisms. This latter correspondence need not be orderly or ' rational '; it may be perfectly well set up at random (i.e. determined by factors

144

outside our present view) provided only that if the presentation of a particular problem P_i got through to some set S_i, then always when P_i is presented again the actions shall again go through to S_i. Such a case would occur if the connexions were, say, electrical and made by plugging connexions at random into a plug-board. Once made, they would ensure that recurrence of P_i would give the same pattern for the selection of S_i; and the change from P_i to some other problem, P_j say, by involving some change in the sensory input to R, would cause some change in the distribution over the step-mechanisms.

In the same way, if nerve-cells were to grow at random (i.e. determined in their growth by local temporary details of oxygen supply, mechanical forces, etc) until their histological details were established, and if the paths taken by impulses depended on the concatentation of stimuli coming in, then the recurrence of P_i would always give access to S_i, and a change from P_i to P_j, by changing the sensory stimuli, would change the distribution.

An easy method by which Γ may be provided is given in S. 16/13.

These details need not detain us. They are mentioned only to show that the basic requirements are easily met, and that the mechanism meeting them may look far less tidy than Figure 10/9/1 might suggest. In this sense the Figure, though helpful in some ways, is apt to be seriously misleading In S. 16/12 we return to the matter.

10/11. In the previous sections, the various situations P_1, P_2, P_3, . . . were arbitrary, and not assumed to have any particular relation between them. A special case, common enough to be of interest, occurs when the situations usually occur in a particular sequence. Thus a young child, reaching across the table for a biscuit, may have first to get his hand past the edge of the table without striking it, then the hand past his cup without spilling it, then past the jam without his sleeve wiping it, and so on: a sequence of actions, each of which calls for some adaptation. Much of life consists of just such sequences.

The system of Figure 10/9/1 can readily give such sequences in which every part is adapted to its own little problem. The situation of ' hand coming past the edge of the table and in danger of striking it ' is P_1, say Adaptation to this situation can occur in the usual way, by the basic method of the ultrastable system.

The sleeve passing near open jam is another situation, P_2; adaptation to this, too, can occur. And the alterations necessary in adaptation to P_2 will not, in our present system, cause loss of the adaptation to P_1.

Whether the whole situation can be adapted to by such a sequence of sub-adaptations (to P_1, to P_2, etc.) depends *on the environment*: only certain types of environment will allow such fragmentation. If such types of environment are frequent in an organism's life, then there will be advantage in evolution if the species changes so that each organism is provided, genetically, with a mechanism similar to that of Figure 10/9/1.

10/12. To amplify the point, we may consider the case of an organism that lives in an environment that consists of many sensorily-different situations, and such that each situation is adequately met by one of two reactions, eat or flee say, so that the organism's problem in life is to allot one of the two reactions to each of many situations. In such an environment, the reacting part R of Figures 7/5/1 or 10/9/1 could be quite small, for it requires only mechanism capable of performing two reflexes. The stores of step-mechanisms, however, would have to be large, and the gating mechanism Γ perhaps elaborate; for here would have to be as many records as there are sensory situations. Each would require its own locus of storage, and the gating mechanism would have to be able to ensure that each situation led to its particular locus. In such a world we would, therefore, expect the organism to have a differently proportioned brain from one that lived in a world such as was presented to the Homeostat.

It should not be beyond the biologist's powers to identify a species with such an environment. Examination of the organism's nervous system might then enable some fundamental identifications to be made.

10/13. The objection may be raised that the specification deduced in this chapter is too vague to be of use to the worker who wants to find the corresponding mechanism in, say, the human brain. The reply must be that the specification is right to be vague; for what is given—that adaptation occurs with accumulation—specifies an extremely broad class of mechanisms, so that a very great diversity of actual machines could all show adaptation with accumulation. If they can all show it, a deduction would be patently wrong if, without further *data*, it proceeded to indicate some one of the class.

What the deduction has shown is that we must give up our naïve conviction that the outstanding behavioural properties of adaptation indicate some unique cerebral mechanism, or that they will provide the unique explanation of the features of the living brain. 'Many of these features cannot be related uniquely to the processes of adaptation, for these processes can go on in systems that lack those neurophysiological features, systems very different from the living brain, such as the modern computer. Only further information, beyond that assumed in this chapter, can take the identification further.

CHAPTER 11

The Fully-joined System

11/1. The Homeostat is, of course, grossly different from the brain in many respects, one of the most obvious being that while the brain has a very great number of component parts the Homeostat has, effectively, only four. This difference does not make the theory of the ultrastable system totally inapplicable, for much of the theory is true regardless of the number of parts, which is simply irrelevant. Nevertheless, we are in danger, after spending so much time getting to know a system of four parts, of developing a set of images, a set of working mental concepts, that is seriously out of proportion if considered as a set of working concepts with which to think about the real brain. Let us therefore consider specifically the properties of the ultrastable system that has a very great number of parts We shall find that one difficulty becomes outstanding, and we shall spend the remainder of the book dealing with it, for it is the main problem in the adaptation of large systems.

Adaptation-time

11/2. Suppose the Homeostat were of a thousand units. Such a size goes only a small fraction of the way to brain-size, but it will serve our purpose. Such a system will have a thousand relays (F, Figure 8/2/3); let us suppose that all but a hundred are shorted out, so that the system is left with one hundred essential variables. This number may be of the same order of size as the number of essential variables in a living organism.

Since these variables are essential, adaptation implies that *all* are to be kept within their proper limits. Let us try a rough preliminary calculation Simplifying the situation further, let us suppose that the step-mechanisms, as they change, give to each essential variable a 50–50 chance of going within, or outside of, its limits, and that the chances are independent. (The case of independence should be considered, by the strategy of S. 2/17,

148

as the case is central) We ask, *how many trials* will, on the average, be required for adaptation ?

Each variable has a probability $\frac{1}{2}$ of being kept within its limits. At any one trial the probability that all of 100 will be kept in is $(\frac{1}{2})^{100}$, and so the average number of trials will be 2^{100}, by S. 22/7. How long will this take, at, say, one per second ? The answer is: about 10^{22} years, a time unimaginably vaster than all astronomically meaningful time ! For practical purposes this is equivalent to never, and so we arrive at our major problem: the brain, though having many components, *does* adapt in a fairly short time—the 1,000-unit Homeostat, though of vastly fewer components, does not. What is wrong ?

It can hardly be that the brain does not use the basic process of ultrastability, for the arguments of S. 7/8 show that *any* system made of parts that obey the ordinary laws of cause and effect must use this method. Further, there is no reason to suppose that the function 2^N, where N is the number of essential variables, is seriously in error, even though it is somewhat uncertain: other lines of reasoning (given below) also lead to the same order of size, a size far too large to be compatible with the known facts. There seems to be little doubt that a 1,000-unit Homeostat would quite fail, by its slowness in getting adapted, to resemble the mammalian brain. Wherein, then, does this system not resemble (in an essential way) the system of brain and environment ?

11/3. In the previous section the dynamic nature of the brain and environment was really ignored, for the calculation was based on a direct relation between step-mechanisms and essential variables, while what connected them was ignored. Let us now ask the question again, ignoring the essential variables but observing the dynamic systems of environment and reacting part (Figure 7/2/1). Two type-cases are worth consideration (by S. 2/17).

The first case occurs when the system is linear, like the Homeostat, so that it has only one state of equilibrium, which can be stable or unstable. In this case, unstable fields are of no use to the organism, for they do not persist; only the stable can be of enduring use, for only they persist. Let us ask then: if a Homeostat had a thousand units, how many trials would be necessary for a *stable* field to be found ? Though the answer to this question is not known, for the mathematical problem has not yet been solved, there is evidence (S. 20/10) suggesting that in some typical cases the number will be of the order of 2^N, where N is the number of variables   There seems to be little doubt that if a Homeostat were made with a thousand units, practically every field would be unstable, and the chance of one occurring in a lifetime would be practically zero. We thus arrive at much the same conclusion as before.

The second case to be considered is that of the system that has the transformation on its states formed at random, so that every state goes equiprobably to every state. Such systems have been studied by Rubin and Sitgreaves. Among their results they find that the modal length of trajectory is $\sqrt{n}$, where n is the number of states. Now if the whole is made of N parts, each of which can take any one of σ states, then the whole can take any one of σ^N. This is n; so the modal length of trajectory is $\sqrt{\sigma^N}$, which can be written as $(\sqrt{\sigma})^N$. Again, if we fill in some plausible numbers, with $N = 1,000$, we find that the length of trajectory, and therefore the time before the system settles to *some* equilibrium, takes a time utterly beyond that ordinarily observed to be taken by the living brain.

11/4. The three functions given by the three calculations are all of the exponential type, in that the number of trials is proportional to some number raised to the *power* of the number of essential variables or parts. Exponential functions have a fundamental peculiarity: they increase with deceptive slowness when the exponent is small, and then develop with breath-taking speed as the exponent gets larger. Thus, so long as the Homeostat has only a few units, the number of trials it requires is not large. Let its size undergo the moderate increase to a thousand parts, however, and the number of trials rushes up to numbers that make even the astronomical look insignificant. In the presence of this exponential form, a mere speeding up of the individual trials, or similar modification, will not bring the numbers down to an ordinary size.

11/5. What had made the processes of the last two sections so excessively time-consuming is that partial successes go for nothing. To see how potent is this fact, consider a simple calculation which will illustrate the point.

Suppose N events each have a probability p of success, and the probabilities are independent. An example would occur if N wheels bore letters A and B on the rim, with A's occupying the fraction p of the circumference and B's the remainder. All are spun and allowed to come to rest; those that stop at an A count as successes. Let us compare three ways of compounding these minor successes to a Grand Success,* which, we assume, occurs only when every wheel is stopped at an A.

Case 1: All N wheels are spun; if all show an A, Success is recorded and the trials ended; otherwise all are spun again, and so on till ' all A's ' comes up at one spin.

Case 2: The first wheel is spun; if it stops at an A it is left there; otherwise it is spun again. When it eventually stops at an A the second wheel is spun similarly; and so on down the line of N wheels, one at a time, till all show A's

Case 3: All N wheels are spun; those that show an A are left to continue showing it, and those that show a B are spun again. When further A's occur they also are left alone. So the number spun gets fewer and fewer, until all are at A's.

Regard each spin (regardless of the number of wheels turned) as one trial. We now ask, how many trials, on the average, will the three cases require ?

Case 1 will require $\left(\dfrac{1}{p}\right)^N$, as in S. 11/2. Case 2 will require, on the average, $1/p$ for the first wheel, then $1/p$ for the second, and so on; and thus N/p for them all. Case 3 is difficult to calculate but will be the average of the longest of a sample of N drawn from the distribution of length of run for one wheel; it will be somewhat larger than $1/p$.

The calculations are of interest not for their quantitative exactness but because when N gets large they tend to widely differing values. Suppose, for instance, that p is $\frac{1}{2}$, that spins occur at one a second, and that N is 1,000. Then if T_1, T_2, and T_3 are the average times to reach Success in Cases 1, 2, and 3 respectively,

$$T_1 = 2^{1000} \text{ seconds,}$$

$$T_2 = \frac{1000}{2} \text{ seconds,}$$

$$T_3 = \text{rather more than } \tfrac{1}{2} \text{ second.}$$

* As we shall have to consider several compoundings of minor events to major events, I shall use the convention of *I. to C.*, S. 13/8, and distinguish them respectively by a lower case, or a capital, initial.

When these values are converted to ordinary quantities, T_1 is about 10^{293} years, T_2 is about 8 minutes, and T_3 is a few seconds. Thus, while getting Success under the rules of Case 1 (all simultaneously) is practically impossible, getting it under Cases 2 and 3 is easy.

The final conclusion—that Case 1 is very different from Cases 2 and 3—does not depend closely on the particular values of p and N. It illustrates the general fact that the exponential function (Case 1) tends to become large at an altogether faster rate than the linear. If the reader likes to try other numbers he is likely to arrive at results showing much the same features.

11/6. Comparison of the three Cases soon shows why Cases 2 and 3 can arrive at Success so much sooner than Case 1: they can benefit by partial successes, which 1 cannot. Suppose, for instance, that, under Case 1, a spin gave 999 A's and 1 B. This is very near complete Success; yet it counts for nothing, and all the A's have to be thrown back into the melting-pot. In Case 3, however, only one wheel would remain to be spun; while Case 2 would perhaps get a good run of A's at the left-hand end and could thus benefit somewhat.

The examples thus show the great, the very great, reduction in time taken that occurs when the final Success can be reached by stages, in which partial successes can be conserved and *accumulated*.

11/7. It is difficult to find a real example which shows in one system the three ways of progression to Success, for few systems are constructed so flexibly. It is, however, possible to construct, by the theory of probability, examples which show the differences referred to. Thus suppose that, as the traffic passes, we note the final digit on each car's number-plate, and decide that we want to see cars go past with the final digits 0, 1, 2, 3, 4, 5, 6, 7, 8, 9, in that order. If we insist that the ten cars shall pass consecutively, as in Case 1, then on the average we shall have to wait till about 10,000,000,000 cars have passed: for practical purposes such an event is impossible. But if we allow success to be achieved by first finding a ' 0 ', then finding a ' 1 ', and so on until a ' 9 ' is seen, as in Case 2, then the number of cars which must pass will be about fifty, and this number makes ' Success ' easily achievable.

11/8. A well-known physical example illustrating the difference is the crystallisation of a solid from solution. When in solution, the molecules of the solute move at random so that in any given interval of time there is a definite probability that a given molecule will possess a motion and position suitable for its adherence to the crystal. Now the smallest visible crystal contains billions of molecules: if a visible crystal could form only when all its molecules happened simultaneously to be properly related in position and motion to one another (Case 1), then crystallisation could never occur: it would be too improbable   But in fact crystallisation can occur by succession (Case 2), for once a crystal has begun to form, a single molecule which happens to possess the right position and motion can join the crystal regardless of the positions and motions of the other molecules in the solution. So the crystallisation can proceed by stages, and the time taken resembles T_2 rather than T_1.

We may draw, then, the following conclusion. *A compound event that is impossible if the components have to occur simultaneously may be readily achievable if they can occur in sequence or independently.*

11/9. It is now becoming apparent in what way the 1,000-unit Homeostat, which takes such an excessively long time to adapt, differs from the living organism, which usually gets adapted in a fraction of its generation-time. The organism, of course, does not reach its full adult adaptation by making trial after trial, all of which count for nothing until suddenly everything comes right ! On the contrary, it conforms more to the rules of Cases 2 or 3, achieving partial successes and then *retaining them* while improving what is still unsatisfactory.

However, before we turn to consider the latter cases we should notice that the 1,000-unit Homeostat is not wholly atypical, for environments *do* exist, though they are rare, that demand that all successes occur simultaneously and against which partial successes count for nothing. When they occur, it is notorious that they give the living organism great difficulty. A trifling example occurs when a trout would take a fly on the surface; the trout must both break the surface at the correct place and must also close its jaws at the right moment; two variables here are essential in the sense that both their values must be within proper limits for success to be achieved; failure in either respect means failure totally.

The example *par excellence* occurs when the burglar, homeostatically trying to earn his daily bread by stealing, faces that particular environment known as the combination lock. This environment has, of course, been selected to be as difficult for him as possible; and its peculiar difficulty lies precisely in the fact that partial successes—getting, say, six letters right out of seven —count for nothing. Thus there can be no progression towards the solution. Thus, confronted with an environment that does not permit use to be made of partial adaptation, human and Homeostat fail alike.

Cumulative adaptation

11/10. In terrestrial environments, however, such problems are not common. Usually the organism has many essential variables, and also it manages to reach an adaptation of all fairly quickly. Let us take these apparently contradictory facts as data, and see what can be deduced from them (following essentially the method of S. 4/12).

Quite a simple example will suffice to show the point. Let us suppose that an organism has three essential variables (marked 1, 2 and 3) all affected by the environment, and all able to veto the stability of the step-mechanisms S, as in Figure 11/10/1.

Let us suppose that the organism has reached the state of being

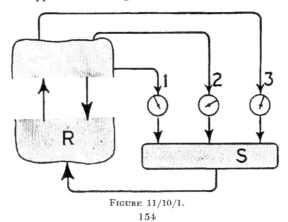

FIGURE 11/10/1.

adapted at essential variables 1 and 2. (More precisely: the disturbance that comes to the environment finds such a set of values on the step-mechanisms S that in the reaction to it, essential variables 1 and 2 never go outside their proper limits.) The reaction does, however, send essential variable 3 outside its limit.

We now take as given that the system will go through a process like that of S. 7/23, and that after it is over the step-mechanisms will be changed to new values such that now essential variable 3 is kept within limits, and also that the other two *still react in the same way as before* (this being necessary if we are to assume that adaptations once formed are held, as we wish to).

To see what this implies, let S_3 be the set of those step-mechanisms that ended with changed values after the trials due to 3's adaptation (some such there must be, or the change of 3's response to the disturbance is an effect without a cause). Now apply the operational test of S. 4/12: as the step-mechanisms in S_3 are changed in value, but the behaviours showing at 1 and 2 are not, it follows that, whatever is shown in Figure 11/10/1, there can be no effective channel of communication from the step-mechanisms S_3 (in S) through R and the environment to 1 and 2.

Next, let M_{12} represent all those parts, in R and the environment, that play a part in determining how the disturbance eventually affects 1 and 2. By M_3 represent similarly the parts on the channel from S_3 through R and the environment to 3. (Nothing is assumed about how M_{12} and M_3 are related.) Now M_3 cannot be void (or S_3 would have no channel to affect 3, and the final adaptation of 3 could not have occurred). Similarly, neither can M_{12} be void. Finally, the earlier deduction that there is no channel from S_3 (through R and environment) to 1 or 2 implies that *there are no common variables to M_{12} and M_3, nor any channel from M_3 to M_{12}* (for otherwise changes at S_3 would show at 1 and 2, contrary to hypothesis).

It has thus been shown that, for adaptations to accumulate, there must *not* be channels from some step-mechanisms (e g. S_3) to some variables (e.g. M_{12}), nor from some variables (e g. M_3) to others (e.g. M_{12}). Thus, for the accumulation of adaptations to be possible the system *must not be fully joined*. The idea so often implicit in physiological writings, that all will be well if only sufficient cross-connexions are available, is, in this context, quite wrong.

155

This is the point. If the method of ultrastability is to succeed within a reasonably short time, then partial successes must be retained   For this to be possible it is necessary that certain parts should *not* communicate to, or have an effect on, certain other parts.

11/11. Now we can see where the Homeostat was misleading. From the beginning of the book (from S. 1/7) we have treated the brain and the environment as richly joined, each within its own parts and each to the other. Thus the Homeostat was built so that every unit did in fact interact with every other unit.   In this way we developed the theory of the system that is integrated totally.

By working throughout with systems which were always assumed to be as richly connected as the reader cared to think them, we avoided the possibility of talking much about integration, and then discussing a mechanism that, in fact, really worked in separate parts. The reacting parts and the environments that we have discussed have so far been integrated in the extreme.

11/12. Nevertheless, it is now clear that one can go too far in this direction. The Homeostat goes too far; it is too well integrated, cannot accumulate adaptations, and thereby takes a quite un-brainlike time in reaching adaptation. What we must discuss now is a system similar to the Homeostat in its ultrastability, but not so richly cross-joined. To what degree, then, should it be cross-joined if it is to resemble the nervous system ?

The views held about the amount of internal connexion in the nervous system—its degree of ' wholeness '—have tended to range from one extreme to the other. The ' reflexologists ' from Bell onwards recognised that in some of its activities the nervous system could be treated as a collection of independent parts   They pointed to the fact, for instance, that the pupillary reflex to light and the patellar reflex occur in their usual forms whether the other reflex is being elicited or not. The coughing reflex follows the same pattern whether the subject is standing or sitting. And the acquirement of a new conditioned response might leave a previously established response largely unaffected. On the other hand, the Gestalt school recognised that many activities of the nervous system were characterised by wholeness, so that what happened at one point was conditional on what was happening at other points. The two sets of facts were sometimes treated as irreconcilable

Yet Sherrington in 1906 had shown by the spinal reflexes that the nervous system was neither divided into permanently separated parts nor so wholly joined that every event always influenced every other   Rather, it showed a richer, and a more intricate picture—one in which interactions and independencies fluctuated. 'Thus, a weak reflex may be excited from the tail of the spinal dog without interference with the stepping-reflex '. . . . 'Two reflexes may be neutral to each other when both are weak, but may interfere when either or both are strong'. . . . ' But to show that reflexes may be neutral to each other in a spinal dog is not evidence that they will be neutral in the animal with its whole nervous system intact and unmutilated.' The separation into many parts and the union into a single whole are simply the two extremes on the scale of ' degree of connectedness '.

Being chiefly concerned with the origin of adaptation and co-ordination, I have tended so far to stress the connectedness of the nervous system.   Yet it must not be overlooked that adaptation may demand independence as well as interaction.   The learner-driver of a motor-car, for instance, who can only just keep the car in the centre of the road, may find that any attempt at changing gear results in the car, apparently, trying to leave the road.   Later, when he is more skilled, the act of changing gear will have no effect on the direction of the car's travel.   Adaptation thus demands not only the integration of related activities but the independence of unrelated activities.

11/13.   From now on, therefore, we will no longer hold the implicit assumption that all parts are richly joined.   This freedom makes possible various modifications that have not so far been explicitly considered, and that give new forms of ultrastable system.   These forms are still ultrastable, for they conform to the definition (which does not involve explicitly the amount of connexion), but they will not be so excessively slow in becoming adapted as the simple form of S. 11/2.   They do this by developing partial, fluctuating, and temporary independencies within the whole, so that the whole becomes an assembly of subsystems within which communication is rich and between which it is more restricted. The study of such systems will occupy the remainder of the book.

CHAPTER 12

Temporary Independence

12/1. SEVERAL times we have used, without definition, the concept of one variable or system being 'independent' of another. It was stated that a system, to be state-determined, must be ' properly isolated ' , and some parameters in S. 6/2 were described as ' ineffective '. So far the simple method of S. 4/12 has been adequate, but as it is now intended to treat of systems that are neither wholly joined nor wholly separated, a more rigorous method is necessary.

The concept of the ' independence ' of two dynamic systems might at first seem simple: is not a lack of material connexion sufficient ? Examples soon show that this criterion is unreliable. Two electrical parts may be in firm mechanical union, yet if the bond is an insulator the two parts may be functionally independent. And two reflex mechanisms in the spinal cord may be inextricably interwoven, and yet be functionally independent.

On the other hand, one system may have no material connexion with another and yet be affected by it markedly: the radio receiver, for instance, in its relation to the transmitter. Even the widest separation we can conceive—the distance between our planet and the most distant nebulae—is no guarantee of functional separation; for the light emitted by those nebulae is yet capable of stirring the astronomers of this planet into controversy. The criterion of physical connexion or separation is thus useless.

12/2. Can we make the test for independence depend on whether one variable (or system) gives energy or matter to the other ? The suggestion is plausible, but experience with simple mechanisms is misleading. When my finger strikes the key of a typewriter, the movement of my finger determines the movement of the type; and the finger also supplies the energy necessary for the type's movement. The diagram

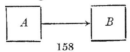

would state, in this case, both that energy, measurable in ergs, is transmitted from A to B, and also that the behaviour of B is determined by, or predictable from, that of A. If, however, power is freely available to B, the transmission of energy from A to B becomes irrelevant to the question of the control exerted. It is easy, in fact, to devise a mechanism in which the flow of both energy and matter is from B to A and yet the control is exerted by A over B. Thus, suppose B contains a compressor which pumps air at a constant rate into a cylinder, creating a pressure that is shown on a dial. From the cylinder a pipe goes to A, where there is a tap which allows air to escape and can thus control the pressure in the cylinder. Now suppose a stranger comes along; he knows nothing of the internal mechanism, but tests the relations between the two variables: A, the position of the tap, and B, the reading on the dial. By direct testing he soon finds that A controls B, but that B has no effect on A. The direction of control has thus no necessary relation to the direction of flow of either energy or matter when the system is such that all parts are supplied freely with energy.

Independence

12/3. The test for independence can, in fact, be built up from the results of primary operations (S. 2/10), without any reference to other concepts or to knowledge of the system borrowed from any other source.

The basic definition simply makes formal what was used intuitively in S. 4/12. To test whether a variable X has an effect on a variable Y, the observer sets the system at a state, allows one transition to occur, and notices the value of Y that follows. (The new value of X does not matter.) He then sets the system at a state that differs from the first only in the value of X (in particular, Y must be returned to its original initial state). Again he allows a transition to occur, and he notices again the value of Y that results. (He thus obtains two transitions of Y from two states that differ only in the value of X.) If these two values of Y are the same, then Y is defined to be **independent** of X so far as the particular initial states and other conditions are concerned.

By **dependent** we shall mean simply 'not independent'.

This operational test provides the ' atom ' of independence Two transitions are needed· the concept of ' independence ' is meaningless with less.

12/4. In general, what happens when the test is applied to one pair of initial states does not restrict what may happen if it is applied to other pairs. The possibility cannot be excluded that the test may give results varying arbitrarily over the possible pairs. Often, however, it happens that, for some given value of all other variables or parameters, Z, W, . . . , Y is independent of X for *all* pairs of initial states that differ only in the value of X. In this case, for that particular field and for that particular value of the other variables and parameters, Y is **independent** of X in a more extended sense. Provided the field and the initial values of Y, Z, W, etc., do not change, Y's transition is unaffected by X's initial value. In this case, Y is independent of X over a region (in the phase space) represented by a line parallel to the X-axis, ' independent ' in the sense that whenever the representative point, moving on a line of behaviour, leaves this region, Y will undergo the same transition.

Sometimes it may happen that Y is independent of X not only for all values of X but also for all values of the other variables and parameters—Z, W, etc. In the previous paragraph a change of Z's value might have changed the field or region so that Y was no longer independent of X. In the present case, Y's transition (from a uniform Y-value) is the same regardless of the initial values of X, Z, W, etc. Y is then **independent** of X unconditionally.

It will be seen that two variables may be ' independent ' to varying degrees: at two points, over a line, over a region, over the whole phase-space, over a *set* of fields. The word is thus capable of many degrees of application. The definitions given above are not intended to answer the question (of doubtful validity) ' what *is* independence *really* ? ' but simply to show how this word must be used if a speaker is to convey an unambiguous message to his audience. Clearly, the word often needs supplementary specification (e.g. does ' Y independent of X ' mean ' over this field ' or ' over all fields ' ?), the supplementary specification must then be given, either by the context or explicitly.

The word ' independent ' is thus similar to the word ' stable ': both words are often useful in that they can convey information

about a system quickly and easily *when the system has a suitable
simplicity* and when it is known that the listener will interpret
them suitably.   But always the speaker must be prepared, if the
system is not simple, to add supplementary details or even to go
back to a description of the transitions themselves; here there is
always security, for here the information is complete.

12/5.   Because there are various degrees of independence, so that
Y may be independent of *X* over a small region of the field but
not independent if the same region is extended, it follows that
one system can give a variety of diagrams of immediate effects—
as many as there are ranges and conditions of independence
considered.   This implication is unpleasant for us; but we cannot
evade the fact.   (Fortunately it commonly happens that the independencies in which we are interested give much the same diagram,
so often one diagram will represent all the significant aspects of
independence.)

12/6.   So far we have discussed *Y*'s independence of *X*.   Whatever this is, it in no way restricts, in general, whether *X* is or is
not independent of *Y*.   If *X* is independent of *Y*, but *Y* is not
independent of *X*, then *X* **dominates** *Y*.

12/7.   The definition given so far refers to independence between
two variables.   It may happen that every variable in a system *A*
is independent of every variable in a system *B*, all possible pairs
being considered.   We then say that system *A* is **independent** of
system B.

   Again, such independence does not, in general, restrict the
possibilities whether *B* is or is not independent of *A*; *A* may
dominate *B*.

12/8.   To illustrate the definition's use, and to show that its
answers accord with common experience, here are some examples.

   If a bacteriologist wishes to test whether the growth of a micro-
organism is affected by a chemical substance, he prepares two
tubes of nutrient medium containing the chemical in different
concentrations (*X*) but with all other constituents equal; he seeds
them with equal numbers of organisms; and he observes how the
numbers (*Y*) change as time goes on.   Then he compares the two

later numbers of organisms after two initial states that differed only in the concentrations of chemical.

To test whether a state-determined system is dependent on a parameter, i.e. to test whether the parameter is 'effective', the observer records the system's behaviour on two occasions when the parameter has different values. Thus, to test whether a thermostat is really affected by its regulator he sets the regulator at some value, checks that the temperature is at its usual value, and records the subsequent behaviour of the temperature; then he returns the temperature to its previous value, changes the position of the regulator, and observes again. A change of behaviour implies an effective regulator.

Finally, an example from animal behaviour. Parker tested the sea-anemone to see whether the behaviour of a tentacle was independent of its connexion with the body.

> 'When small fragments of meat are placed on the tentacles of a sea-anemone, these organs wind around the bits of food and, by bending in the appropriate direction, deliver them to the mouth.'

(He has established that the behaviour is regular, and that the system of tentacle-position and food-position is approximately state-determined. He has described the line of behaviour following the initial state: tentacle extended, food on tentacle.)

> 'If, now, a distending tentacle on a quiet and expanded sea-anemone is suddenly seized at its base by forceps, cut off and held in position so that its original relations to the animal as a whole can be kept clearly in mind, the tentacle will still be found to respond to food brought in contact with it and will eventually turn toward that side which was originally toward the mouth.'

(He has now described the line of behaviour that follows an initial state identical with the first except that the parameter 'connexion with the body' has a different value. He observed that the two behaviours of the variable 'tentacle-position' are identical.) He draws the deduction that the tentacle-system is, in this aspect, independent of the body-system·

> 'Thus the tentacle has within itself a complete neuromuscular mechanism for its own responses.'

The definition, then, agrees with what is usually accepted· Though clumsy in simple cases, it has the advantage in complex cases of providing a clear and precise foundation. By its use the independencies within a system can be proved by primary operations only.

12/9. The definition makes 'independence' depend on how the system behaves over a single unit of time (over a single step if changing in steps, or over an infinitesimal time if changing continuously). The dependencies so defined between all pairs of variables give, as defined in S. 4/12, the diagram of *immediate* effects.

In general, this diagram is not restricted: all geometrically drawable forms may occur in a wide enough variety of machines. This freedom, however, is not always possible if we consider the relation between two variables over an extended period of time. Thus, suppose Z is dependent on Y, and Y dependent on X, so that the diagram of immediate effects contains arrows:

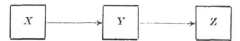

X may have no *immediate* effect on Z, but over two steps the relation is not free; for two different initial values of X will lead, one step later, to two different values of Y; and these two different values of Y will lead (as Z is dependent on Y) to two different values of Z. Thus after *two* steps, whether X has an immediate effect on Z or not, changes at X will give changes at Z; and thus X does have an effect on Z, though delayed.

Another sort of independence is thus possible: whether changes at X are followed at *any* time by changes at Z. These relations can be represented by a **diagram of ultimate effects.** It must be carefully distinguished from the diagram of immediate effects. It is related to the latter in that it can be formed by taking the diagram of immediate effects and adding further arrows by the rule that if any two arrows are joined head to tail,

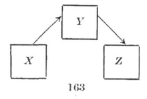

a third arrow is added from tail to head, thus

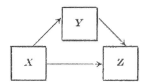

The rule is applied repeatedly till no further addition of arrows is possible. Thus the diagram of immediate effects **I** in Figure 12/9/1 would yield the diagram of ultimate effects **II**.

FIGURE 12/9/1.

The diagram of ultimate effects shows at once the dependencies in the case when we allow time for the effects to work round the system. Thus from II of the Figure we see that variable 1 is permanently independent of 2, 3, and 4, and that the latter three are all ultimately dependent on each other.

The effects of constancy

12/10. Suppose eight variables have been joined, by the method of *S.* 6/6, to give the diagram of immediate effects shown in Figure 12/10/1. We now ask: what *behaviour* at the three

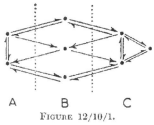

A   B   C

FIGURE 12/10/1.

variables in *B* will make *A* and *C* independent, in the ultimate sense, and also leave both *A* and *C* state-determined? That is, what behaviour at *B* will sever the whole into independent parts, giving the diagram of immediate effects of Figure 12/10/2:

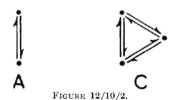

FIGURE 12/10/2.

The question has not only theoretical but practical importance. Many experiments require that one system be shielded from effects coming from others. Thus, a system using magnets may have to be shielded from the effects of the earth's magnetism; or a thermal system may have to be shielded from the effects of changes in the atmospheric temperature; or the pressure which drives blood through the kidneys may have to be kept independent of changes in the pulse-rate.

A first suggestion might be that the three variables B should be removed. But this conceptual removal corresponds to no physical reality the earth's magnetic field, the atmospheric temperature, the pulse-rate cannot be 'removed' In fact the answer is capable of proof (S. 22/14): *that A and C should be independent and state-determined it is necessary and sufficient that the variables B should be null-functions.* In other words, A and C must be separated by a *wall of constancies.*

It also follows that if the variables B can be sometimes fluctuating and sometimes constant (i.e. if they behave as part-functions), then A and C can be sometimes functionally joined and sometimes independent, according to B's behaviour.

12/11. Here are some illustrations to show that the theorem accords with common experience.

(*a*) If A (of Figure 12/10/1) is a system in which heat-changes are being studied, B the temperatures of the parts of the container, and C the temperatures of the surroundings, then for A to be isolated from C and state-determined, it is necessary and sufficient for the B's to be kept constant. (*b*) Two electrical systems joined by an insulator are independent, if varying slowly, because electrically the insulator is unvarying (*c*) The centres in the spinal cord are often made independent of the activities in the brain by a transection of the cord; but a break in physical continuity is not necessary: a segment may be poisoned, or anaesthetised, or frozen; what is necessary is that the segment should be unvarying.

Physical separation, already noticed to give no certain independence, is sometimes effective because it sometimes creates an intervening region of constancy.

12/12. The example of Figure 12/10/1 showed one way in which the behaviour of a set of variables, by sometimes fluctuating and sometimes being constant, could affect the independencies within a system. The range of ways is, however, much greater.

To demonstrate the variety we need a rule by which we can make the appropriate modifications in the diagram of ultimate effects when one or more of the variables is held constant. The rule is:—Take the diagram of immediate effects. If a variable V is constant, remove all arrows whose heads are at V; then, treating this modified diagram as one of immediate effects, complete the diagram of ultimate effects, using the rule of S. 12/9. The resulting diagram will be that of the ultimate effects when

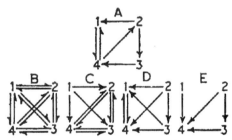

FIGURE 12/12/1 : If a four-variable system has the diagram of immediate effects A, and if 1 and 2 are part-functions, then its diagram of ultimate effects will be B, C, D or E as none, 1, 2, or both 1 and 2 become inactive, respectively.

V is constant. (It will be noticed that the effect of making V constant cannot be deduced from the original diagram of ultimate effects alone.) Thus, if the system of Figure 12/12/1 has the diagram of immediate effects A, then the diagram of ultimate effects will be B, C, D or E according as none, 1, 2, or both 1 and 2 are constant, respectively.

It can be seen that with only four variables, and with only two of the four possibly becoming constant, the patterns of independence show a remarkable variety. Thus, in C, 1 dominates 3; but in D, 3 dominates 1. As the variables become more numerous so does the variety increase rapidly.

12/13. The multiplicity of inter-connexions possible in a tele-phone exchange is due primarily to the widespread use of temporary constancies. The example serves to remind us that ' switching ' is merely one of the changes producible by a re-distribution of constancies. For suppose a system has the

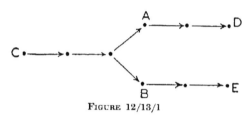

FIGURE 12/13/1

diagram of immediate effects shown in Figure 12/13/1. If an effect coming from C goes down the branch AD only, then, for the branch BE to be independent, B must be constant. How the constancy is obtained is here irrelevant. When the effect from C is to be ' switched ' to the BE branch, B must be freed and A must become constant. Any system with a ' switching ' process must use, therefore, an alterable distribution of constancies. Conversely, *a system whose variables can be sometimes fluctuating and sometimes constant is adequately equipped for switching.*

The effects of local stabilities

12/14. The last few sections have shown how important, in any system that is to have temporary independencies, are variables that temporarily go constant. As such variables play a funda-mental part in what follows, let us examine them more closely

Any subsystem (including the case of the single variable) that stays constant is, by definition, at a state of equilibrium. If the subsystem's surrounding conditions (parameters) are constant, the subsystem evidently has a state of equilibrium in the corresponding field; if it stays constant while its parameters are changing, then that state is evidently one of equilibrium in all the fields occurring. Thus, constancy in a subsystem's state implies that the state is

167

one of equilibrium, and constancy in the presence of small impulsive disturbances implies stability.

The converse is also true. If a subsystem is at a state of equilibrium, then it will stay at that state, i.e. hold a constant value (so long as its parameters do not change value).

Constancy, equilibrium, and stability are thus closely related.

12/15. Are such variables (or subsystems) common? Later (S. 15/2) it will be suggested that they are extremely common, and examples will be given. Here we can notice two types that are specially worth notice.

One form, uncommon perhaps in the real world but of basic importance as a type-form in the strategy of S. 2/17, is that in which the subsystem has a definite probability p that any particular state, selected at random, is equilibrial. We shall be concerned with this form in S. 13/2. (In explanation, it should be mentioned that the sample space for the probabilities is that given by a *set* of subsystems, each a machine with input and therefore determinate in whether a given state, with given input-value, is or is not equilibrial.) The case would arise when the observer faced a subsystem that was known (or might reasonably be assumed) to be a determinate machine with input, but did not know which subsystem, out of a possible set, was before him; the sample space being provided by the set suitably weighted, the observer could legitimately speak of the probability that *this* system, at *this* state, and with *this* input, should be in equilibrium.

The other form, very much commoner, is that which shows ' threshold ', so that *all* states are equilibrial when some parametric function is less than a certain value, and few or none are equilibrial when it exceeds that value. Well-known examples are that a weight on the ground will not rise until the lifting force exceeds a certain value, and a nerve will not respond with an impulse until the electric intensity, in some form, rises above a certain value.

What is important for us here is to notice that threshold, by readily giving constancy, can readily give what is necessary for the connexions between variable and variable to be temporary. Thus the changes in the diagram of Figure 12/12/1 could readily be produced by parts showing the phenomenon of threshold

12/16. These deductions can now be joined to those of S. 12/10. If three subsystems are joined so that their diagram of immediate effects is

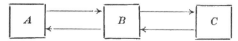

and if B is at a state that is equilibrial for all values coming from A and C, then A and C are (unconditionally) independent. Thus, B's being at a state of equilibrium *severs the functional connexion between A and C.*

Suppose now that B's states are equilibrial for some states of A and C, but not for others. As A and C, on some line of behaviour of the whole system, pass through various values, so will they (according to whether B's state at the moment is equilibrial or not) be sometimes dependent and sometimes independent.

Thus we have achieved the first aim of this chapter: to make rigorously clear, and demonstrable by primary operations, what is meant by ' temporary functional connexions ', when the control comes from factors within the system, and not imposed arbitrarily from outside.

12/17. The same ideas can be extended to cover any system as large and as richly connected as we please. Let the system consist of many parts, or subsystems, joined as in S. 6/6, and thus provided with basic connexions. If some of the variables or subsystems are constant for a time, then during that time the connexions through them are reduced functionally to zero, and the effect is as if the connexions had been severed in some material way during that time.

If a high proportion of the variables go constant, the severings may reach an intensity that cuts the whole system into subsystems that are (temporarily) quite independent of one another. Thus a whole, connected system may, if a sufficient proportion of its variables go constant, be temporarily equivalent to a set of unconnected subsystems. *Constancies*, in other words, *can cut a system to pieces.* (*I. to C.*, S. 4/20, gives an illustration of the fact.)

12/18. The field of a state-determined system whose variables often go constant has only the peculiarity that the lines of behaviour often run in a sub-space orthogonal to the axes. Thus,

169

over an interval in which all variables but one are constant, the corresponding line of behaviour must run as a straight line parallel to the axis of the variable that is changing. If all but two are

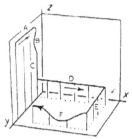

inactive (along some line of behaviour), that line in the phase-space may curve but it must remain in the two-dimensional plane parallel to the two corresponding axes; and so on. If all the variables are constant, the line naturally becomes a point—at the state of equilibrium. Thus a three-variable system might give the line of behaviour shown in Figure 12/18/1.

FIGURE 12/18/1. In the different stages the active variables are : A, y ; B, y and z ; C, z ; D x ; E y ; F x and z.

In the interval before they reach equilibrium, such variables will, of course, behave as part-functions. Through the remaining chapters they will show their importance. For convenience of description, a part-function (described in time by a variable) will be said to be **active** or **inactive** (at a given point on a line of behaviour) according to whether the variable is changing or remaining constant.

CHAPTER 13

The System with Local Stabilities

13/1. HAVING examined what is meant by a system that has ' partial, fluctuating, and temporary independencies within the whole ' we can now consider some of the properties that a system of such a type will show in its behaviour.

In saying ' a system of such a type ' we have not, of course, defined a system with precision: we have only defined a set or class of systems. How shall we achieve precision ? Two ways are open to us.

One way is to add further details until we have defined a particular system with full precision, so that its behaviour is determinate and uniquely defined; we then follow the behaviour in all detail. Such a study would give us an exact conclusion, but it would give us far more detail than we require, or can conveniently handle, in the remaining chapters.

Another way is to talk about such systems ' in general '. Here nothing is easier than to relax our grasp and to talk vaguely about what will ' usually ' happen, regardless of the fact that whether particular properties (such as linearity, or the presence of threshold) are ' usually ' present differs widely in the systems of the sociologist, the neurophysiologist, and the physicist. Rigour and precision *are* possible while speaking of systems ' in general ' provided two requirements are met: the *set* of systems under discussion must be defined precisely, and statements made must be precise statements about the properties of *the set*. In other words, we give up the aim of being precise about the individual system, and accept the responsibility of being precise about the set. This second way is the method we shall largely follow in the remaining chapters.

Having changed to the new aim, we shall often find that the argument about the set is conducted most readily in terms of some individual system that is followed in detail; when this happens, the individual system must be understood to have

171

importance only as a typical, generic, or ' random ' element of the set it belongs to. Though the argument will often appear verbally to be focused on an individual system, it is directed really at the properties of the set, the individual system being introduced only as a means to an end.

We shall have much to do, in what follows, with systems constructed in some ' random ' way. The word will always mean that we are discussing some *generic* system so as to find its *typical* properties, and thus to arrive at some precise deduction about the defined *set* of systems.

13/2. A set of systems of special importance for the later chapters is the set of those systems that are made of parts that have a high proportion of their states equilibrial, and are made by the parts being joined at random.

More precisely. assume that we have before us a very great number of parts, assumed to be fairly homogeneous, so that there is a defined ' universe ', or distribution, of them. Each is assumed to be state-determined, and thus to have in it *no randomness whatever*. As a little machine with input, if it is at a certain state and in certain conditions it will do a certain thing; and it will do this thing whenever the state and conditions recur.

We now take a sample of these parts by some clearly defined sampling process and thus arrive at some particular set of parts. (It is not assumed that all parts have an equal probability of being taken.) Again we take a sample from the possible ways of joining them, taking it by a clearly defined sampling process, and thus arrive at some one way of joining them.

The particular set of parts, joined in the particular way, now gives the final system.

This particular final system, be it noticed, is state-determined. It is *not* stochastic in the sense of being able, from a given state and in given conditions, to undergo various transitions with various probabilities. Thus the *particular* system is not random at all The randomness enters with the observer or experimenter; he is little interested in the particular system taken by the sampling, but is much interested in the population from which the particular system has come, as the neurophysiologist is interested in the set of mammalian brains. The ' randomness ' comes in because the observer faces a system that interests him only because it is typical of the set. With the population as his sample space (derived from the two primary sample spaces) he may then legitimately speak of the *probability* of the system showing a certain event, or having a certain property.

If to this specification we add the restriction that the original parts are rich in states of equilibrium (e.g. as in S. 12/15), we get a type of system that will be referred to frequently in what follows. For lack of a better name I shall call it a **polystable** system. Briefly, it is any system whose parts have many equilibria and that has been formed by taking parts at random and joining them at random (provided that these words are understood in the exact sense given above).

Definitions can only be justified ultimately, however, by their works. The remainder of the book will demonstrate something of the properties of this interesting type of system, a key-system in the strategy of S. 2/17.

13/3. In such demonstrations we shall not be discussing one particular system, specified in all detail: we shall be discussing a set. When a set is discussed we must be careful to keep an important distinction in mind, and *we* must make the distinction arbitrarily: (1) are we discussing what *can* happen?—a question which focuses attention on the extreme possibilities, and therefore on the rare and exceptional; or (2) are we discussing what *usually* happens?—which focuses attention on the central mass of cases, and therefore on the common and ordinary. Both questions have their uses; but as the answers are often quite different, we must be careful not to confuse them.

13/4. A property shown by *all* state-determined systems, and one that will be important later is the following. In a state-determined system, if a subsystem has been constant and then commences to show changes in its variables, we can deduce that

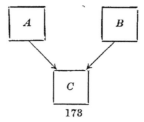

among its parameters must have been, when it started changing, at least one that was itself changing. Picturesquely one might say that change can come only from change. The reason is not difficult to see. If variable or subsystem C is affected immediately only by parameters A and B, and if A and B are constant over some interval, and if, within this interval, C has gone from a state c to the same state (i.e. if c is a state of equilibrium), then for C to be consistent in its behaviour it must continue to repeat the transition 'c to c' so long as A and B retain their values, i.e. so long as A and B remain constant. If C is state-determined, a transition from c to some other state can occur only after A or B, for whatever reason, has changed *its* value.

Thus a state-determined subsystem that is at a state of equilibrium and is surrounded by constant parameters (variables of other subsystems perhaps) is, as it were, trapped in equilibrium. Once at the state of equilibrium it cannot escape from it until an external source of change allows it to change too. The sparks that wander in charred paper give a vivid example of this property, for each portion, even though combustible, is stable when cold; one spark can become two, and various events can happen, but a cold portion cannot develop a spark unless at least one adjacent point has a spark. So long as one spark is left we cannot put bounds to what may happen; but if the whole should reach a state of 'no sparks', then from that time on it is unchanging.

Progression to equilibrium

13/5. Let us now consider how a polystable system will move towards its final state of equilibrium From one point of view there is nothing to discuss, for if the parts are state-determined and the joining defined, the whole is a state-determined system that, if released from an initial state, will go to a terminal cycle or equilibrium by a line of behaviour exactly as in any other case.

The fact, however, that the polystable system has parts with many equilibria, which will often stay constant for a time, adds special features that deserve attention; for, as will be seen later, they have interesting implications in the behaviours of living organisms.

13/6. A useful device for following the behaviour of these somewhat complex wholes is to find the value of the following index.

At any given moment, the whole system is at a definite state, and therefore so is each variable, the state of each variable either is or is not a state of equilibrium for that variable (in the conditions given by the other variables). The *number of variables* that are at a state of equilibrium will be represented by i. If the whole is of n variables then obviously i must lie in the range of 0 to n.

If i equals n, then every variable is at a state of equilibrium in the conditions given by the others, so the whole is at a state of equilibrium (S. 6/8). If i is not equal to n, the other variables, $n - i$ in number, will change value at the next step in time. A new state of the whole will then occur, and i will have a new value. Thus, as the whole moves along a line of behaviour, i will change in value; and we can get a useful insight into the behaviour of the whole by considering how i will behave as time progresses.

13/7. The behaviour of i is strictly determinate once the system and its initial state have been given. In a set of systems, however, the behaviour of i is difficult to characterise except at the two extremes, where its behaviour is simple and clear. Comparison of what happens at the extremes will give us an insight that will be invaluable in the later chapters, for it will go a long way towards answering the fundamental problem of Chapter 11. (By establishing what happens in the two specially simple and clear cases we are following the strategy of S 2/17.)

13/8. At one extreme is the polystable system that has been joined very richly, so that almost every variable is joined to almost every other. (Such a system's diagram of immediate effects would show that almost all of the $n(n - 1)$ arrows were present.) Let us consider the case in which, as in S. 12/15, every subsystem has a high probability p of being at a state of equilibrium, and in which the probabilities are all independent. How will i behave ? (Here we want to know what will usually happen; what *can* happen is of little interest.)

The probability of each part being at a state of equilibrium is p, and so, if independence (of probability) holds, the probability that the whole (of n variables) is at a state of equilibrium will be p^n (by S. 6/8). If p is not very close to 1, and n is large, this quantity will be extremely small (S. 11/4). i will usually have a value not far from np (i.e. about a fraction p of the total will be

at equilibrium at any moment). Then the line of behaviour
will perform a sort of random walk around this value, the whole
reaching a state of equilibrium if and only if i should chance on
the extreme value of n. Thus we get essentially the same picture
as we got in S. 11/3: a system whose lines of behaviour are long
and complex, and whose chance of reaching an equilibrium in a
fairly short time is, if n is large, extremely small. In this case
the time taken by the whole to arrive at a state of equilibrium
will be extremely long, like T_1 of S. 11/5.

13/9. Particularly worth noting is what happens if i should
happen to be large but not quite equal to n. Suppose, for instance, i were 999 in a 1,000-variable system of the type now being
considered. The whole is now near to equilibrium, but what will
happen ? One variable is not at equilibrium and will change.
As the system is richly connected, most of the 999 other variables
will, at the next instant (or step), find themselves in changed
conditions; whether the state each is at is *now* equilibrial will
depend on factors such that (by hypothesis) $999p$ will still be
equilibrial, and thus i is likely to drop back simply to its average
value. Thus the richly-joined form of the polystable system,
even if it should get very near to equilibrium (in the sense that
most of its parts are so) will be unable to retain this nearness but
will almost certainly fall back to an average state   Such a system
is thus typically unable to retain partial or local successes.

13/10. With the number n still large, and the probabilities p
still independent, contrast the behaviour of the previous section
(in which the system was assumed to be richly or completely
joined) with that of the polystable system in which the primary
joins between variables are scanty. (A similar system also occurs
if p is made very near to 1; for, by S. 12/17, as most of the variables
will be at states of equilibrium, and thus constant for most of the
time, the functional connexions will also be scanty.) How will i
behave in this case, especially as the scantiness approaches its
limit ?

Consider the case in which the scantiness has actually reached
its limit. The system is now identical with one of n variables
that has no connexions between any of them; it is a 'system'
only in the nominal sense. In it, any part that comes to a state

of equilibrium must remain there, for no disturbance can come to it. So if two states of the whole, earlier and later, are compared, all parts contributing to i in the earlier will contribute in the later; so *the value of i cannot fall with time.* It will, of course, usually increase. Thus, this type of system goes to its final state of equilibrium *progressively* Its progression, in fact, is like that of Case 3 of S. 11/5, for the final equilibrium has only to wait for the part that takes longest. The time that the whole takes will therefore be like T_3, and thus not excessively long.

13/11.   The two types of polystable system are at opposite poles, and systems in the real world will seldom be found to correspond precisely with either. Nevertheless, the two types are important by the strategy of S. 2/17, for they provide clear-cut types with clear-cut properties; if a real system is similar to either, we may legitimately argue that its properties will approximate to those of the nearer.

Polystable systems midway between the two will show a somewhat confused picture. Subsystems will be formed (e.g. as in S. 12/17) with kaleidoscopic variety and will persist only for short times; some will hold stable for a brief interval, only to be changed and to disintegrate as delimitable subsystems. The number of variables stable, i, will keep tending to climb up, as a few subsystems hold stable, only to fall back by a larger or smaller amount as they become unstable. Oscillations will be large, until one swing happens to land i at the value n, where it will stick.

More interesting to us will be the systems nearer the limit of disconnexion, when i's tendency to increase cumulatively is better marked, so that i, although oscillating somewhat and often slipping back a little, shows a recognisable tendency to move to the value n. This is the sort of system that, after the experimenter has seen i repeatedly return to n after displacement, is apt to make him feel that i is 'trying' to get to n.

13/12.   So far we have discussed only the first case of S. 12/15; what if the polystable system were composed of parts that all had their states of equilibrium characterised by a threshold ? This question will specially interest the neurophysiologist, though it will be of less interest to those who are intending to work with adapting systems of other types.

177

The presence of threshold precludes the previous assumption of independence in the probabilities; for now a variable's chance of being at a state of equilibrium will vary in some correspondence with the values of the variable's parameters. In the case of two or more neurons, the correspondence will be one way if the effect is excitatory, and inversely if it is inhibitory. (If there is a mixture of excitatory and inhibitory modes, the outcome may be an approximation to the independent form) To follow the subject further would lead us into more detail than is appropriate in this survey; and at the present time little can be said on the matter.

13/13. To sum up· The polystable system, if composed of parts whose states of equilibrium are distributed independently of the states of their inputs, goes to a final equilibrium in a way that depends much on the amount of functional connexion.

When the connexion is rich, the line of behaviour tends to be complex and, if n is large, exceedingly long; so the whole tends to take an exceedingly long time to come to equilibrium. When the line meets a state at which an unusually large number of the variables are stable, it cannot retain the excess over the average.

When the connexion is poor (either by few primary joins or by many constancies in the parts), the line of behaviour tends to be short, so that the whole arrives at a state of equilibrium soon. When the line meets a state at which an unusually large number of the variables are stable, it tends to retain the excess for a time, and thus to progress to total equilibrium by an accumulation of local equilibria.

Dispersion

13/14. The polystable system shows another property that deserves special notice.

Take a portion of any line of behaviour of such a system. On it we can notice, for every variable, whether it did or did not change value along the given portion. Thus, in Figure 12/18/1, in the portion indicated by the letters B and C both y and z change but x does not. In the portion indicated by F, x and z change but y does not. By **dispersion** I shall refer to the fact that the active variables (y and z) in the first portion are not identical with those (x and z) of the second. (In the example the portions come from the same line, but the two portions may also come from different lines.) As the example shows, it is not implied that the two sets shall contain no common element, only that the two sets are not identical.

The importance of dispersion will be indicated in S. 13/17. Here we should notice the essential feature: though the two portions may start from points that differ only in one, or a few, variables (as in S. 12/3) the changes that result may distribute the activations (S. 12/18) to different sets of variables, i.e. to different places in the system. Thus, the important phenomenon of different *patterns* (or *values*) at one place leading to activations in different *places* in the system demands no special mechanism. any polystable system tends to show it.

13/15. If the two places are to have minimal overlap, and if the system is not to be specially designed for the separation of particular patterns of input, then all that is necessary is that the parts should have almost all their states equilibrial. Then the number active will be few; if the fraction of the total number is usually about r, and if the active variables are distributed independently, the fraction that will be common to the two sets (i.e. the overlap) will be about r^2. This quantity can be as small as one pleases by a sufficient reduction in the value of r, which can be done by making the parts such that the proportion of states equilibrial is almost 1. Thus the polystable system may respond, to two different input states, with two responses on two sets of variables that have only small overlap.

13/16. It will be proposed later that dispersion is used widely in the nervous system. First we should notice that it is used widely in the sense-organs.

The fact that the sense-organs are not identical enforces an initial dispersion. Thus if a beam of radiation of wave-length $0.5\ \mu$ is directed to the face, the eye will be stimulated but not the skin; so the optic nerve will be excited but not the trigeminal. But if the wave-length is increased beyond $0.8\ \mu$, the excitation changes from the optic nerve to the trigeminal. Dispersion has occurred because a change in the stimulus has moved the excitation (activity) from one set of anatomical elements (variables) to another.

In the skin are histologically-distinguishable receptors sensitive to touch, pain, heat, and cold. If a needle on the skin is changed from lightly touching it to piercing it, the excitation is shifted from the ' touch ' to the ' pain ' type of receptor; i.e. dispersion occurs.

Whether a change in colour of a stimulating light changes the excitation from one set of elements in the retina to another is at present uncertain. But dispersion clearly occurs when the light changes its position in space; for, if the eyeball does not move, the excitation is changed from one set of elements to another. The lens is, in fact, a device for ensuring that dispersion occurs: from the primitive light-spot of a Protozoon dispersion cannot occur.

It will be seen therefore that a considerable amount of dispersion is enforced before the effects of stimuli reach the central nervous system: the different stimuli not only arrive at the central nervous system different in their qualities but they often arrive by different paths, and excite different groups of cells.

13/17. The sense organs evidently have as an important function the achievement of dispersion. That it occurs or is maintained in the nervous system is supported by two pieces of evidence.

The fact that neuronic processes frequently show threshold, and the fact that this property implies that the functioning elements will often be constant (S. 12/15) suggest that dispersion is *bound* to occur, by S. 12/16.

More direct evidence is provided by the fact that, in such cases as are known, the tracts from sense-organ to cortex at least maintain such dispersion as has occurred in the sense organ. The point-to-point representation of the retina on the visual cortex, for instance, ensures that the dispersion achieved in the retina will at least not be lost. Similarly the point-to-point representation now known to be made by the projection of the auditory nerve on the temporal cortex ensures that the dispersion due to pitch will also not be lost. There are therefore good reasons for believing that dispersion plays an important part in the nervous system.

Localisation in the polystable system

13/18. How will responses to a stimulus be localised in a poly-stable system?—how will the set of the active variables be distributed over the whole set ?

In such a system, the reaction to a given stimulus, from a given state, will be regular and reproducible, for the whole is state-determined. To this extent its behaviour is lawful. But when the observer notices *which* variables have shown the activity it will probably seem lawless, for the details of where the activation spreads to have been determined by the sampling process, and the activated variables will probably be scattered over the system apparently haphazardly (subject to S. 13/4). Thus the question ' Is the reaction localised ? ' is ambiguous, for two different answers can be given. In the sense that the activity is restricted to certain variables of the whole system, the answer is ' yes '; but in the sense that these variables occur in no simply describable way, the answer is ' no '.

An illustration that may be helpful is given by the distribution over a town of the chimneys that ' smoke ' (suffer from a forced down-draught) when the wind blows from a particular direction. The smoking or not of a particular chimney will be locally determinate; for a wind of a particular force and direction, striking the adjacent roofs at a particular angle, will regularly produce the same eddies, which will determine the smoking or not of the chimney. But geographically the smoking chimneys are not distributed with any simple regularity, for if a plan of the town is marked with a black dot for every chimney that smokes in an east wind, and a red dot for every one that smokes in a west wind, the black and red dots will probably be mixed irregularly. The phenomenon of ' smoking ' is thus determined in detail yet distributed geographically at random.

13/19. Such is the ' localisation ' shown by a polystable system. In so far as the brain, and especially the cerebral cortex, corresponds to the polystable, we may expect it to show ' localisation ' of the same type. On this hypothesis we would expect the brain to behave as follows.

The events in the environment will provide a continuous stream of information which will pour through the sense organs into the nervous system. The set of variables activated at one moment will usually differ from the set activated at a later moment; and the activity will spread and wander with as little apparent orderliness as the drops of rain that run, joining and separating, down a window-pane. But though the wanderings seem disorderly, the whole is reproducible and state-determined; so that if the same reaction is started again later, the same initial stimuli will meet the same local details, will develop into the same patterns, which will interact with the later stimuli as they did before, and the behaviour will consequently proceed as it did before.

This type of system would be affected by removals of material in a way not unlike that demonstrated by many workers on the cerebral cortex. The works of Pavlov and of Lashley are typical. Pavlov established various conditioned responses in dogs, removed various parts of the cerebral cortex, and observed the effects on the conditioned responses. Lashley taught rats to run through mazes and to jump to marked holes, and observed the effects of similar operations on their learned habits. The results were complicated, but certain general tendencies showed clearly. Operations involving a sensory organ or a part of the nervous system first traversed by the incoming impulses are usually severely destructive to reactions that use that sensory organ. Thus, a conditioned response to the sound of a bell is usually abolished by destruction of the cochleae, by section of the auditory nerves, or by ablation of the temporal lobes. Equally, reactions involving some type of motor activity are apt to be severely upset if the centre for this type of motor activity is damaged. But removal of cerebral cortex from other parts of the brain gave vague results. Removal of almost any part caused some disturbance, no matter from where it was removed or what type of response or habit was being tested; and no part could be found whose removal would destroy the response or habit specifically.

These results have offered great difficulties to many theories of cerebral mechanisms, but are not incompatible with the theory put forward here. For in a large polystable system the whole reaction will be based on activations that are both numerous and widely scattered. And, while any exact statement would have to be carefully qualified, we can see that, just as England's paper-making industry is not to be stopped by the devastation of any single county, so a reaction based on numerous and widely scattered elements will tend to have more immunity to localised injury than one whose elements are few and compact.

13/20. Lashley had noticed this possibility in 1929, remarking that the memory-traces might be localised individually without conflicting with the main facts, provided there were many traces and that they were scattered widely over the cerebral cortex, unified functionally but not anatomically. He did not, however, develop the possibility further; and the reason is not far to seek when one considers its implications.

Such a localisation would, of course, be untidy; but mere untidiness as such matters little. Thus, in a car factory the spare parts might be kept so that rear lamps were stored next to radiators, and ash-trays next to grease guns; but the lack of obvious order would not matter if in some way every item could be produced when wanted. More serious in the cortex are the effects of adding a second reaction; for merely random dispersion provides no means for relating their locations. It not only allows related reactions to activate widely separated variables, but it has no means of keeping unrelated reactions apart; it even allows them to use common variables. We cannot assume that unrelated reactions will always differ sufficiently in their sensory forms to ensure that the resulting activations stay always apart, for two stimuli may be unrelated yet closely similar. Nor is the differentiation trivial, for it includes the problem of deciding whether a few vertical stripes in a jungle belong to some reeds or to a tiger.

Not only does random dispersion lead to the intermingling of subsystems, with abundant chances of random interaction and confusion, but even more confusion is added with every fresh act of learning. Even if some order has been established among the previous reactions, each addition of a new reaction is preceded by a period of random trial and error which will necessarily cause the changing of step-mechanisms which were already adjusted to previous reactions, which will be thereby upset. At first sight, then, such a system might well seem doomed to fall into chaos. Nevertheless, I hope to show, from S. 15/4 on, that there are good reasons for believing that its tendency will actually be towards ever-increasing adaptation.

CHAPTER 14

Repetitive Stimuli and Habituation

14/1. THIS chapter continues the study of the polystable system but is something of a digression; and the reader who proceeds directly to Chapter 15 will lose nothing of the logical thread. Nevertheless, it has been included for two reasons.

The first is that it will give us practice in understanding the polystable system, and will show how systems of that type can be discussed in terms that are both general and precise.

A second reason is that it gives another example of the thesis that pervades the book:—When a system ' runs to equilibrium ' one's first impression is that what is interesting has now come to an end—an impression that is often valid when the system is simple, and the equilibrium that of a run-down clock. What has been largely overlooked, and what this book attempts to display, is that when a *complex* system runs to equilibrium, the equilibrium necessarily implies a complex relationship between the states of the various parts. When the relationship between the states of the parts is examined, they will show unusual and striking features, features that are of peculiar interest to the student of behaviour. Thus Chapter 8, on the Homeostat, showed ' only ' a system running to equilibrium (e.g. Figure 8/5/1); yet because the system and conditions were structured, interesting relations could be traced between the actions and interactions of the various parts at and around the terminal equilibrium. These relations are what we identified in Chapter 5 as ' adaptation '. The present chapter will give another example of how a system, ' merely ' running to equilibrium under a complex repetitive input, also produces behaviour of psychological and physiological interest.

14/2. First a definition. When there are many states of equilibrium in a field, then as every line of behaviour must end at *some* state of equilibrium (or cycle), the lines of behaviour collect into sets, such that the lines in one set come to one common termination (cycle or state of equilibrium). The whole field is thus divisible into regions (each a **confluent**) such that each region contains one and only one state of equilibrium or cycle, to which every line of behaviour in it eventually comes. The chief property of a confluent is that the representative point, if released from any point within it, (*a*) cannot leave the confluent, (*b*) will go to the state of equilibrium or cycle, where it will remain so long as the parametric conditions persist.

The division of the whole field into confluents is not peculiar to machines of special type, but is common to all systems that are state-determined and that have more than one state of equilibrium or cycle.

Habituation

14/3. Consider now what will happen if a polystable system be subjected to an impulsive (S. 6/5) stimulus S repetitively, the stimulus being unvarying, and with intervals between its applications sufficiently long for the system to come to equilibrium before the next application is made.

By S. 6/5, the stimulus S, being impulsive, will displace the representative point from any given state to some definite state. Thus the effect of S (acting on the representative point at a state of equilibrium by the previous paragraph) is to transfer it to some

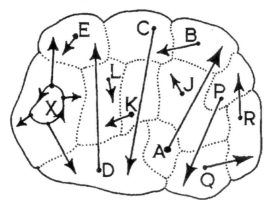

FIGURE 14/3/1 : Field of system with twelve confluents, each containing a state of equilibrium (shown as a dot), or a cycle (X at the left). The arrows show the displacements caused by S when it is applied to the representative point at any state of equilibrium or on X.

definite state in the field and there to release it. The possibilities sketched in Figure 14/3/1 will illustrate the process sufficiently.

Suppose the system is in equilibrium at *A*. *S* is applied; its effect is to move the representative point to the end of the arrow, in this example moving it into another confluent   The system is now, by hypothesis, left alone until it has settled: this means that the basic field operates, carrying it, in this example, to the state of equilibrium *B*. Here it will remain until the next application of *S*, which in this example, again moves it to a new confluent; here the basic field takes it to the state of equilibrium *C*. So does the alternation of *S* and the basic field take it from equilibrium to equilibrium till it arrives at *E*. From this state, *S* moves it only to within the same confluent and the ' leaving alone ' results in its coming back to *E*. *S* (having by hypothesis a unique effect) now takes it to the arrow head, and again it comes back to *E*. This state of affairs is now terminal, and the representative point is trapped within the *E*-confluent.

It can now be seen that the process is *selective*; the representative point ends in a confluent such that the *S*-displacement carries it to some point *within* the confluent. Confluents such as *A*, *C*, and *D*, with the *S*-displacement going outside, cannot hold the representative point under the process considered; confluents such as *E*, *J*, and *L* can trap it.

14/4. The diagram shows two complications that must be considered for completeness' sake.

The first is that the events of the right-hand side may occur, where the process considered takes the representative point cyclically through confluents *P*, *Q*, *R*, *P*, *Q*, *R*, *P*, . . .

The second is shown on the left at *X*, where the confluent comes to a cycle. From this cycle a variety of displacements may be caused by *S*, depending on the precise moment at which *S* is applied (i e. on just where the representative point happens to be).

Whether such cycles (between or within confluents) are common in the nervous system is a question to be settled by experiment. The cycle *within* the confluent, as at *X*, will hardly disturb the conclusions below; for either all *S*-displacements fall within the confluent (in which case it is trapped as stated above) or it will sooner or later leave the confluent (and we are no longer concerned with the cycle). Thus in the Figure, unless the period of the cycle bears some exact simple relation to that of the applications of S (an event of zero probability if they can vary continuously), the representative point will in fact leave X and eventually be trapped at E. (The cycle around P, Q, R adds complications that can be dealt with in a more detailed discussion.)

14/5. The description given is not rigorous, but can easily be made so. It is intended only to illustrate the thesis that under repetitive applications of a stimulus (with sufficient delay between the applications for the system to come to equilibrium) the polystable system is *selective*, for it sticks sooner or later at a state *from whose confluent the stimulus cannot shift it*. And, if there is a metric and continuity over the phase space, this distance that the stimulus S finally moves the point will be *less than the average distance*, for short arrows are favoured. Thus the amounts of change caused by the successive applications of S change from average to less than average.

We need not attempt here to formulate calculations about the exact amount: they can be left to those specially interested. What we should notice is that the outcome of the process is *not symmetric*. When we think of a randomly assembled system of random parts we are apt to deduce that its response to repetitive stimulation will be equally likely to decrease or to increase. The argument shows that this is not so: there is a fundamental tendency for the response to get smaller.

There is a line of argument, much weaker, which may help to make the conclusion more evident. We may take it as axiomatic that large responses tend to cause more change (or are associated with more change) within the system than small. If the responses have any action back on their own causes, then large responses tend to cause a large change in what made them large; but the small only act to small degree on the factors that made them small. Thus factors making for smallness have a fundamentally better chance of surviving than those that make for largeness. Hence the tendency to smallness.

(If the point requires illustration, we could consider the question: Of two boys making their own fireworks, who has the better chance of survival ?—the boy who is trying to produce the biggest firework ever, or the boy who is trying to produce the tiniest !)

14/6. The process can readily be demonstrated, almost in truistic form, on the Homeostat (which is here treated as a system whose variables include ' position of uniselector ' so that it has many states of equilibrium, differing from one another according to the uniselector's position).

The process is shown in Figure 14/6/1. Two units were joined

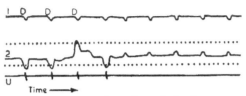

FIGURE 14/6/1 : Homeostat tracing. At each D, 1's magnet is displaced by the operator through a fixed angle. 2 receives this action through its uniselector. When the uniselector's value makes 2's magnet meet the critical state (shown dotted) the value is changed. After the fourth change the value causes only a small movement of 2, so the value is retained permanently.

$1 \longrightarrow 2$. The effect of 1 on 2 was determined by 2's uniselector, which changed position if 2 exceeded its critical states. The operator then repeatedly disturbed 2 by moving 1, at D. As often as the uniselector transmitted a large effect to 2, so often did 2 shift its uniselector. But as soon as the uniselector arrived at a position that gave a transmission insufficient to bring 2 to its critical states, that position was retained. So under constant stimulation by D the amplitude of 2's response changed from larger to smaller.

The same process in a more complex form is shown in Figure 14/6/2. Two units are interacting: $1 \rightleftarrows 2$. Both effects go

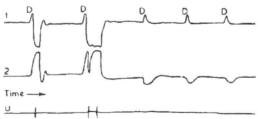

FIGURE 14/6/2 : Homeostat arranged as ultrastable system with two units interacting. At each D the operator moved 1's magnet through a fixed angle. The first field such that D does not cause a critical state to be met is retained permanently.

through the uniselectors, so the whole is ultrastable. At each D the operator displaced 1's magnet through a constant distance. On the first 'stimulation', 2's response brought the system to its critical states, so the ultrastability found a new terminal field. The second stimulation again evoked the process. But the new terminal field was such that the displacement D no longer caused 2 to reach its critical states; so this field was retained. Again under constant stimulation the response had diminished.

14/7. In animal behaviour the phenomenon of ' habituation ' is met with frequently: if an animal is subjected to repeated stimuli, the response evoked tends to diminish. The change has been considered by some to be the simplest form of learning. Neuronic mechanisms are not necessary, for the Protozoa show it clearly:

> '*Amoebae* react negatively to tap water or to water from a foreign culture, but after transference to such water they behave normally.'
> ' If *Paramecium* is dropped into $\frac{1}{2}\%$ sodium chloride it at once gives the avoiding reaction . . . If the stimulating agent is not so powerful as to be directly destructive, the reaction ceases after a time, and the *Paramecia* swim about within the solution as they did before in water.' (Jennings.)

Fatigue has sometimes been suggested as the cause of the phenomenon, but in Humphrey's experiments it could be excluded. He worked with the snail, and used the fact that if its support is tapped the snail withdraws into its shell. If the taps are repeated at short intervals the snail no longer reacts. He found that when the taps were light, habituation appeared early; but when they were heavy, it was postponed indefinitely. This is the opposite of what would be expected from fatigue, which should follow more rapidly when the heavier taps caused more vigorous withdrawals.

A variety of special explanations have been put forward to explain its origin, but the almost universal distribution of its occurrence in living organisms should warn us that the basis must be some factor much more widely spread than the neurophysiological. The argument of this chapter suggests that it is to be expected to some degree in all polystable systems when they are subjected to a repetitive stimulus or disturbance.

Minor disturbances

14/8. Exactly the same type of argument—of looking for what can be terminal—can be used when S is not an accurately repeated stimulus but is, on each application, a sample from a set of disturbances having some definite distribution. In this case, Figure 14/3/1, for example, would remain unchanged in its confluents and states of equilibrium, but the arrow going from each state of equilibrium would lose its uniqueness and become a cluster or distribution of arrows from which, at each disturbance, some one would be selected by some process of sampling.

The outcome is similar. The equilibrium whose arrows all go far away to other confluents is soon left by the representative point; while the equilibrium whose arrows end wholly within its own confluent acts as a trap for it. Thus the polystable system (if free from cycles) goes selectively to such equilibria as are immune to the action of small irregular disturbances.

14/9. The fields (of the main variables) selected by the ultrastable system are subject to this fact. Thus, consider the three fields of Figure 14/9/1 as they might have occurred as terminal fields in Figure 7/23/1. In fields A and C the undisturbed representa-

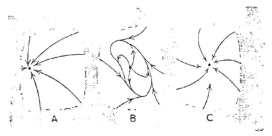

FIGURE 14/9/1 : Three fields of an ultrastable system, differing in their liability to change when the system is subjected to small random disturbances. (The critical states are shown by the dots)

tive points will go to, and remain at, the states of equilibrium. When they are there, a leftwards displacement sufficient to cause the representative point of A to encounter the critical states may be insufficient if applied to C; so C's field may survive a displacement that destroyed A's. Similarly a displacement applied to the representative point on the cycle in B is more likely to change the field than if applied to C. A field like C, therefore, with its state of equilibrium near the centre of the region, tends to have a higher immunity to displacement than fields whose states of equilibrium or cycles go near the edge of the region.

14/10. How would this tendency show itself in the behaviour of the living organism ?

The processes of S. 7/23 allow a field to be terminal and yet to show all sorts of bizarre features: cycles, states of equilibrium near the edge of the region, stable and unstable lines mixed, multiple states of equilibrium, multiple cycles, and so on. These possibilities obscured the relation between a field's being terminal and its being suitable for keeping essential variables within normal limits. But a detailed study was not necessary; for we have just seen that all such bizarre fields tend selectively to be destroyed when the system is subjected to small, occasional, and random disturbances. Since such disturbances are inseparable from practical existence, the process of ' roughing it ' tends to cause their replacement by fields that look like C of Figure 14/9/1 and act simply to keep the representative point well away from the critical states.

CHAPTER 15

Adaptation in Iterated and Serial Systems

15/1. THE last three chapters have been concerned primarily with technique, with the logic of mechanism, when the mechanism shows partial, fluctuating and temporary divisions into subsystems within the whole; they have considered specially the case when the subsystems are rich in states of equilibrium. We can now take up again the thread left at S. 11/13, and can go on to consider the problem of how a large and complex organism can adapt to a large and complex environment without taking the almost infinite time suggested by S. 11/5.

The remaining chapters will offer evidence that the facts are as follows.

(1) The ordinary terrestrial environment has a distribution of properties very different from the distribution assumed when the estimate of S. 11/2 came out so high.

(2) Against the actual distribution of terrestrial environments the process of ultrastability can often give adaptation in a reasonably short time.

(3) When particular environments do get more complex, the time of adaptation goes up, not only in theoretical ultrastable systems but in real living ones.

(4) When the environment is excessively complex and close-knit, the theoretical ultrastable system and the real living fail alike.

In this chapter and the next we will examine environments of gradually increasing complexity. (What is meant by 'complexity' will appear as we proceed.)

15/2. In S. 11/11 it was suggested that the Homeostat (i.e. the two units or so marked off to represent 'environment') is not typical of the terrestrial environment because in the Homeostat every variable is joined directly to every other variable, so that what happens at each variable is conditional, at that moment, on the values of *all* the other variables in the system. What, then, does characterise the ordinary terrestrial environments from this point of view ?

Common observation shows that the ordinary terrestrial environment usually shows several features, which are closely related :

(1) Many of the variables, often the majority, are *constant* over appreciable intervals of time, and thus behave as part-functions. Thus, the mammal stands on ground that is almost always immobile; tree-trunks keep their positions, a cup placed on a table will stay there till a force of more than a certain amount arrives. If one looks around one, only in the most chaotic surroundings will all the variables be changing. This constancy, this commonness of part-functions, must, by S. 12/14, be due to commonness of states of equilibrium in the parts that compose the terrestrial environment. Thus the environment of the living organism tends typically to consist of parts that are rich in states of equilibrium.

(2) Associated with this constancy (naturally enough by S. 12/17) is the fact that most variables of the environment have an immediate effect on only a few of the totality of variables. At the moment, for instance, if I dip my pen in the ink-well, hardly a single other variable in the room is affected. Opening of the door may disturb the positions of a few sheets of paper, but will not affect the chairs, the electric light, the books on the shelves, and a host of others.

We are, in fact, led again to consider the properties of a system whose connexions are fluctuating and conditional—the type encountered before in S. 11/12, and therefore treatable by the same method. I suggest, therefore, that most of the environments encountered on this earth by living organisms contain many part-functions. Conversely, a system of part-functions adequately represents a very wide class of commonly occurring environments.

As a confirmatory example, here is Jennings' description of an hour in the life of *Paramecium*, with the part-functions indicated as they occur.

(It swims upwards and) '. . . thus reaches the surface film.'

The effects of the surface, being constant at zero throughout the depths of the pond, will vary as part-functions. A discontinuity like a surface will generate part-functions in a variety of ways.

'Now there is a strong mechanical jar—someone throws a stone into the water perhaps.'

Intermittent variations of this type will cause variations of part-function form in many variables.

(The *Paramecium* dives) '. . . this soon brings it into water that is notably lacking in oxygen.'

The content of oxygen will vary sometimes as part-, sometimes as full-, function, depending on what range is considered. Jennings, by not mentioning the oxygen content before, was evidently assuming its constancy.

'   . it approaches a region where the sun has been . . . heating the water.'

Temperature of the water will behave sometimes as part-, sometimes as full-, function.

(It wanders on) '. . . into the region of a fresh plant stem which has lately been crushed. The plant-juice, oozing out, alters markedly the chemical constitution of the water.'

Elsewhere the concentration (at zero) of these substances is constant.

'Other *Paramecia* . . . often strike together' (collide).

The pressure on the *Paramecium's* anterior end varies as a part-function.

'The animal may strike against stones.'

Similar part-functions.

'Our animal comes against a decayed, softened, leaf'

More part-functions.

'. . till it comes to a region containing more carbon dioxide than usual.'

Concentration of carbon dioxide, being generally uniform with local increases, will vary in space as a part-function.

'Finally it comes to the source of the carbon dioxide—a large mass of bacteria, embedded in zoogloea.'

Another part-function due to contact.

It is clear that the ecological world of *Paramecium* contains many part-functions, and so too do the worlds of most living organisms.

A total environment, or universe, that contains many part-functions, will show dispersion, in that the set of variables active at one moment will often be different from the set active at another. The pattern of activity *within the environment* will therefore tend, as in S. 13/18, to be fluctuating and conditional rather than invariant. As an animal interacts with its environment, the observer will see that the activity in the environment is limited now to this set, now to that. If one set persists active for a long time and the rest remains inactive and inconspicuous, the observer may, if he pleases, call the first set ' the ' environment. And if later the activity changes to another set he may, if he pleases, call it a ' second ' environment. It is the presence of part-functions and dispersion that makes this change of view reasonable.

An organism that tries to adapt to an environment composed largely of part-functions will find that the environment is composed of subsystems which sometimes are independent but which from time to time show linkage. The alternation is shown clearly when one learns to drive a car. The beginner has to struggle with several subsystems: he has to learn to control the steering-wheel and the car's relation to road and pedestrian; he has to learn to control the accelerator and its relation to engine-speed, learning neither to race the engine nor to stall it; and he has to learn to change gear, neither burning the clutch nor stripping the cogs. On an open, level, empty road he can ignore accelerator and gear and can study steering as if the other two systems did not exist; and at the bench he can learn to change gear as if steering did not exist. But on an ordinary journey the relations vary. For much of the time the three systems

$$\text{driver} + \text{steering wheel} + \ldots$$
$$\text{driver} + \text{accelerator} + \ldots$$
$$\text{driver} + \text{gear lever} + \ldots$$

could be regarded as independent, each complete in itself. But from time to time they interact. Not only may any two use common variables in the driver (in arms, legs, brain) but some linkage is provided by the machine and the world around. Thus, any attempt to change gear must involve the position of the accelerator and the speed of the engine; and turning sharply round a corner should be preceded both by a slowing down and by a change of gear. The whole system thus shows that temporary and conditional division into subsystems that is typical of the whole that is composed largely of part-functions.

Thus the terrestrial environment conforms largely to the poly-stable type.

15/3. To study how ultrastability will act when the environment is not fully joined, we shall have to use the strategy of S. 2/17 and pick out certain cases as type-forms. We will therefore consider environments with four degrees of connectedness.

First we will consider (in S. 15/4–7) the ' whole ' in which the connexion between the parts is actually zero—the limiting case as the connexions get less and less.　　'

In S. 15/8–11 we will consider the case in which actual connexions exist, but in which the subsystems are connected in a chain, without feedback between subsystems. These two cases will suffice to demonstrate certain basic properties.

In the next chapter we will consider the more realistic case in which the subsystems are joined unrestrictedly in direction, so that feedback occurs between the subsystems. This case will be considered in two stages. first, in S. 16/2–4 we will dispose of the case in which the connexions are rich; and then, from S. 16/5 onwards, we will consider the most interesting case, that in which the connexions are in all directions, so that feedback occurs between the subsystems, but in which the connexions are not rich so that the whole can be regarded as formed from subsystems each of which is richly connected internally, joined by connexions (between the subsystems) that are much poorer—the case, in fact, of the system that is neither richly joined nor unjoined.

Adaptation in iterated systems

15/4. The first case to be considered is that in which the whole system, of organism and environment, is actually divided into subsystems that (at least during the time of observation) do not have any effective action on one another. Thus instead of A in Figure 15/4/1 we are considering B. (For simplicity, the diagram shows lines instead of arrows.) If the whole system consists of organism and environment, the actual division between

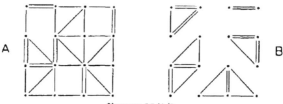

FIGURE 15/4/1.

the two might be that shown in Figure 15/4/2. Such an arrangement would be shown functionally by any organism that deals with its environment by several independent reactions. Such a whole will be said to consist of **iterated** systems.

Environment

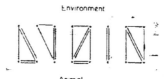

Animal

FIGURE 15/4/2 : Diagrammatic representation of an animal of eight variables interacting with its environment as five independent systems

S. 13/10 exemplified the argument applicable to such a ' whole '. If i is the number of subsystems that are at a state of equilibrium at any particular moment, then in an iterated set i cannot fall, and will usually rise. As subsystem after subsystem reaches equilibrium so will each stay there; and thus the whole will change cumulatively towards total equilibrium.

15/5. Whether the feedbacks in Figure 15/4/2 are first order or second (S. 7/5) is here irrelevant. the whole still moves to equilibrium progressively. Thus, if each subsystem has essential variables and step-mechanisms as in Figure 7/5/1, the stability of the second order will develop as in S. 7/23, and thus the *adaptation* of the whole to this environment will also develop cumulatively and progressively.

In this case, the processes of learning by trial and error will go on in one subsystem independently of what is going on in the others. That such independent, localised learning can occur within one animal was shown by Parker in the following experiment:

' If a sea-anemone is fed from one side of its mouth, it will

197

take in, by means of the tentacles on that side, one fragment of food after another. If now bits of food be alternated with bits of filter paper soaked in meat juice, the two materials will be accepted indiscriminately for some eight or ten trials, after which only the meat will be taken and the filter paper will be discharged into the sea water without being brought to the mouth   If, after having developed this state of affairs on one side of the mouth, the experiment is now transferred to the opposite side, both the filter paper and the meat will again be taken in till this side has also been brought to a state of discriminating '

15/6. What of the time taken by the iterated set to become adapted ? T_3 (of S. 11/5) is applicable here; so the extremeness of T_1 is not to be feared. Thus, however large the whole, if it should actually consist of iterated subsystems, then the time it takes to get adapted may be expected to be of the same order as that taken by one of its subsystems. If this time is fairly short, the whole may be very large and yet become adapted in a fairly short time.

15/7. If Figure 15/4/2 is re-drawn so as to show explicitly its relation to the system of Figure 7/5/1 the result is that shown in Figure 15/7/1 (where the subsystems have been reduced to three for simplicity in the diagram).

At once the reader may be struck by the fact that the three reacting parts in the organism (in its brain usually) are represented as having no connexion between them: is this not a fatal flaw ?

The subject is discussed more thoroughly in S. 17/2; here a partial answer can be given. Let us compare the course of adaptation as it would proceed (1) with the two left-hand sub-systems wholly unconnected as shown, and (2) with the reacting part of subsystem A having some immediate effect on subsystem B.

The first case is straightforward: each subsystem is a little ultrastable system, homologous with that of S. 7/5/1, and each would proceed to adaptation in the usual way.

When B is joined so as to be affected by A, however, the whole course is somewhat changed. A is unaffected, so it will proceed to adaptation as before; but B, previously isolated, is now affected by one or more parameters that need no longer be constant. The effect on B will depend on whether the effect comes to B from A's reacting part or from A's step-mechanisms. If from the step-

Environment

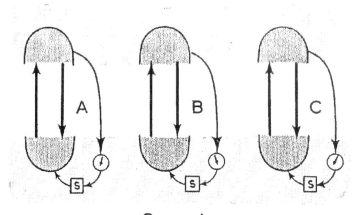

Organism

FIGURE 15/7/1 : Sketch of the diagram of immediate effects of an organism adapting to an environment as three separate subsystems. (Compare Figures 15/8/1 and 16/6/1.)

mechanisms, B can achieve no permanent adaptation until A has reached adaptation, for their values will keep changing. However, once A's step-mechanisms have reached their terminal values, B's parameters will be constant, and B can *then* commence profitably its own search, undisturbed by further changes. Thus the join from A's step-mechanisms will about double the time taken for the whole to reach adaptation.

If, however, the effect comes to B from A's reacting part, then even after A has reached adaptation, every time that A shows its adaptation (by responding appropriately to a disturbance to its environment), the lines of behaviour that A's reacting part follow will provide B with a varying set of values at its parameters. B is thus in a situation homologòus to that of the Homeostat in S. 8/10, except that B may be subject to parameter-values many more than two. The time that B will take to reach adaptation under *all* these values is thus apt to resemble T_1 (S. 11/5), and thus to be excessively long. Thus a joining from the reacting part of A to that of B may have the effect of postponing the whole's adaptation almost indefinitely.

These remarks are probably sufficient for the moment to show that the absence of connexions between organismal subsystems in Figure 15/7/1 does not condemn the representation off-hand. There is more to this matter of joining than is immediately evident. (The topic is resumed in S. 17/2.)

Serial adaptation

15/8. By S. 15/3, our second stage of connectedness in the system occurs when the parts of the environment are joined as a chain. Figure 15/8/1 illustrates the case.

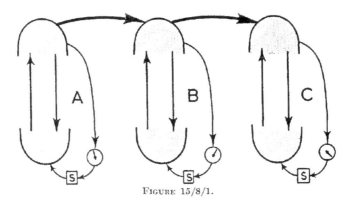

FIGURE 15/8/1.

Without enquiring at the moment into exactly what will happen, it is obvious, by analogy with the previous section, that adaptation must occur in the sequence—*A* first, then *B*, then *C*. Thus we are considering the case of the organism that faces an environment whose parts are so related that the environment can be adapted to only by a process *that respects its natural articulation.*

15/9. Such environments are of common occurrence. A puppy can learn rabbit-catching only after it has learned how to run: the environment does not allow the two reactions to be learned in the opposite order. A great deal of learning occurs in this way. Mathematics, for instance, though too vast and intricate for one all-comprehending flash, can be mastered by stages. The stages have a natural articulation which must be respected if mastery is to be achieved. Thus, the learner can proceed in the order ' Addition, long multiplication, . . .' but not in the order ' Long multiplication, addition, . . .' Our present knowledge of mathematics has in fact been reached only because the subject contains such stage-by-stage routes.

As a clear illustration of such a process, here is Lloyd Morgan on the training of a falcon:

> ' She is trained to the lure—a dead pigeon . . —at first with the leash. Later a light string is attached to the leash, and the falcon is unhooded by an assistant, while the falconer, standing at a distance of five to ten yards, calls her by shouting and casting out the lure. Gradually day after day the distance is increased, till the hawk will come thirty yards or so without hesitation; then she may be trusted to fly to the lure at liberty, and by degrees from any distance, say a thousand yards. This accomplished, she should learn to stoop to the lure. . . . This should be done at first only once, and then progressively until she will stoop backwards and forwards at the lure as often as desired. Next she should be entered at her quarry . . .'

The same process has also been demonstrated more formally. Wolfe and Cowles, for instance, taught chimpanzees that tokens could be exchanged for fruit: the chimpanzees would then learn to open problem boxes to get tokens; but this way of getting fruit (the ' adaptive ' reaction) was learned only if the procedure for the exchange of tokens had been well learned first. In other words, the environment was beyond their power of adaptation if presented as a complex whole—they could not get the fruit— but if taken as two stages in a particular order, could be adapted to.

'. . . the growing child fashions day by day, year by year, a complex concatenation of acquired knowledge and skills, adding one unit to another in endless sequence ', said Culler. I need not further emphasise the importance of serial adaptation.

15/10. To see the process in more detail, consider the following example. A young animal has already learned how to move about the world without colliding with objects. (Though this learning is itself complex, it will serve for illustration, and has the advantage of making the example more vivid.) This learning process was due to ultrastability: it has established a set of values on the step-mechanisms which give a field such that the system composed of eyes, muscles, skin-receptors, some parts of the brain, and hard external objects is stable and always acts so as to keep within limits the mechanical stresses and pressures caused by objects in contact with the skin-receptors (S. 5/4). The diagram of immediate effects will therefore resemble Figure 15/10/1. This system will be referred to as part *A*, the ' avoiding ' system.

FIGURE 15/10/1 . Diagram of immediate effects of the ' avoiding ' system. Each word represents many variables

As the animal must now get its own food, the brain must develop a set of values on step-mechanisms that will give a field in which the brain and the food-supply occur as variables, and which is stable so that it holds the blood-glucose concentration within normal limits. (This system will be referred to as part *B*, the ' feeding ' system.) This development will also occur by ultrastability; but while this is happening the two systems will interact.

The interaction will occur because, while the animal is making trial-and-error attempts to get food, it will repeatedly meet objects with which it might collide. The interaction is very obvious when a dog chases a rabbit through a wood. Further, there is the possibility that the processes of dispersion within brain and environment may allow the two reactions to use common variables. When the systems interact, the diagram of immediate effects will resemble Figure 15/10/2.

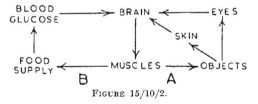

FIGURE 15/10/2.

Let us assume at this point (simply to get a clear discussable case) that the step-mechanisms affecting *A* are, for whatever reason, not changeable while the adaptation to *B* is occurring (compare S. 10/8). As the ' avoiding ' system *A* is not subject to further step-function changes, its field will not alter, and it will at all times react in its characteristic way. So the whole system is equivalent to an ultrastable system B interacting with an 'environment' A. It would also be equivalent to an ultra-stable system interacting with an inborn reflex, as in S. 3/12 B will therefore change its step-mechanism values until the whole has a field which is stable and which holds within limits the variable (blood-glucose concentration) whose extreme deviations cause the step-mechanisms to change. We know from S. 8/11 that, whatever the peculiarities of A, B's terminal field will be adapted *to them*.

It should be noticed that the seven sets of variables (Figure 15/10/2) are grouped in one way when viewed anatomically and in a very different way when viewed functionally. The anatomical point of view sees five sets in the animal's body and two sets in the outside world. The functional point of view sees the whole as composed of two parts· an 'adapting' part B, to which A is 'environment'.

It is now possible to predict how the system will behave after the above processes have occurred. Because part A, the 'avoiding' system, is unchanged, the behaviour of the whole will still be such that collisions do not occur; and the reactions to the food supply will maintain the blood-glucose within normal limits. But, in addition, because B became adapted to A, the getting of food will be modified so that it does not involve collisions, for all such variations will have been eliminated.

15/11. What of the time required for adaptation of all the essential variables when the environment is so joined in a chain ?

The dominating subsystem A will, of course, proceed to adaptation in the ordinary way. B, however, even when A is adapted may still be disturbed to some degree by changes coming to it from A, changes that come ultimately from the disturbances to A that A must adapt against. C also may get upset by some of these disturbances, transmitted through B, and so on. Thus each subsystem down the chain is likely to be disturbed by all the disturbances that come to the subsystems that dominate it, and also by the reactive, adaptive changes made by the same dominating subsystems.

It is now clear how important is the channel-capacity of the connexions that transmit disturbances down the chain. If their capacity is high, so much disturbance may be transmitted to the lower members of the chain that their adaptations may be postponed indefinitely. If their capacity is low, the attenuation may be so rapid that C, though affected by B, may be practically unaffected by what happens at A; and a further subsystem D may be practically unaffected by those at B; and so on. Thus, as the connexions between the subsystems get weaker, so does adaptation tend to the sequential—first A, then B, then C, and so on. (The limit, of course, is the iterated set.)

If the adaptation is sequential, the behaviour corresponds to that of Case 2 (S. 11/5). The time of adaptation will then be that of the moderate T_2 rather than that of the excessively long T_1. Thus adaptation, even with a large organism facing a large environment, may be achievable in a moderate time if the environment consists of subsystems in a chain, with only channels of small capacity between them.

CHAPTER 16

Adaptation in the Multistable System

16/1. Continuing our study of types of environment we next consider, after Figures 15/7/1 and 15/8/1, the case in which the subsystems of the environment are connected unrestrictedly in direction, so that feedbacks occur between them. This type of environment may vary according to the *amounts* of communication (variety) that are transmitted between subsystem and subsystem. Two degrees are of special interest as types:

(1) those in which it is near the maximum—the richly joined environment. (The exposition is more convenient if we consider this case first, as it can be dismissed briefly.)
(2) those in which the amount is small.

The richly joined environment

16/2. When a set of subsystems is richly joined, each variable is as much affected by variables in other subsystems as by those in its own. When this occurs, the division of the whole into subsystems ceases to have any natural basis.

The case of the richly joined environment thus leads us back to the case discussed in Chapter 11.

16/3. Examples of environments that are both large and richly connected are not common, for our terrestrial environment is widely characterised by being highly subdivided (S. 15/2). A richly connected environment would therefore intuitively be perceived as something unusual, or even unnatural. The examples given below are somewhat *recherché*, but they will suffice to make clear what is to be expected in this case.

The combination lock was mentioned in S. 11/9. Though not vigorous dynamically, its parts, so far as they affect the output at the bolt, are connected in that the relations between them are highly conditional. Thus, if there are seven dials that allow the bolt to move only when set at RHOMBUS, then the effect of the first dial going to R on the movement of the bolt is conditional on the positions of all the other six; and similarly for the second and remaining letters.

A second example is given by a set of simultaneous equations, which can legitimately be regarded as the temporary environment of a professional computer if he is paid simply to get correct answers. Sometimes they come in the simplest form, e.g.

$$\left.\begin{array}{l} 2x = 8 \\ 3y = -7 \\ \tfrac{1}{2}z = 3 \end{array}\right\}$$

Then they correspond to the iterated form; and each line can be treated without reference to the others, as in S 15/4

Sometimes they are rather more complex, e.g

$$\left.\begin{array}{rl} 2x & = 3 \\ 3x - 2y & = 2 \\ x + y - z & = 0 \end{array}\right\}$$

This form can be solved serially, as in S. 15/8; for the first line can be treated without reference to the other two; then when the first process has been successful the second line can be treated without reference to the last; and so to the end. The peculiarity of this form is that the value of x is *not conditional* on the values of the coefficients in the second and third lines.

Sometimes the forms are more complex, e.g.

$$\left.\begin{array}{rl} 2x + y - 3z = 2 \\ x - y + 2z = 0 \\ -x - 3y + z = 1 \end{array}\right\}$$

Now the value of x is conditional on the values of *all* the coefficients; and in finding x, no coefficient can be ignored. The same is true of y and z. Thus if we regard the coefficients as the environment and the values of x, y and z as output, correctness in the answer demands that, in getting any part of the answer (any one of the three values), *all* the environment must be taken into account.

A third, and more practical, example of a richly connected environment (now, thank goodness, no more) faced the experimenter in the early days of the cathode-ray oscilloscope Adjusting the first experimental models was a matter of considerable complexity An attempt to improve the brightness of the spot might make the spot also move off the screen. The attempt to bring it back might alter its rate of sweep and start it oscillating vertically An attempt to correct this might make its line of sweep leave the horizontal; and so on. This system's variables (brightness of spot, rate of sweep, etc.) were dynamically linked in a rich and complex manner. Attempts to control it through the available parameters were difficult precisely because the variables were richly joined.

16/4. How long will an ultrastable system that includes such an environment take to get adapted ?

This is the question of S. 11/2. Unless a large fraction of the outcomes are acceptable, the time taken tends to be like T_1 of S. 11/5. As the system is made larger, so does the time of adaptation tend to increase beyond all bounds of what is practical; in other words, the ultrastable system probably fails. But this failure does not discredit the ultrastable system as a model of the brain (S. 8/17), for such an environment is one that is also likely to defeat the living brain. That the living organism is notoriously apt to find such environments difficult or impossible for adaptation is precisely the reason why the combination lock is relied on for protection.

Even when a skilled thief defeats the combination lock he supports, rather than refutes, the thesis. Thus if he can hear, as each dial moves, a tumbler fall into position, then the environment is to him a serial one (S. 15/8); for he can get the first dial-setting right without reference to the others, then the second, and so on. The time of its opening is thus made vastly shorter. Thus the skilled thief does not really adapt successfully to the richly joined environment—he demonstrates that what to others is richly joined is to him joined serially.

Thus the first answer to the question: how does the ultrastable system, or the brain, adapt to a richly joined environment ? is—it doesn't. After the reasonableness of this answer has been made clear, we may then notice that sometimes there are ways in which an environment, apparently too complex for adaptation, may eventually be adapted to; perhaps by the discovery of ways of getting through the necessary trials much faster, or perhaps by the discovery that the environment is not really as complex as it looks. (*I. to C.*, S. 13/4, discusses the matter.)

The poorly joined environment

16/5. We will finally consider the case in which the environment consists of subsystems joined so that they affect one another only weakly, or occasionally, or only through other subsystems. It was suggested in S. 15/2 that this is the common case in almost all natural terrestrial environments.

If the degree of interaction between the subsystems varies, its limits are: at the lower end, the iterated systems of S. 15/4 (as the communication between subsystems falls to zero), and at the upper end, the richly connected systems of S. 16/2 (as the communication rises to its maximum).

When the communication *between* subsystems falls much below that *within* subsystems, the subsystems will show naturally and prominently (S. 12/17).

If such an environment acts within an ultrastable system, what will happen ? Will adaptation occur ? As the discussion below will show, the number of cases is so many, and the forms so various, that no detailed and exhaustive account is possible. We must therefore use the strategy of S. 2/17, getting certain type-forms quite clear, and then covering the remainder by some appeal to continuity: that so far as other forms resemble the type-forms in their construction, to a somewhat similar degree will they resemble the type-forms in their behaviour.

16/6. To obtain a secure basis for the discussion of this most important case, let us state explicitly what is now assumed:

(1) The environment is assumed to be as described in S. 15/2, so that it consists of large numbers of subsystems that have many states of equilibrium. The environment is thus assumed to be polystable.

(2) Whether because the primary joins between the subsystems are few, or because equilibria in the subsystems are common, the interaction between subsystems is assumed to be weak.

(3) The organism coupled to this environment will adapt by the basic method of ultrastability, i.e. by providing second-order feedbacks that veto all states of equilibrium except those that leave each essential variable within its proper limits.

(4) The organism's reacting part is itself divided into sub-systems between which there is no direct connexion. Each sub-

system is assumed to have its own essential variables and second order feedback. Figure 16/6/1 illustrates the connexions, but somewhat inadequately, for it shows only three subsystems. (It should be compared with Figures 15/7/1 and 15/8/1.)

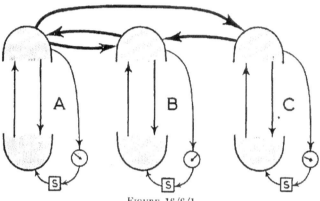

FIGURE 16/6/1.

Such a system is essentially similar to the **multistable** system defined in the first edition. (The system defined there allowed more freedom in the connexions between the main variables, e.g. from reacting part to reacting part, and between reacting part and an environmental subsystem other than that chiefly joined to it; these minor variations are a nuisance and of little importance— in the next chapter we shall be considering such variations.)

16/7. To trace the behaviour of the multistable system, suppose that we are observing two of the subsystems, e.g. *A* and *B* of Figure 16/6/1, that their main variables are directly linked so that changes of either immediately affects the other, and that for some reason all the other subsystems are inactive.

The first point to notice is that, as the other subsystems are inactive, their presence may be ignored; for they become like the ' background ' of S. 6/1. Even if some are active, they can still be ignored if the two observed subsystems are separated from them by a wall of inactive subsystems (S. 12/10).

The next point to notice is that the two subsystems, regarded as a unit, *form a whole which is ultrastable*. This whole will therefore proceed, through the usual series of events, to a terminal field. Its behaviour will not be essentially different from that recorded in Figure 8/4/1. If, however, we regard the same series of events as occurring, not within one ultrastable whole, but as interactions between a minor environment and a minor organism, each of two subsystems, then we shall observe behaviours homologous with those observed when interaction occurs between ' organism ' and ' environment '. In other words, *within a multistable system, subsystem adapts to subsystem in exactly the same way as animal adapts to environment.* Trial and error will appear to be used, and, when the process is completed, the activities of the two parts will show co-ordination to the common end of maintaining the essential variables of the double system within their proper limits.

Exactly the same principle governs the interactions between three subsystems. If the three are in continuous interaction, they form a single ultrastable system which will have the usual properties.

As illustration we can take the interesting case in which two of them, A and C say, while having no immediate connexion with each other, are joined to an intervening system B, intermittently but not simultaneously. Suppose B interacts first with A: by their ultrastability they will arrive at a terminal field. Next let B and C interact. If B's step-mechanisms, together with those of C, give a stable field to the main variables of B and C, then that set of B's step-mechanism values will persist indefinitely; for when B rejoins A the original stable field will be re-formed. But if B's set with C's does not give stability, then it will be changed to another set. It follows that B's step-mechanisms will stop changing when, and only when, they have a set of values which forms fields stable with both A and C. (The identity in principle with the process described in S. 8/10 should be noted.)

16/8. The process can be illustrated on the Homeostat. Three units were connected so that the diagram of immediate effects was $2 \rightleftarrows 1 \rightleftarrows 3$ (corresponding to A, B, and C respectively). To separate the effects of 2 and 3 on 1, bars were placed across the potentiometer dishes (Figure 8/2/2) of 2 and 3 so that they could move only in the direction recorded as downwards in Figure 16/8/1, while 1 could move either upwards or downwards. If 1 was above the central line (shown broken), 1 and 2 interacted, and 3 was independent; but if 1 was below the central line, then

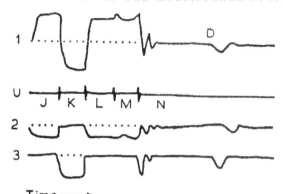

FIGURE 16/8/1 : Three units of the Homeostat interacting. Bars in the central positions prevent 2 and 3 from moving in the direction corresponding here to upwards. Vertical strokes on U record changes of uniselector position in unit 1. Disturbance D, made by the operator, demonstrates the whole's stability.

1 and 3 interacted, and 2 was independent. 1 was set to act on 2 negatively and on 3 positively, while the effects $2 \rightarrow 1$ and $3 \rightarrow 1$ were uniselector-controlled.

When switched on, at J, 1 and 2 formed an unstable system and the critical state was transgressed. The next uniselector connexions (K) made 1 and 2 stable, but 1 and 3 were unstable. This led to the next position (L) where 1 and 3 were stable but 1 and 2 became again unstable. The next position (M) did not remedy this; but the following position (N) happened to provide connexions which made both systems stable. The values of the step-mechanisms are now permanent; 1 can interact repeatedly with both 2 and 3 without loss of stability.

It has already been noticed that if A, B and C should form from time to time a triple combination, then the step-mechanisms of all three parts will stop changing when, and only when, the triple combination has a stable field. But we can go further than that. If A, B and C should join intermittently in various ways, sometimes joining as pairs, sometimes as a triple, and sometimes remaining independent, then their step-mechanisms will stop changing when, and only when, they arrive at a set of values which gives stability to all the arrangements.

Clearly the same line of reasoning will apply no matter how many subsystems interact or in what groups or patterns they join. Always we can predict that *their step-mechanisms will stop changing when, and only when, the combinations are all stable.* Ultrastable systems, whether isolated or joined in multistable systems, act always selectively towards those step-mechanism values which provide stability.

16/9. At the beginning of the preceding section it was assumed, for simplicity, that the process of dispersion was suspended, for we assumed that the two subsystems interacting remained the same two (e.g. *A* and *B* of Figure 16/6/1) during the whole process. What modifications must be made when we allow for the fact that in a multistable system the number and distribution of subsystems active at each moment may fluctuate by dispersion ?

The progression to equilibrium of the whole, to a terminal field, and thus to adaptation of the whole, will occur whether dispersion occurs or not. The effect of dispersion is to destroy the individuality of the subsystems considered in the previous section. There two subsystems were pictured as going through the complex processes of ultrastability, their main variables being repeatedly active while those of the surrounding subsystems remained inactive. This permanence of individuality can hardly occur when dispersion occurs. Thus. suppose that a multistable system's field of all its main variables is stable, and that its representative point is at a state of equilibrium *R*. If the representative point is displaced to a point *P*, the lines from this point will lead it back to *R*. As the point travels back from *P* to *R*, subsystems will come into action, perhaps singly, perhaps in combination, becoming active and inactive in kaleidoscopic variety and apparent confusion. Travel along another line to *R* will also activate various combinations of subsystems; and the set made active in the second line may be very different from that made active by the first.

In such conditions it is no longer profitable to observe particular sybsystems when a multistable system adapts. What will happen is that so long as some essential variables are outside their limits, so long will change at step-mechanisms cause combination after combination of subsystems to become active. But when a stable field arises not causing step-mechanisms to change, it will, as usual, be retained. If now the multistable system's adaptation be tested by displacements of its representative point, the system will be found to respond by various activities of various subsystems, all co-ordinated to the common end. But though co-ordinated in this way, there will, in general, be no simple relation between the actions of subsystem on subsystem: knowing which subsystems were activated on one line of behaviour, and how they interacted, gives no certainty about which will be activated on some other line of behaviour, or how they will interact.

Later I shall refer again to 'subsystem A adapting to, or interacting with, subsystem B', but this will be only a form of words, convenient for description: it is to be understood that what is A and what is B may change from moment to moment.

16/10. This new picture answers the objection to Figure 16/6/1 (and the others) that it shows a tidiness nowhere evident when the organism (or the environment) is examined anatomically or histologically. The Figures are diagrams of immediate effects, and are intended purely as an aid to easier thinking about functional and behavioural relationships. They must be regarded as showing only *functional* connexions, and of these only those between variables that are active over some small interval of time. Figure 16/6/1 is thus apt to mislead both by suggesting a permanence of structure that does not exist when dispersion occurs, and by suggesting an actual two-dimensional form that may well have no anatomical or histological existence. Nevertheless, the functional relationships are indisputable, and the Figure represents them. How they are related to variables physically identifiable in the brain has yet to be discovered.

16/11. Though the multistable system may look chaotic in action, as the activity fluctuates over the subsystems with the same apparent lack of order as that shown by the smoking chimneys of S. 13/18, yet the tendency is always towards ultimate equilibrium and adaptation. So the next question to ask is that of Chapter 11: will the adaptation take an excessively long time ?

Clearly, following the arguments of the previous chapter, much will depend on the richness of connexion between the subsystems —on how much disturbance comes to each subsystem from the others.

At the limit, when the transfers of disturbance are all zero, the whole system becomes identical with the iterated systems of

S. 15/6, and the whole will progress to adaptation similarly. In this case the time taken to reach adaptation will be the moderate time of T_3, rather than the excessive time of T_1.

As the connexions become richer, whether by more basic joins or by the subsystems having fewer states of equilibrium, so will the system move towards the richly-connected type of S. 16/4; and so will the time required for adaptation increase towards that of T_1.

Summary. We are now in a position to summarise the answer, given by the intervening chapters, to the objection, raised in S. 11/2, that ultrastability cannot be the mode of adaptation used by living organisms because it would take too long. We can now appreciate that the objection was unwittingly using the assumption that the organism and the environment were richly joined both within themselves and to each other. Evidence has been given, in S. 15/2, that the *actual* richness is by no means high. Then Chapters 15 and 16 have shown that when it is not high, adaptation by ultrastability can occur in a time that is no longer impossibly long. Thus the objection has been answered, at least in outline.

There we must leave the matter, for a closer examination would have to depend on measurements of actual brains adapting to actual environments. The study of the matter should not be beyond the powers of the present-day experimenter.

Retroactive inhibition

16/12. The suggestion now before the reader is that the system of Figure 7/5/1, when looked at more closely in the forms in which it occurs in actual organisms and environments, will be found to break up into parts more like those of Figure 16/6/1—the multistable system. Let us trace out some of the properties of this system—*extra* to those it possesses by being basically ultrastable and only a particular form of Figure 7/5/1—and see how they accord with what is known of the living organism.

A first question to be asked about the multistable system is whether it can take advantage of the recurrent situation, a matter considered earlier in Chapter 10. Thus, after a multistable system has adapted to a parameter's taking the value P_2, then to its value P_8, will it, when given P_2 again, retain anything of its first adaptation ?

Before attempting the answer, let us recall that, in any poly-stable system, any two different lines of behaviour will give changes in two sets of variables (S. 13/14) which may or may not overlap. Each set will be distributed over the system somewhat as the smoking chimneys of S. 13/18 were distributed over the town. Two disturbances (D_1 and D_2), to a polystable system, will give two sets of active variables, as two winds (W_1 and W_2), to a town, would give two sets of smoking chimneys.

Of the chimneys in the town, what fraction will smoke with both the winds ? The precise answer would depend on precise conditions; but we can see as a first approximation (as in S. 13/15) that if only a small fraction smoke under W_1, and a small fraction under W_2, then if the two fractions are independent, the fraction smoking under both will be the product of the single fractions, and thus much smaller than either. Thus if a random 1 per cent smoke under W_1 and another random 1 per cent under W_2, those that smoke under both will be only $\frac{1}{100}$ of 1 per cent.

The independence, and the smallness of the overlap, can occur only if W_1 and W_2 are well separated in direction. If W_2 should be very close to W_1's direction, it will probably cause smoking in many of W_1's chimneys (in the limit, of course, as it matches W_1's direction, it will make all W_1's chimneys smoke).

Thus a polystable system (subject to certain conditions of statistical independence which would require detailed examination) will respond to two parameter-values (or disturbances, or stimuli) with two sets of variables whose overlap depends on:—(1) the amount of activation that each causes, and (2) the resemblance between the parameter-values.

Suppose now that the parameter values correspond, as in S. 10/8, to environments that have to be adapted to (or to problems that have to be solved). Since the multistable system is also polystable, what has just been said will be true of the multistable system. Here the two lines of behaviour will include trials and will cause changes in the step-mechanisms as well as in the main variables. The degree to which the two sets of activated step-mechanisms overlap will again depend on what fraction of all step-mechanisms are activated and on the degree of resemblance of the parameter-values (or environments). In particular, if the lines of behaviour overlap on only a few step-mechanisms, the second set of trials may cause little change in the step-mechanisms that have an effect on the first reaction, and thus little loss in the first adaptation. Thus *the multistable system*, without further *ad hoc* modification, *will tend to take advantage of the recurrent situation*.

16/13. It is of interest to notice that when two stimuli (or parameter-values) are widely different, the multistable system will tend to direct the activations to widely different sets of step-mechanisms. It thus provides, without further *ad hoc* modification, a functional equivalent of the gating mechanism Γ of S. 10/9.

16/14. Conversely, as the two disturbances (or stimuli, or parameter-values) tend to equality, so will the overlap of the two activated sets tend to increase. A large overlap in the step-mechanisms will mean that the second set of trials will be severely destructive to the first adaptation. Now the tendency for new learning to upset old is by no means unknown in psychology; and an examination of the facts shows that the details are strikingly similar to those that would be expected to occur if the nervous system and its environment were multistable. In experimental psychology ' retroactive inhibition ' has long been recognised The evidence is well known and too extensive to be discussed here, so I will give simply a typical example. Muller and Pilzecker found that if a lesson were learned and then tested after a half-hour interval, those who passed the half-hour idle recalled 56 per cent of what they had learned, while those who filled the half-hour with new learning recalled only 26 per cent. Hilgard and Marquis, in fact, after reviewing the evidence, consider that the phenomenon is sufficiently ubiquitous to justify its elevation to a ' principle of interference '. There can therefore be no doubt that the phenomenon is of common occurrence. New learning does tend to destroy old.

In a multistable system, the more the stimuli used in new learning resemble those used in previous learning, the more will the new tend to upset the old; for, by the method of dispersion assumed here, the more similar are two stimuli the greater is the chance that the dispersion will lead them to common variables and to common step-mechanisms. In psychological experiments it has repeatedly been found that the more the new learning resembled the old the more marked was the interference. Thus

Robinson made subjects learn four-figure numbers, perform a second task, and then attempt to recall the numbers; he found that maximal interference occurred when the second task consisted of learning more four-figure numbers. Similarly Skaggs found that after learning five-men positions on the chessboard, the maximal failure of memory was caused by learning other such arrangements. The multistable system's tendency to be disorganised by new reactions is thus matched by a similar tendency in the nervous system.

16/15. It should be noticed that the demands that a brain model should show both retroactive inhibition and the ability to accumulate adaptations are opposed; for retroactive inhibition demands that later adaptations *shall* be destructive to earlier adaptations, while the power to accumulate adaptations demands that the later *shall not* be destructive to the earlier. The Homeostat showed retroactive inhibition at maximal intensity (S. 10/5), for any later adaptation destroyed the earlier totally. A set of iterated systems, with some suitable gating-mechanism, shows the maximal power of accumulating adaptations. A multistable system of some intermediate degree can show both features partially, and will thus resemble the living organism.

CHAPTER 17

Ancillary Regulations

17/1. Our study of adaptation has led us to the ultrastable system, and then to some difficulties, in S. 11/2, about how long an ultrastable system would take to get adapted. These difficulties have been largely resolved by our identification of the multistable system. (This is not to say that the topic of adaptation is exhausted, for it extends to innumerable special cases that deserve particular study.) In this chapter and the next we will consider some other objections that may be raised to the thesis that the brain is to a major degree multistable. In dealing with them we shall encounter some new aspects of the subject that are worthy of attention.

Communication within the brain

17/2. If it is accepted from here onwards that the formulation of S. 16/6 and its Figure (the multistable system) solves, at least in its major features, the problem posed in Chapter 1, there arises the question why Figure 16/6/1 shows, in the lower part (the organism), no joins between subsystem and subsystem. Does not this absence make the representation a travesty of the facts ?— a brain with no communication between its parts !

17/3. In this matter let us dispose once for all of the idea, fostered in almost every book on the brain written in the last century, that the more communication there is within the brain the better. It will suffice if we remember the three following ways in which we have already seen that some function can be successful only if certain pairs of variables are *not* allowed to communicate, or between which the communication must not be allowed to increase beyond a certain degree.

(1) In S. 8/15 we saw that when an organism is adapting by discrete trials, the essential variables must change the step-mechanisms at a rate much slower than the rate at which the

main variables change. Too rapid a change at the step-mechanisms means that the appropriateness (or not) of a set of values does not have time to be communicated round, through the brain and environment as they carry out the trial, to the essential variables, which would thus be acting before the arrival of their necessary information. If it takes ten seconds for the goodness of a trial to be tested, then alterations should obviously not be made more frequently than at about eleven-second intervals. And if it takes ten years to observe adequately the effect of a profound re-organisation of a Civil Service, then such re-organisations ought not to occur more frequently than at eleven-year intervals. The amount of communication from essential variables to step-functions can thus become harmful if excessive.

(2) In Chapter 10 we considered how the organism could take advantage of the recurrent situation, so that if, having adapted first to A and then to B, A were presented again, it could produce the behaviour appropriate to A at once. It was shown in S. 10/8 that during the adaptation to B, the step-mechanisms concerned with the adaptation to A *must not* be affected by what happens at the essential variables. The allowing of such communication would thus be harmful.

(3) In S. 16/11 it was shown that a multistable system's chance of getting adapted in a reasonably short time is closely related to its approximation to the iterated form. Thus every addition of channels of communication takes the system further from the iterated form and, whatever else it may do, increases the time taken to arrive at adaptation.

Thus, *in adapting systems, there are occasions when an increase in the amount of communication can be harmful.*

17/4. It may still be objected that Figure 16/6/1 should show connexions directly between the reacting parts, because such connexions are necessary for co-ordination to be achieved between part and part. The objection in fact is mistaken; connexions are not *necessary*. Let me explain.

First we can dismiss at once the case in which the parts of the environment (as in Figure 15/7/1) are not joined, for then the threats to the various essential variables come independently and can be responded to independently. In this case the necessity for co-ordination between parts does not arise.

What of the case of Figure 16/6/1, when the parts of the environment *are* joined, and when what is done by, say, the reacting part of *A* may affect, through the part *B* of the environment, what happens at the second (*B*) essential variable ? In this case co-ordination between the actions of the two reacting parts is certainly necessary, for the desirable state of *all* essential variables being kept within limits can be achieved only by each part's actions being properly related to what the others are doing; for all actions meet in the common environment.

Given, then, that co-ordination between the reacting parts is demanded, does this imply that the reacting parts must be in direct communication ? It does not; for communication between them is already available (in the case considered) *through the environment*.

The anatomist may be excused for thinking that communication between part and part in the brain can take place only through some anatomically or histologically demonstrable tract or fibres. The student of function will, however, be aware that channels are also possible through the environment. An elementary example occurs when the brain monitors the acts of the vocal cords by a feedback that passes, partly at least, through the air before reaching the brain.

As the matter is of considerable importance in the general theory of how organism and environment interact, and as it has hitherto received little attention (though S. 5/13 touched on it), let us consider an example that shows how functioning parts of the brain may sometimes be co-ordinated by a channel of communication that passes through the environment.

Consider the player serving at tennis. His left arm makes a movement that projects the ball into the air; a moment later, his right arm makes a movement that, we will assume, strikes the ball correctly into the opposite court. We will also assume that the movements of the left arm are (for whatever reason) not invariable but are subject to small random variations between service and service. We assume that these variations are appreciable, so that unless the movements of the right arm are also varied, and properly paired to those of the left, the ball is likely to go out. Nevertheless we are assuming that the right arm's movements *are* so paired that the ball arrives safely in the proper place (' position of the ball's arrival ' is the essential variable, and its normal limits are the bounds of the opposite court).

For the co-ordination to occur, there *must* be some channel from the source of the left arm's variations to the right arm's movements (*I. to C.*, S. 11/11; the pairing proves as much by S. 4/13 above). Our question now is: must this channel lie within the brain ?

Not only it need not, it usually does not; as the following argument will show. Consider the situation at the moment when the ball is in mid-air: is the right arm's developing movement now guided by messages from the left arm's centre* or from the position of the ball in the air ? The operational test (of S. 4/12 and 12/3) is decisive: let the left arm's movements remain unaltered but assume now that the position of the ball be altered, by a sharp gust say; is the right arm's movement altered? The normal player, if the ball should be affected by a gust, will at once modify his right-arm movements accordingly. These modifications, by the basic operational test, show that the right arm is immediately

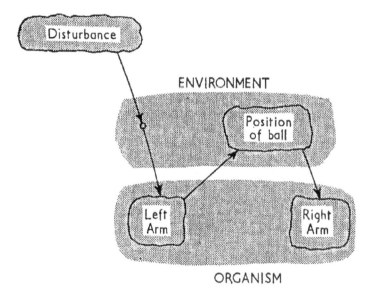

FIGURE 17/4/1.

* We must avoid the tangles caused by the fact that the right arm is controlled by the left motor cortex, and vice versa.

affected, in part at least, by the position of the ball in the air.
Thus the server at tennis normally co-ordinates his left and right
arms' movements by the method: Left arm throws up the ball
with imperfect accuracy, then the position of the ball in the air
(through vision) guides the right arm.   The diagram of immediate
effects is (to show the correspondence with Figure 16/6/1) as
shown in Figure 17/4/1.

Thus, within the assumptions bounding this example, *co-
ordination between parts can take place through the environment;
communication within the nervous system is not always necessary.*

17/5.   After these observations, one may begin to wonder why
the brain should have connexions between its parts at all.   There
are at least two reasons.

The first comes from the fact that, in the organism's life-long
struggle to defend its essential variables against disturbance, there
is a fundamental advantage in getting information about the
disturbance early.   (The fact can either be accepted as obvious,
or proved more formally, as in *I. to C.*, S. 12/5.)   Now while
many of the disturbances that threaten an essential variable come
ultimately from the environment, some of them may come from
other parts of the same organism.   Thus every child that is
learning to feed itself discovers that its lip may be hurt both by
environmental objects and also by its own attempt to pass a
spoonful of food into its closed mouth.   If the lip is not to be
struck, the mouth must be opened in advance of the spoon's
arrival; for this to be possible, information that the spoon is
approaching must get to the 'mouth centre' before the spoon
arrives.   Sometimes the information may come through the
environment (by the child watching the spoon), with the diagram
of immediate effects:

But if, for whatever reason, communication from hand to mouth
is not possible through the environment, then communication
within the brain, from hand-centre to mouth-centre, is *necessary*
if the mouth is to be opened before the spoon arrives.   Thus

communication within the brain can clearly be necessary or advantageous.

17/6. A second reason why communication within the brain may be desirable can be discussed rigorously only in the concepts of *I. to C.*, S. 7/7, but the reason can be sketched here.

When a system is described, it starts by being a member of a large class of possible forms; as each specification is added, so does the class that it may belong to shrink. Start with a system restricted only by having the states possible to it fixed at a certain number. If now is added the further specification 'its diagram of immediate effects contains all possible arrows ', the possibilities in its fields are restricted only slightly. But had it been added that the diagram contained *few* arrows, the possibilities in the fields would have been restricted severely.

Thus, other things being equal, the fewer the joins, the fewer are the modes of behaviour available to the system. From this point of view, extra connexions within the brain can be advantageous, for *they make possible a greater repertoire of behaviours.*

Another way by which the same fact can be seen is to consider the reacting parts before they were joined. The parameters used in the joining must, before the joining, have had fixed values (for otherwise the parts would not have been state-determined) Thus before the joining each parameter must have been fixed at some *one* of its possible values; after the joining the parameter would be capable of variation as it was affected by the other part. With the variation would have come, to the part, a corresponding variety in its fields, and ways of behaving (S 6/8). Thus joining, by mobilising parameters that would otherwise be fixed, adds to the variety of possible behaviours.

It can now be admitted, without misunderstanding, that Figure 16/6/1 would have been more realistic with some connexions drawn between the reacting parts. The presentation and discussion at S. 16/6, however, was simpler without them.

17/7. If increased connexions between the reacting parts in the organism bring in the two advantages just described, they also bring in, as S. 16/4 showed, the disadvantage of lengthening, perhaps to a very great degree, the time required for adaptation. Doubtless there are even more factors to be reckoned in the balance, but what we have seen is sufficient to show that *richness of connexion between the parts in the brain has both advantages and disadvantages.* Clearly the organism must develop so that its brain finds, in this respect, an optimum.

It is not suggested that what is wanted is the optimum in the strict sense. Finding an optimum is a much more complex operation than finding a value that is acceptable (according to a given criterion). Thus, suppose a man comes to a foreign market containing a hundred kinds of fruit that are quite new to him. To find the *optimum* for his palate he must (1) taste all the hundred, (2) make at least ninety-nine comparisons, and (3) remember the results so that he can finally go back to the optimal form. On the other hand, to find a fruit that is acceptable he need merely try them in succession or at random (taking no trouble to remember the past), stopping only at the first that passes the test. To demand the optimum, then, may be excessive; all that is required in biological systems is that the organism finds a state or value *between given limits.*

Thus, for the organism to adapt with some efficiency against the terrestrial environment, it is necessary that the degree of connexion between the reacting parts lie between certain limits.

Ancillary regulations

17/8. ' Between certain limits '—we have heard that phrase before ! Are we arguing in a circle ? Not really, for two different adaptations are involved, of two types or levels or orders.

To see the two adaptations and their relation, recall that we started (S. 3/14) by assuming that certain essential variables were to be kept within limits. Call them E_1, E_2, E_3, and E_4; in Figure 8/2/1 they are clearly evident; keeping *them* within limits is one adaptation. In Chapter 11 we added another essential variable F the *time* taken by the four E's to get stable within their limits; keeping *it* within limits is another adaptation This F is quite distinct from a fifth E, which would enter the system in quite a different way. Yet F does come to the whole as an essential variable, for from S. 11/2 onwards we have consistently discussed the case in which it has certain limits which we do not want it to exceed (The possibility of various classes of essential variables was mentioned in S. 3/15.)

The E's—the four relays on the Homeostat say—are clearly

homologous and equivalent; but F comes into the whole in a different way. To see how, suppose that it is most desirable (for some major essential variable $\mathscr{E}$) that success, on some lesser essential variable E, be achieved in fewer than a hundred trials (i.e. F is to be less than 100). E, making trials, will cause change after change to occur on its corresponding step-mechanisms; at the same time F (increasing exhaustion perhaps) is steadily mounting to its limit. What is to happen if F passes its limit of 100 ? If $\mathscr{E}$ is such that the organism dies, nothing remains to be said; but if $\mathscr{E}$ is not totally essential, the organism is in the condition of having made many trials in some way that has failed to bring success quickly (the situation discussed in Chapter 11). What is to be done ? By the method of ultrastability, F's passing beyond its limit must induce changes, but clearly these changes should not be simply in the same step-mechanisms that E has been working on, or the action by F is no different from a hundred-and-first trial by E. For F to have an appropriately effective action, its passage beyond the limit must induce changes in those conditions that have continued *unchanged* throughout E's hundred trials. E's trials must not consist of further samples from the same set, but must change to samples from a new set. Thus if the organism is a cat in a box, and if it has made 100 trials of manipulating the levers and objects without success, now is the time for it to make trials from a new statistical population—to change perhaps to various forms of mewing and calling.

Thus the improvement of the E's speed of adaptation by the selection of an appropriate value for the step-mechanisms under F's control is not the same as making a selection on the step-mechanisms that E itself should make. Providing an examinee with pen, paper, and a quiet room may be called ' helping the examinee ', but it is clearly quite distinct from the ' help ' that would show him how to answer the individual question. F ' helps ' the E's only in the first sense, not the second.

Thus the conclusion of S. 17/7—that if an organism is to adapt with reasonable speed, certain parameters will have to be brought within certain limits—does not involve a circular appeal, for the two selections are working at different levels, i.e. on different sets.

17/9.   It is not for a moment suggested that all naturally occurring organisms have essential variables that divide neatly into distinct levels: E's, F's, and so on. Would that it were so! When it occurs, the whole act of adaptation (really life-long as we saw in S. 10/2) can be divided into portions; then the practical scientist can study the system portion by portion, level by level, and can thus greatly simplify its study. The Homeostat was designed partly so as to enable two levels to be obviously distinguishable. (1) the four continuous variables at the magnets and (2) the discontinuous variables on the uniselectors. *When* a system has this natural internal division, the observer can take advantage of the fact to describe the somewhat complex whole in three stages, each considerably simpler: the continuous system and its properties, the discontinuous system and *its* properties, and the interaction between them. But when the whole system is not so divisible it remains merely a fearfully complex whole, not capable of reduction, and therefore as intractable to the scientist as the examples in S. 16/3.

This book inevitably concerns itself with the case in which the essential variables are divisible clearly into levels: the primary levels (of E_1, E_2, E_3, E_4) in Chapters 7 to 10, and then a sharply differentiated F in Chapters 11 to the present. In this it was again following the strategy of S. 2/17, getting a clear grasp of the manageable cases so that they could serve as a basis for at least a distant survey of the unmanageable. The reader will now appreciate that the simplicity of the earlier chapters was essentially a didactic device, not resembling the actual complexity of actual organisms. In fact, their real complexity is greater, by many orders of size, than that considered here. Thus, the reacting part R of Figure 7/5/1, which looks so simple, may not only contain the complexities of the multistable system (Figure 16/6/1) but also, in the higher organisms, many subsystems of the form of Figure 7/5/1 itself, each with its own little sub-essential variables and sub-adaptations; for much adaptation to long-term goals is achieved by finding suitable sets of sub-goals, perhaps in complex sequences of timing and conditionality. Thus once we have used the carefully simplified forms of Figures 7/5/1 and 16/6/1 to establish our understanding, we must be prepared to admit that in the real brain the same principles work in a complexity that is of an altogether higher order, one that may well prove to be for ever beyond the *detailed* comprehension of the human scientist, who has an I.Q. limited, for all practical purposes, to something below 200.

With this admitted, let us continue to examine those cases in which some division into levels, and some easy understanding, are possible.

17/10. In Chapter 7 it was shown that the simple ultrastable system would solve the basic problem of getting the primary essential variables stable within their limits. But in Chapter 11 we recognised that adaptation, though it occurs in a purely logical sense, may occur at such a low degree of efficiency as to be useless for practical purposes If we are to find the mechanism that resembles the living, and especially the human, brain we must find one that adapts, not merely in a nominal sense but with really high efficiency.   In S. 17/7 we found that such efficiency implies adjustment of the degree of intra-cerebral connectivity to within certain limits.

We can now notice explicitly that there are other parameters that will also have to be adjusted if the degree of adaptation is to be more than merely nominal.   Several of these have already been noticed in passing:

(1) In S. 8/15 we noticed that the *duration of trial* demanded adjustment.   In that section, the adjustment was, of course, made by the operator before the tracings of the Homeostat's behaviour were taken; but nothing has yet been said about how this adjustment is to be made *automatically* in the organism.

(2) In S. 7/7 it was demanded that the essential variables should act on the step-mechanisms in the particular way hunt at ' bad ' and stick at ' good '.   Nothing was said about how this particular relation was to be provided in the organism.

(3) In S. 10/8 it was shown that if an ultrastable system was to adapt efficiently to a recurrent situation, a certain *gating-mechanism* was necessary; but nothing was said about how the organism should acquire one.

(4) S. 13/11 showed how important is the value of the para-meter · richness of equilibria among the states of the parts. Nothing was said about how this parameter should be adjusted to within satisfactory limits.

Doubtless there are others that we have not yet noticed.   One other of outstanding importance deserves a section to itself.

Distribution of feedback

17/11. Another adjustment that is necessary, if the adaptation is to be more than merely nominal, has already been made in Figure 16/6/1, which thereby begged an important question. In the Figure, if we start in the environment at any subsystem and trace a route through the essential variable that it affects, on through the corresponding step-mechanism, reacting part, and so back to the environment, we arrive at the same subsystem as the one we started at. The Figure thus implies that if an essential variable, E_1 say, is being upset by a part of the environment, E_1's actions will eventually affect the very part of the environment that is the cause of the trouble.

The correspondence undoubtedly favours efficiency in adaptation, as may be seen by tracing explicitly what would happen otherwise. (The argument is clearest when the systems are iterated, Figure 15/7/1.) Suppose, in it, that the second-order loops were severed and then re-connected in some random way: so that the essential variable of A affected the reacting part of B, say A disturbance to A that A is not adapted to would now result in changes at B's step-mechanisms, though the set of values here might be perfectly adapted to dealing with whatever disturbance came to B. Thus without proper distribution of the second-order feedbacks the effects from the essential variables would only change at random, destroying in the process minor adaptations already established. Thus without appropriate distribution of the second-order feedbacks there cannot be that conservation of correct adaptations in the subsystems, and the cumulative progression to adaptation that Chapter 10 treated as of major importance. The system would still adapt as a Homeostat does, but it would take the excessive time of T_1 rather than the moderate time of T_3 (S. 11/5).

The distribution of second-order feedbacks cannot be settled once for all, for a part of each circuit is determined by, or supplied by, the environment, and is thus subject to change. To this the organism must make counter-adjustments, if the distribution is to remain appropriate.

A well-known example that illustrates the necessity for finding *where* to apply a correction is given by the aspiring chess-player who has just-lost a game and who is considering how his strategy

should be altered for the future. Often he is acutely aware of
the fact that he is not sure *where* to apply the correction. Should
he examine the last few moves and alter his tactics ? Should he,
in future, avoid that sort of middle-game ? Or, maybe, should
he stop opening with P—Q4 and change to P—K4 ? The young
chess-player has not only to solve the problems of what move to
make next but also that of where to feed back the corrections.
Thus, there may well be players today who are weak simply
because, when they lose a game, they change their opening rather
than their end-game.

(In this example the ' parts ' to be modified are strung out in
time: the modification has to find the right place in the sequence.
The example serves to remind us that a diagram of immediate
effects (such as Figure 16/6/1) represents *functional*, not structural
or anatomical relations.)

17/12. The last two sections have shown that at least five ancillary
regulations have to be made if the basic process of ultrastability
is to bring adaptation with reasonable efficiency and speed. The
next question thus is: how are these **ancillary** regulations to be
achieved ?

17/13. The answer can be given with some assurance, for all
processes of regulation are dominated by the law of requisite
variety. (It has been described in *I. to C.*, Chapter 11 ; here will
be given only such details as are necessary.)

This law (of which Shannon's theorem 10 relating to the sup-
pression of noise is a special case) says that if a certain *quantity*
of disturbance is prevented by a regulator from reaching some
essential variables, then that regulator must be capable of exerting
at least that quantity of selection. (Were the law to be broken,
we would have a case of appropriate effects without appropriate
causes, such as an examinee giving correct answers before he has
been given the questions (S. 7/8). Scientists work on the assumption that such things do not happen; and so far they have found
no fact that would make them question the assumption.) The
provision of the ancillary regulations thus demands that a process
of selection, of appropriate intensity, exist. Where shall we find
this process ?

The biologist, of course, can answer the question at once; for the work of the last century, and especially of the last thirty years, has demonstrated beyond dispute that natural, Darwinian, selection is responsible for all the selections shown so abundantly in the biological world. Ultimately, therefore, these ancillary regulations are to be attributed to natural selection. They will, therefore, come to the individual (to our kitten perhaps) either by the individual's gene-pattern or they develop under an ultra-stability of their own. There is no other source.

17/14. The subject of adaptation in brain-like mechanisms, how-ever, today interests an audience much wider than the biological. I will, therefore, give a brief account of these processes of selection so that the reader whose training has not been biological can see just how the ancillary regulations must be developed in brains other than the living

The account will also serve a second purpose. So far, the book has followed the method of starting, in Chapter 1, with the fact of adaptation as an effect, and has argued back to its causes. This is not the natural direction for argument, which goes alto-gether more simply and clearly if we just take an initial state and then ask: what will happen from now on ? I propose, therefore, to sketch the process in its natural direction, showing that, given a certain very general starting point, adaptation as an outcome is inevitable.

CHAPTER 18

Amplifying Adaptation

Selection in the state-determined system

18/1. The origin of selections ceases to be a problem as soon as it is realised that selection, far from being a rarity, is performed to greater or less degree by *every* isolated state-determined system (*I. to C.*, S. 13/19). In such a system, as two lines of behaviour may become one, but one line cannot become two, so *the number of states that it can be in can only decrease.*

This selection is well known, but in simple systems it shows only in trivial form The spring-driven clock, for instance, is selective for the run-down state: start it at any state of partial winding and it will make its way to the run-down state, where it will remain. The often-made observation that machines run to an equilibrium expresses the same property.

In simple systems the property seems trivial, but as the system becomes more complex so does this property become richer and more interesting. The Homeostat, for instance, can be regarded simply as a system, with magnets and uniselectors, that runs to a partial equilibrium, where it sticks. But the equilibrium is only partial, and therefore richer in content than that of the run-down clock. The uniselectors are motionless but the magnets may still move, and the partial equilibrium manifests a dynamic homeostasis that has been *selected* by the uniselector's process of running to equilibrium. Thus the Homeostat begins to show something of the richness of properties that emerge when the system is complex enough, or large enough, to show: (1) a high intensity of selection by running to equilibrium, and also (2) that this selected set of states, though only a small fraction of the whole, is still large enough in itself to give room for a wide range of dynamic activities. Thus, *selection for complex equilibria, within which the observer can trace the phenomenon of adaptation, must not be regarded as an exceptional and remarkable event*. **it is the rule.** The chief reason why we have failed to see this fact in the past is that our terrestrial

231

world is grossly bi-modal in its forms: either the forms in it are extremely simple, like the run-down clock, so that we dismiss them contemptuously, or they are extremely complex, so that we think of them as being quite different, and say they have Life.

18/2. Today we can see that the two forms are simply at the extremes of a single scale. The Homeostat made a start at the provision of intermediate forms, and modern machinery, especially the digital computers, will doubtless enable further forms to be interpolated, until we can see the essential unity of the whole range.

Further examples of intermediate forms are not difficult to invent. Here is one that shows how, in *any* state-determined dynamic system, some properties will have a greater tendency to persist, or 'survive', than others. Suppose a computer has a hundred stores, labelled 00 to 99, each of which initially holds one decimal digit, i.e. one of 0, 1, 2, . . . , 9, chosen at random, independently and equiprobably. It also has a source of random numbers (drawn, preferably, from molecular, thermal, agitation). It now repeatedly performs the following operation:

Take two random numbers, each of two digits; suppose 82 and 07 come up. In this case multiply together the numbers in stores 82 and 07, and replace the digit in the first store (no. 82) by the right-hand digit of the product.

Now Even × Even gives Even, and Odd × Odd gives Odd; but Odd × Even gives Even, so the number in the first store can change from Odd to Even, but not from Even to Odd. As a result, the stores, which originally contained Odds and Evens in about equal numbers, will change to containing more and more Evens, the Odds gradually disappearing. The biologist might say that in the 'struggle' to occupy the stores and survive the Evens have an advantage and will inevitably exterminate the Odds.

In fact, among the Evens themselves there are degrees of ability to survive. For the Zeros have a much better chance than the other Evens, and, as the process goes on, so will the observer see the Zeros spread over the stores. In the end they will exterminate their competitors completely.

18/3. This example is easily followed, but is uncomfortably close to the trivial. More complex examples could easily be set up, but they would tell us nothing of the principles at work (though they would provide most valuable and convincing examples). What all would show is that when a single-valued operation is performed repeatedly on a set of states (this operation being the 'laws' of the system), the system tends to such states as are not affected by the operation, or are affected to less than usual degree. In other words, *every single-valued operation tends to select forms that are peculiarly able to resist its change-inducing action*. In simple systems this fact is almost truistic, in complex systems anything but. And when it occurs on the really grand scale, on a system with millions of variables and over millions of years, then the states selected are likely to be truly remarkable and to show, *among their parts*, a marked *co-ordination* tending to make them immune to the operation.

The development of life on earth must thus *not* be seen as something remarkable. On the contrary, it was inevitable. It was inevitable in the sense that if a system as large as the surface of the earth, basically polystable, is kept gently simmering dynamically for five thousand million years, then nothing short of a miracle could keep the system away from those states in which the variables are aggregated into intensely self-preserving forms. The *amount* of selection performed by this system, of which we know only one example, is of an order of size so vastly greater than anything that we experience as individuals, that we not unnaturally have some difficulty in grasping that the process is really the same as that seen so trivially in our everyday systems. Nevertheless it is so; the greater extension in space enables a vastly greater number of forms to be tested, and the greater extension in time enables the forms to be worked up to a vastly greater degree of intricate co-ordination.

We can thus trace, from a perfectly natural origin, the gene-patterns that today inhabit the earth; we are not surprised that the earth has developed forms that show, in conjunction with their environments, the most remarkable power of being resistant to the change-inducing actions of the world around them. They are resistant, not in the static and uninteresting way that a piece of granite, or a run-down clock, is resistant, but in the dynamic and much more interesting way of forming intricate dynamic systems around themselves (their so-called 'bodies', with extensions such as nests and tools) so that the whole is homeostatic and self-preserving by *active* defences.

18/4. What concerns us in this book is the fact that the active defences can be *direct* or *indirect*. The *direct* were considered only in S. 1/3   They include all the regulatory mechanisms that are specified *in detail* by the gene-pattern.   They are adapted because the conditions that insisted on them have been constant over many generations

The earlier forms of gene-pattern adapted in this way only.   The later forms, however, have developed a specialisation that can give them a defence against a class of disturbances to which the earlier were vulnerable   This class consists of those disturbances that, though not constant over a span of many generations (and thus not adaptable to by the gene-pattern, for the change is too rapid) are none the less constant over a span of a single generation. When disturbances of this class are frequent, there is advantage in the development of an adapting mechanism that is (1) controlled in its outlines by the gene-pattern (for the same outlines are wanted over many generations), and (2) controlled in details by the details applicable to that particular generation.

This is the learning mechanism.   Its peculiarity is that the gene-pattern delegates part of its control over the organism to the environment.   Thus, it does not specify in detail how a kitten shall catch a mouse, but provides a learning mechanism and a tendency to play, so that it is *the mouse* which teaches the kitten the finer points of how to catch mice.

This is regulation, or adaptation, by the indirect method.   The gene-pattern does not, as it were, dictate, but puts the kitten into the way of being able to form its own adaptation, guided in detail by the environment.

18/5. We can now answer the question raised in S. 17/12, and can see how the law of requisite variety is to be applied to the question of how the ancillary regulations are to be achieved, i.e. how the necessary parameters are to be brought to their appropriate values.

Some may be adjusted by the direct action of the gene-pattern, so that the organism is born with the correct values.   For this to be possible, the environmental conditions must have been constant for a sufficiently long time, and the processes of natural selection must have been intense enough and endured long enough for the total selection exerted to satisfy the law.

Some ancillary regulations may be adjusted by the gene-pattern at one remove. In this case the gene-pattern would establish values that would result in the appearance of a mechanism, actually a regulator, that would then proceed, by *its own* action, to bring the parameters to appropriate values.

Other ancillary regulators might be adjusted by the gene-pattern at two removes; but we need not trace the matter further, as real systems will seldom be arranged neatly in distinct levels (S. 17/9). All we need notice here is that adaptation can be achieved by the gene-pattern either directly or indirectly.

Amplifying adaptation

18/6. The method of adaptation by learning is the only way of achieving adaptation when what is adaptive is constant for too short a time for adaptation of the gene-pattern to be achieved. For this reason alone we would expect the more advanced organisms to show it. The method, however, has also a peculiar advantage that is worth notice, particularly when we consider the limitation implied by the law of requisite variety, and ask *how much* regulation the gene-pattern can achieve in the two cases.

Direct and indirect regulation occur as follows Suppose an essential variable X has to be kept between limits x' and x''. Whatever acts directly on X to keep it within the limits is regulating directly. It may happen, however, that there is a mechanism M available that affects X, and that will act as a regulator to keep X within the limits x' and x'' provided that a certain parameter P (parameter to M) is kept within the limits p' and p''. If, now, any selective agent acts on P so as to keep it between p' and p'', the end result, after M has acted, will be that X is kept between x' and x''

Now, in general, the quantities of regulation required to keep P in p' and p'' and to keep X in x' to x'' are independent. The law of requisite variety does not link them. Thus it may happen that a *small* amount of regulation supplied to P may result in a much larger amount of regulation being shown by X.

When the regulation is direct, the amount of regulation that can be shown by X is absolutely limited to what can be supplied to it (by the law of requisite variety); when it is indirect, however, *more regulation may be shown by X than is supplied to P*. Indirect regulation thus permits the possibility of *amplifying* the amount of regulation; hence its importance.

18/7. Living organisms came across this possibility aeons ago, for the gene-pattern is a channel of communication from parent to offspring: 'Grow a pair of eyes,' it says, 'they'll probably come in useful; and better put haemoglobin into your veins—carbon monoxide is rare and oxygen common.' As a channel of communication it has a definite, finite capacity, Q say. If this capacity is used directly, then, by the law of requisite variety, the amount of regulation that the organism can use as defence against the environment cannot exceed Q. To this limit, the non-learning organisms must conform. If, however, the regulation is done indirectly, then the quantity Q, used appropriately, may enable the organism to achieve, against its environment, an amount of regulation much greater than Q. Thus the learning organisms are no longer restricted by the limit.

The possibility of such 'amplification' is well known in other ways. If a child wanted to discover the meanings of English words, and his father had only ten minutes available for instruction, the father would have two possible modes of action. One is to use the ten minutes in telling the child the meanings of as many words as can be described in that time. Clearly there is a limit to the number of words that can be so explained. This is the direct method. The indirect method is for the father to spend the ten minutes showing the child how to use a dictionary. At the end of the ten minutes the child is, in one sense, no better off; for not a single word has been added to his vocabulary. Nevertheless the second method has a fundamental advantage; for in the future the number of words that the child can understand is no longer bounded by the limit imposed by the ten minutes. The reason is that if the information about meanings has to come through the father directly, it is limited to ten-minutes' worth; in the indirect method the information comes partly through the father and partly through another channel (the dictionary) that the father's ten-minute act has made available.

In the same way the gene-pattern, when it determines the growth of a learning animal, expends part of its resources in forming a brain that is adapted not only by details in the gene-pattern but also by details in the environment. The environment acts as the dictionary.   While the hunting wasp, as it attacks its prey, is guided in detail by its genetic inheritance, the kitten is taught how to catch mice by the mice themselves.   Thus in the learning organism the information that comes to it by the gene-pattern is much *supplemented* by information supplied by the environment; so the total adaptation possible, after learning, can exceed the quantity transmitted directly through the gene-pattern.

Summary

The primary fact is that *all* isolated state-determined dynamic systems are selective : from whatever state they have initially, they go towards states of equilibrium. The states of equilibrium are always characterised, in their relation to the change-inducing laws of the system, by being *exceptionally resistant.*

(Specially resistant are those forms whose occurrence leads, by whatever method, to the occurrence of further replicates of the same form—the so-called ' reproducing ' forms.)

If the system permits the formation of local equilibria, these will take the form of dynamic subsystems, exceptionally resistant to the disruptive effects of events occurring locally.

When such a stable dynamic subsystem is examined internally, it will be found to have parts that are *co-ordinated* in their defence against disturbance.

If the class of disturbance changes from generation to generation but is constant within each generation, even more resistant are those forms that are born with a mechanism such that the *environment* will make it act in a regulatory way against the particular environment—the ' learning ' organisms.

This book has been largely concerned with the last stage of the process. It has shown, by consideration of specially clear and simple cases, how the gene-pattern can provide a mechanism (with both basic and ancillary parts) that, when acted on by any given environment, will inevitably tend to adapt to that particular environment.

APPENDIX

CHAPTER 19

The State-determined System

19/1. THE mathematics necessary for the study of adaptation does not consist simply of the solution of a particular mathematical problem. The problem, to the bio-mathematician, ranges from the identification of the basic logic necessary for the representation of the basic concept of mechanism, through its development into various branches (such as from the discrete to the continuous and from the non-metric to the metric), to the eventual use of specialised techniques for special particular problems.

Since the problems that interest the biologist usually come from systems of very great complexity, in which treatment of *all* the facts is not possible, special importance must be given to methods, such as that of topology, that allow simple answers to be given to simple questions, even though the basic facts are complex. The mathematical basis should therefore be sufficiently general to allow specialisation into the methods of topology. Here we have been greatly aided by the magnificent work of the French school that writes, collectively, under the pseudonym of N. Bourbaki. In their great *Eléments de Mathématiques* this school has shown how the theory of sets, in a simple basic form, can be gradually extended and developed, without the least loss of precision or the least change in the fundamental concepts, into the realms of topology, algebra, geometry, theory of functions, differential equations, and all the various branches of mathematics.

How the theory of sets, essentially in the form used by Bourbaki, gives a secure basis for the logic of mechanism, has already been displayed in Part I of *I to C*. (That book does not use Bourbaki's symbols explicitly, but his concepts are used throughout and in exactly his form; so the reader who wishes to correlate *I. to C.* with Bourbaki's work will find that the correlation is in most places obvious.)

The logic of mechanism

19/2. Our starting-point is the idea, much more than a century old, that a 'machine' is that which, whenever it is in given conditions and at a given internal state, goes always to a particular state (i.e. not to different states on different occasions). This definition at once shows its formal correspondence with Bourbaki's 'algebraic law of external composition'. For if the external conditions can be at any one of a set Ω, and the internal states of the machine at any one of a set E, then the machine defines, by its behaviour, a mapping (Bourbaki's '*application*') of $\Omega \times E$ into E. The concept of 'machine' thus corresponds *exactly* to one of the most basic concepts in mathematics.

After this basic identification many others follow at once. The mapping of E into E given by holding the value of Ω constant corresponds to the machine when isolated. An element of E that is invariant in the algebra (for some value of Ω) corresponds to a state of equilibrium of the machine when the input (or surrounding conditions) is held constant (i.e. for a given field). The compatibility (or not) of an equivalence relation with an external law of composition corresponds to whether or not a proposed simplification of a state-determined system leaves the new system still state-determined. If it does, then the algebraic quotient-law corresponds to the new, simplified, canonical representation. And so on, in a manner that deserves extensive treatment.

It is not my intention here to develop the subject *ab initio* and extensively As this book is concerned primarily with the brain and with systems in which continuity is common, we need only notice that Bourbaki has shown how the basic concepts, stated in discrete form, can be specialised to the continuous forms and to those with a metric. In this Appendix we will deal only with such forms as are continuous and provided with a metric.

(*N.B.* Throughout this chapter the emphasis is on the system that is isolated and left alone to show what it will do, apart from occasional interferences from the experimenter The statements made should be interpreted accordingly. Chapter 21 deals explicitly with the system that is being subjected to changes in its conditions, or at its input.)

19/3. A **variable** is a function of the time. A **system** of n variables will usually be represented by $x_1, x_2, \ldots, x_n$, or sometimes more briefly by x. The case where $n = 1$ is not excluded. It will be assumed throughout that n is finite; a system with an infinite number of variables (e.g. that of S 19/17) will be replaced by a system in which i is discontinuous and n finite, and which differs from the original system by some amount that is negligible.

Each variable x_i is a function of the time t; it will sometimes be written as $x_i(t)$ for emphasis. It must be single-valued, but need not be continuous. A constant may be regarded as a variable which undergoes zero change.

19/4. The **state** of a system at a time t is the set of numerical values of $x_1(t), \ldots, x_n(t)$. Two states $(x_1, \ldots, x_n)$ and $(y_1, \ldots, y_n)$ are **equal** if $x_i = y_i$ for all i.

19/5. A **transition** can be specified only after an interval of time, finite and represented by Δt or infinitesimal and represented by dt, has been specified. It is represented by the pair of states, one at time t and one at the specified time later.

A **line of behaviour** is specified by a succession of states and the time-intervals between them. Two lines of behaviour are **equal** if all the corresponding states and time-intervals along the succession are equal. (So two lines of behaviour that differ only in the absolute times of their origin are equal.)

19/6. A **primary operation** is a physical event, not a mathematical, requiring a real machine and a real operator or experimenter. He selects an initial state $(x_1^0, \ldots, x_n^0)$, and then records the transition that occurs as the system changes in accordance with its own internal drives and laws.

19/7. If, on repeatedly applying primary operations, he finds that all the lines of behaviour that follow an initial state S are equal, and if a similar equality occurs after every other state $S', S'', \ldots$, then the system is **regular**.

Such a system can be represented by equations of form

$$x_1 = F_1(x_1^0, \ldots, x_n^0; \ t)$$

$$\cdot\ \cdot\ \cdot\ \cdot\ \cdot\ \cdot\ \cdot\ \cdot$$

$$x_n = F_n(x_1^0, \ldots, x_n^0; \ t)$$

in which the F's are single-valued functions of their arguments but are otherwise quite unrestricted. Obviously, if the initial state is at $t = 0$, we must have

$$F_i(x_1^0, \ldots , x_n^0 ; \ 0) = x_i^0 \qquad (i = 1, \ldots , n)$$

19/8.   Theorem : *The lines of behaviour of a state-determined system define a group.*

Let the initial state of the variables be x^0, where the single symbol represents all n, and let time t' elapse so that x^0 changes to x'. With x' as initial state let time t'' elapse so that x' changes to x''. As the system is state-determined, the same total line of behaviour will be followed if the system starts at x^0 and goes on for time $t' + t''$. So

$$x_i'' = F_i(x_1', \ldots , x_n' ; \ t'') = F_i(x_1^0, \ldots , x_n^0 ; \ t' + t'')$$
$$(i = 1, \ldots , n)$$

But

$$x_i' = F_i(x_1^0, \ldots , x_n^0; \ t') \qquad (i = 1, \ldots , n)$$

giving

$$F_i\{F_1(x^0; \ t'), \ldots , F_n(x^0; \ t'); \ t''\} = F_i(x_1^0, \ldots , x_n^0; \ t' + t'')$$
$$(i = 1, \ldots , n)$$

for all values of x^0, t', and t'' over some given region; and this is one way of defining a one-parameter finite continuous group.

The converse is not true. Thus $x = (1 + t)x^0$ defines a group (with $n = 1$); but the times do not combine by addition, and the system is not state-determined.

Example : The system with lines of behaviour given by

$$x_1 = x_1^0 + x_2^0 t + t^2$$
$$x_2 = x_2^0 + 2t$$

is state-determined, but that with lines given by

$$x_1 = x_1^0 + x_2^0 t + t^2$$
$$x_2 = x_2^0 + t$$

is not.

Canonical representation

19/9.   Theorem: *That a system $x_1, \ldots , x_n$ should be state-determined it is necessary and sufficient that the x's, as functions of t, should satisfy equations*

$$\left.\begin{aligned}
\frac{dx_1}{dt} &= f_1(x_1, \ldots, x_n) \\
&\quad\cdot\cdot \\
\frac{dx_n}{dt} &= f_n(x_1, \ldots, x_n)
\end{aligned}\right\} \qquad \cdot \qquad \cdot \qquad \cdot \quad (1)$$

where the f's are single-valued, but not necessarily continuous, functions of their arguments; in other words, the fluxions of the set $x_1, \ldots, x_n$ can be specified as functions of that set and of no other functions of the time, explicit or implicit. The equations, in this form, are said to be the **canonical representation** *of the system.*

(The equations will sometimes be written

$$dx_i/dt = f_i(x_1, \ldots, x_n) \qquad (i = 1, \ldots, n) \quad . \quad (2)$$

and may be abbreviated even to $x = f(x)$ if the context makes the meaning clear.)

(1) Let the system be state-determined. Start it at $x_1^0, \ldots, x_n^0$ at time $t = 0$ and let it change to $x_1, \ldots, x_n$ at time t, and then on to $x_1 + dx_1, \ldots, x_n + dx_n$ at time $t + dt$. Also start it at $x_1, \ldots, x_n$ at time $t = 0$ and let time dt elapse By the group property (S. 19/8) the final states must be the same. Using the same notation as S. 19/8, and starting from x_i^0, x_i changes to $F_i(x^0; t + dt$ and starting at x_i it gets to $F_i(x; dt)$. Therefore

$$F_i(x^0, t + dt) = F_i(x, dt) \qquad (i = 1, \ldots, n).$$

Expand by Taylor's theorem and write $\dfrac{\partial}{\partial b}F_i(a; b)$ as $F_i'(a; b)$. Then

$$F_i(x^0; t) + dt \cdot F_i'(x^0; t) = F_i(x; 0) + dt \; F_i'(x; 0)$$
$$(i = 1, \ldots, n)$$

But both $F_i(x^0; t)$ and $F_i(x; 0)$ equal x_i.

Therefore $\quad F_i'(x^0, t) = F_i'(x; 0) \qquad (i = 1, \ldots, n) \qquad . \; (3)$

But $\qquad\qquad x_i = F_i(x^0; t) \qquad (i = 1, \ldots, n)$

so $\qquad\qquad \dfrac{dx_i}{dt} = \dfrac{\partial}{\partial t}F_i(x^0; t)$

$$= F_i'(x^0; t)$$

so by (3), $\qquad \dfrac{dx_i}{dt} = F_i'(x; 0) \qquad (i = 1, \ldots, n)$

which proves the theorem, since $F_i'(x; 0)$ contains t only in $x_1, \ldots, x_n$ and not in any other form, either explicit or implicit.

Example 1· The state-determined system of S. 19/8, treated in this way, yields the differential equations, in canonical form.

$$\left.\begin{array}{l} \dfrac{dx_1}{dt} = x_2 \\[2ex] \dfrac{dx_2}{dt} = 2 \end{array}\right\}$$

The second system may not be treated in this way as it is not state-determined and the group property does not hold.

Corollary·

$$f_i(x_1, \ldots, x_n) \equiv \left[\frac{\partial}{\partial t} F_i(x_1, \ldots, x_n; t)\right]_{t=0} \qquad (i = 1, \ldots, n)$$

(2) Given the differential equations, they may be written

$$dx_i = f_i(x_1, \ldots, x_n).dt \qquad (i = 1, \ldots, n)$$

and this shows that a given set of values of $x_1, \ldots, x_n$, i.e. a given state of the system, specifies completely what change, dx_i, will occur in each variable, x_i, during the next time-interval, dt. By integration this defines the line of behaviour from that state. The system is therefore state-determined.

Example 2· By integrating

$$\left.\begin{array}{l} \dfrac{dx_1}{dt} = x_2 \\[2ex] \dfrac{dx_2}{dt} = 2 \end{array}\right\}$$

the group equations of the example of S. 19/8 are regained.

19/10. *Definition.* The system is **linear** when the functions $f_1, \ldots, f_n$ are all linear functions of the arguments $x_1, \ldots, x_n$.

19/11. *Example 3·* The equations of the Homeostat may be obtained thus.—If x_i is the angle of deviation of the i-th magnet from its central position, the forces acting on x_i are the momentum, proportional to $\dot{x}_i$, the friction, also proportional to $\dot{x}_i$, and the four currents in the coil, proportional to x_1, x_2, x_3 and x_4. If linearity is assumed, and if **all four** units are constructionally identical, we have

$$\frac{d}{dt}(m\dot{x}_i) = -kx_i + l(p - q)(a_{i1}x_1 + \ldots + a_{i4}x_4)$$

$$(i = 1, 2, 3, 4)$$

where p and q are the potentials at the ends of the trough, l depends on the valve, k depends on the friction at the vane, and m depends on the moment of inertia of the magnet. If $h = l(p - q)/m$ and $j = k/m$, the equations may be written

$$\left.\begin{aligned}dx_i/dt &= x_i \\ d\dot{x}_i/dt &= h(a_{i1}x_1 + \ldots + a_{i4}x_4) - jx_i\end{aligned}\right\} \quad (i = 1, 2, 3, 4)$$

which shows the 8-variable system to be state-determined and linear

They may also be written

$$\left.\begin{aligned}\frac{dx_i}{dt} &= \dot{x}_i \\ \frac{d\dot{x}_i}{dt} &= \frac{k}{m}\left\{\frac{l(p-q)}{k}(a_{i1}x_1 + \ldots + a_{i4}x_4) - x_i\right\}\end{aligned}\right\} \quad (i = 1, 2, 3, 4)$$

Let $m \to 0$ $d\dot{x}_i/dt$ becomes very large, but not dx_i/dt. So $\dot{x}_i$ tends rapidly towards

$$\frac{l(p-q)}{k}(a_{i1}x_1 + \ldots + a_{i4}x_4)$$

while the x's, changing slowly, cannot alter rapidly the value towards which $\dot{x}_i$ is tending. In the limit,

$$\frac{dx_i}{dt} = \dot{x}_i = \frac{l(p-q)}{k}(a_{i1}x_1 + \ldots + a_{i4}x_4) \quad (i = 1, 2, 3, 4)$$

Change the time-scale by $\tau = \dfrac{l(p-q)}{k}t$, and

$$dx_i/d\tau = a_{i1}x_1 + \ldots + a_{i4}x_4 \quad (i = 1, 2, 3, 4)$$

showing the system x_1, x_2, x_3, x_4 to be state-determined and linear The a's are now the values set by the input controls of Figure 8/2/3.

19/12. The theorems of the preceding sections show that the following properties are equivalent, in that the possession of any one implies the possession of the remainder.

(1) The system is state-determined.
(2) From any point of the field departs only one line of behaviour.
(3) The lines of behaviour are specifiable by equations of form:

$$dx_i/dt = f_i(x_1, \ldots, x_n) \quad (i = 1, \ldots, n)$$

in which the right-hand side contains no functions of t except those whose fluxions are given on the left.

19/13. A simple example of a system which is regular but not state-determined is given by the following apparatus. A table top is altered so that instead of being flat, it undulates irregularly but gently like a putting-green (Figure 19/13/1). Looking down

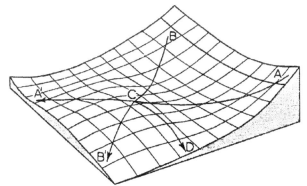

FIGURE 19/13/1.

on it from above, we can mark across it a grid of lines to act as co-ordinates. If we place a ball at any point and then release it, the ball will roll, and by marking its position at, say, every one-tenth second we can determine the lines of behaviour of the two-variable system provided by the two co-ordinates.

If the table is well made, the lines of behaviour will be accurately reproducible and the system will be regular. Yet the experimenter, if he knew nothing of forces, gravity, or momenta, would find this two-variable system unsatisfactory. He would establish that the ball, started at A, always went to A'; and started at B it always went to B'. He would find its behaviour at C difficult to explain. And if he tried to clarify the situation by starting the ball at C itself, he would find it went to D! He would say that he could make nothing of the system; for although each line of behaviour is accurately reproducible, the different lines of behaviour have no simple relation to one another. He will, therefore reject this two-variable system and will not rest till he has discovered, either for himself or by following Newton, a system that *is* state-determined. In my theory I insist on the systems being state-determined because I agree with the experimenter who, in his practical work, is similarly insistent.

Transformations of the canonical representation

19/14. Sometimes systems that are known to be isolated and complete are treated by some method not identical with that used here   In those cases some manipulation may be necessary to convert the other form into ours.   Some of the possible manipulations will be shown in the next few sections.

19/15. Systems can sometimes be described better after a change of co-ordinates. This means changing from the original variables $x_1, \ldots, x_n$ to a new set $y_1, \ldots, y_n$, equal in number to the old and related by *single-valued* functions ϕ_i:

$$y_i = \phi_i(x_1, \ldots, x_n) \qquad (i = 1, \ldots, n)$$

If we think of the variables as being represented by dials, the change means changing to a new set of dials each of which indicates some function of the old.   If the functions ϕ_i are unchanging in time (as functions of their arguments), the new system will remain state-determined.

19/16. In the ' Homeostat ' example of S. 19/11 a fluxion was treated as an independent variable. I have found this treatment to be generally advantageous: it leads to no difficulty or inconsistency, and gives a beautiful uniformity of method.

For example, if we have the equations of a state-determined system we can write them as

$$x_i - f_i(x_1 \quad \ldots, x_n) = 0 \qquad (i = 1, \ldots, n)$$

treating them as n equations in $2n$ algebraically independent variables $x_1, \ldots, x_n, \dot{x}_1, \ldots, \dot{x}_n$ Now differentiate all the equations q times, getting $(q + 1)n$ equations with $(q + 2)n$ variables and derivatives. We can then select n of these variables arbitrarily, and noticing that we also want the next higher derivatives of these n, we can eliminate the other qn variables, using up qn equations. If the variables selected were $z_1, \ldots, z_n$ we now have n equations, in $2n$ variables, of type

$$\Phi_i(z_1, \ldots, z_n, \dot{z}_1, \ldots, \dot{z}_n) = 0 \qquad (i = 1, \ldots, n)$$

where the z's are the selected x's, and z's the corresponding $\dot{x}$'s. These have only to be solved for $z_1, \ldots, z_n$ in terms of $z_1, \ldots, z_n$ and the equations are in canonical form. So the new system is also state-determined (by S. 19/9).

This transformation implies that *in a state-determined system we can avoid direct reference to some of the variables provided we use derivatives of the remaining variables to replace them.*

Example:
$$\left.\begin{array}{l} \dot{x}_1 = x_1 - x_2 \\ \dot{x}_2 = 3x_1 + x_2 \end{array}\right\}$$

can be changed to omit direct reference to x_2 by using x_1 as a new independent variable. It is easily converted to

$$\left.\begin{array}{l} dx_1/dt = \qquad\quad \dot{x}_1 \\ dx_1/dt = -4x_1 + 2\dot{x}_1 \end{array}\right\}$$

which is in canonical form in the variables x_1 and x_1.

19/17. Systems which are isolated but in which effects are transmitted from one variable to another with some finite delay may be rendered state-determined by adding derivatives as variables. Thus, if the effect of x_1 takes 2 units of time to reach x_2, while x_2's effect takes 1 unit of time to reach x_1, and if we write $x(t)$ to show the functional dependence,

then
$$\left.\begin{array}{l} dx_1(t)/dt = f_1\{x_1(t),\ x_2(t-2)\} \\ dx_2(t)/dt = f_2\{x_1(t-1),\ x_2(t)\} \end{array}\right\}$$

This is not in canonical form; but by expanding $x_1(t-1)$ and $x_2(t-2)$ in Taylor's series and then adding to the system as many derivatives as are necessary to give the accuracy required, we can obtain a state-determined system which resembles it as closely as we please.

19/18. If a variable depends on some cumulative effect so that, say, $\dot{x}_1 = f\left\{\int_a^t \phi(x_2)dt\right\}$, then if we put $\int_a^t \phi(x_2)dt = y$, we get the equivalent form

$$\begin{array}{l} dx_1/dt = f(y) \\ dy/dt = \phi(x_2) \\ dx_2/dt = \ldots \text{ etc.} \end{array}$$

which is in canonical form.

19/19. If a variable depends on velocity effects so that, for instance

$$\frac{dx_1}{dt} = f_1\!\left(\frac{dx_2}{dt}, \; x_1, \; x_2\right)$$

$$\frac{dx_2}{dt} = f_2(x_1, \; x_2)$$

then if we substitute for $\dfrac{dx_2}{dt}$ in $f_1(. \ . \ .)$ we get the canonical form

$$\left.\begin{aligned}
dx_1/dt &= f_1\{f_2(x_1,x_2), \; x_1, \; x_2\} \\
dx_2/dt &= f_2(x_1, \; x_2)
\end{aligned}\right\}$$

19/20. If one variable changes either instantaneously or fast enough to be so considered without serious error, then its value can be given as a function of those of the other variables, and it can therefore be eliminated from the system.

19/21. Explicit solutions of the canonical equations

$$dx_i/dt = f_i(x_1, \; . \; . \; . \; , \; x_n) \qquad (i = 1, \; . \; . \; . \; . \; n)$$

will seldom be needed in our discussion, but some methods will be given as they will be required for the examples.

(**1**) A simple symbolic solution, giving the first few terms of x_i as a power series in t, is given by

$$x_i = e^{tX} x_i^0 \qquad (i = 1, \; . \; . \; . \; , \; n) \qquad\qquad . \qquad (1)$$

where X is the operator

$$f_1(x_1^0, \; . \; . \; . \; , \; x_n^0)\frac{\partial}{\partial x_1^0} + \; . \quad . + f_n(x_1^0, \; . \; . \; . \; , \; x_n^0)\frac{\partial}{\partial x_n^0} \; . \quad (2)$$

and

$$e^{tX} = 1 + tX + \frac{t^2}{2!} X^2 + \frac{t^3}{3!} X^3 + \; . \; . \; . \qquad\qquad . \qquad (3)$$

It has the important property that any function $\Phi(x_1, \; . \; . \; . \; , \; x_n)$ can be shown as a function of t, if the x's start from $x_1^0, \; . \; . \; . \; , \; x_n^0$,

by

$$\Phi(x_1, \; . \; . \; . \; , x_n) = e^{tX}\Phi(x_1^0, \; . \; . \; . \; , \; x_n^0) \quad . \qquad . \qquad (4)$$

(**2**) If the functions f_i are linear so that

$$\left.\begin{aligned}
dx_1/dt &= a_{11}x_1 + a_{12}x_2 + \; . \; . \quad + a_{1n}x_n + b_1 \\
&\quad . \; . \; . \; . \; . \; . \; . \\
dx_n/dt &= a_{n1}x_1 + a_{n2}x_2 + \; . \; . \; . + a_{nn}x_n + b_n
\end{aligned}\right\} \quad . \quad (5)$$

then if the b's are zero (as can be arranged by a change of origin) the equations may be written in matrix form as

$$\dot{x} = Ax \qquad . \qquad . \qquad . \qquad (6)$$

where $\dot{x}$ and x are column vectors and A is the square matrix $[a_{ij}]$. In matrix notation the solution may be written

$$x = e^{tA}x^0 \qquad . \qquad . \qquad (7)$$

(3) Most convenient for actual solution of the linear form is the recently developed method of the Laplace transform. The standard text-books should be consulted for details.

19/22. Any comparison of a state-determined system with the other types of system treated in physics and thermodynamics must be made with caution. Thus, it should be noticed that the concept of the state-determined system makes no reference to energy or its conservation, treating it as irrelevant. It will also be noticed that the state-determined system, whatever the ' machine ' providing it, is essentially irreversible. This can be established either by examining the behaviour representation of S 19/7, the canonical representation of S. 19/9, or, in a particular case, by examining the field of the common pendulum in Figure 2/15/1.

CHAPTER 20

Stability

20/1. As will be seen in S. 21/14, the canonical representation contains *all* the information that the real 'machine' can give relative to the selected system. By selecting a particular system the experimenter has already acknowledged that he can obtain only a finite amount of information from the infinite amount that exists in the real 'machine'; yet even this reduction is often insufficient, for the canonical representation of the behavioural properties of $x_1, \ldots, x_n$ may still convey an unmanageably large amount of information. Take the case, for instance, of the cluster of 20,000 stars, about which the astronomer asks· will the cluster condense to a ball, or will it disperse? The canonical representation *can* be set up (it has 120,000 variables), and it contains the answer; but the labour of extracting it is so prohibitively great that astronomers, and others in like position, have looked for methods that do not use all the information available in the canonical representation. Hence the introduction into science of statistical and topological methods, and the use of concepts such as independence (S. 12/4) which may, *if the case is suitable*, enable us to get a simple answer to a simple question without the necessity for our going into every detail.

Prominent among such concepts is that of stability. Its basic elements have been given in *I. to C.*, Chapter 5. Here we shall treat it only in the form suitable for continuous systems, and only with such rigour as is necessary for our main purpose.

20/2. Given a state-determined system in unvarying conditions, so that it has one field, and given a region in the field and a point in the region, a line of behaviour from the point is **stable**, with respect to that field and region and point, if it never leaves the region

20/3. If all the lines within a given region are stable from all points within the region, and if all the lines meet at one point, the system has **normal** stability.

20/4. A state of equilibrium can be defined in several ways. In the field it is a terminating point of a line of behaviour. In the equations of S. 19/7 the state of equilibrium $X_1, \ldots, X_n$ is given by the equations

$$X_i = \underset{t \to \infty}{\mathrm{Lim}}\, F_i(x^0;\ t) \qquad (i = 1, \ldots, n) \qquad . \quad (1)$$

if the n limits exist. In the canonical equations the values satisfy

$$f_i(X_1, \ldots, X_n) = 0 \qquad (i = 1, \ldots, n) \qquad . \quad (2)$$

A state of equilibrium is an invariant of the group, for a change of t does not alter its value.

If the Jacobian of the f's, i.e. the determinant $\left|\dfrac{\partial f_i}{\partial x_j}\right|$, which will be symbolised by J, is not identically zero, then there will be isolated states of equilibrium. If $J \equiv 0$, but not all its first minors are zero, then the equations define a curve, every point of which is a state of equilibrium. If $J \equiv 0$ and all first minors but not all second minors are zero, then a two-way surface exists composed of states of equilibrium; and so on.

20/5. Theorem: *If the f's are continuous and differentiable, a state-determined system tends to the linear form (S. 19/10) in the neighbourhood of a state of equilibrium.*

Let the system, specified by

$$dx_i/dt = f_i(x_1, \ldots, x_n) \qquad (i = 1, \ldots, n)$$

have a state of equilibrium $X_1, \ldots, X_n$, so that

$$f_i(X_1, \ldots, X_n) = 0 \qquad (i = 1, \ldots, n).$$

Put $x_i = X_i + \xi_i$ $(i = 1, \ldots, n)$ so that x_i is measured as a deviation ξ_i from its equilibrial value. Then

$$\frac{d}{dt}(X_i + \xi_i) = f_i(X_1 + \xi_1, \ldots, X_n + \xi_n) \qquad (i = 1, \ldots, n)$$

Expanding the right-hand side by Taylor's theorem, noting that $dX_i/dt = 0$ and that $f_i(X) = 0$, we find, if the ξ's are infinitesimal, that

$$\frac{d\xi_i}{dt} = \frac{\partial f_i}{\partial \xi_1}\xi_1 + \ldots + \frac{\partial f_i}{\partial \xi_n}\xi_n \qquad (i = 1, \ldots, n).$$

The partial derivatives, taken at the point $X_1, \ldots, X_n$, are numerical constants. So the system is linear.

20/6. In general the only test for stability is to observe or compute the given line of behaviour and to see what happens as $t \to \infty$. For the linear system, however, there are tests that do not involve the line of behaviour explicitly. Since, by the previous section, many systems approximate to the linear within the region in which we are interested, the methods to be described are often applicable.

Let the linear system be

$$dx_i/dt = a_{i1}x_1 + a_{i2}x_2 + \ldots + a_{in}x_n \qquad (i = 1, \ldots, n) \quad (1)$$

or, in the concise matrix notation (S. 19/21)

$$\dot{x} = Ax \qquad . \qquad . \qquad . \qquad . \qquad (2)$$

Constant terms on the right-hand side make no difference to the stability and can be ignored. If the determinant of A is not zero, there is a single state of equilibrium. The determinant

$$\begin{vmatrix} a_{11} - \lambda & a_{12} & \ldots & a_{1n} \\ a_{21} & a_{22} - \lambda & \ldots & a_{2n} \\ \ldots & \ldots \ldots & \ldots \ldots & \ldots \\ a_{n1} & a_{n2} & \ldots & a_{nn} - \lambda \end{vmatrix}$$

when expanded, gives a polynomial in λ of degree n which, when equated to 0, and, if necessary, multiplied by -1, gives the **characteristic equation** of the matrix A:

$$\lambda^n + m_1\lambda^{n-1} + m_2\lambda^{n-2} + \ldots + m_n = 0.$$

Each coefficient m_i is the sum of all i-rowed principal (co-axial) minors of A, multiplied by $(-1)^i$. Thus,

$$m_1 = -(a_{11} + a_{22} + \ldots + a_{nn}); \; m_n = (-1)^n |A|.$$

Example: The linear system

$$\begin{aligned} dx_1/dt &= -5x_1 + 4x_2 - 6x_3 \\ dx_2/dt &= 7x_1 - 6x_2 + 8x_3 \\ dx_3/dt &= -2x_1 + 4x_2 - 4x_3 \end{aligned} \Bigg\}$$

has the characteristic equation

$$\lambda^3 + 15\lambda^2 + 2\lambda + 8 = 0.$$

Of this equation, the roots $\lambda_1, \ldots, \lambda_n$ are the **latent roots** of A. The integral of the canonical representation gives each x_i as a linear function of the exponentials $e^{\lambda_1 t}, \ldots, e^{\lambda_n t}$. For the sum to be convergent, every real part of $\lambda_1, \ldots, \lambda_n$ must be negative, and this criterion provides a test for the stability of the system.

Example· The equation $\lambda^3 + 15\lambda^2 + 2\lambda + 8 = 0$ has roots $- 14\cdot902$ and $- 0\cdot049 \pm 0\cdot729 \sqrt{-1}$, so the system is stable.

20/7. A test which avoids finding the latent roots is Hurwitz'. a necessary and sufficient condition that the linear system is stable is that the series of determinants

$$m_1, \quad \begin{vmatrix} m_1 & 1 \\ m_3 & m_2 \end{vmatrix}, \quad \begin{vmatrix} m_1 & 1 & 0 \\ m_3 & m_2 & m_1 \\ m_5 & m_4 & m_3 \end{vmatrix}, \quad \begin{vmatrix} m_1 & 1 & 0 & 0 \\ m_3 & m_2 & m_1 & 1 \\ m_5 & m_4 & m_3 & m_2 \\ m_7 & m_6 & m_5 & m_4 \end{vmatrix}, \text{ etc.}$$

(where, if $q > n$, $m_q = 0$), are all positive.

Example: The system with characteristic equation

$$\lambda^3 + 15\lambda^2 + 2\lambda + 8 = 0$$

yields the series

$$+ 15, \quad \begin{vmatrix} 15 & 1 \\ 8 & 2 \end{vmatrix}, \quad \begin{vmatrix} 15 & 1 & 0 \\ 8 & 2 & 15 \\ 0 & 0 & 8 \end{vmatrix}.$$

These have the values $+ 15$, $+ 22$, and $+ 176$. So the system is stable, agreeing with the previous test.

20/8. Another test, related to Nyquist's, states that a linear system is stable if, and only if, the polynomial

$$\lambda^n + m_1\lambda^{n-1} + m_2\lambda^{n-2} + \ldots + m_n$$

changes in amplitude by $n\pi$ when λ, a complex variable ($\lambda = a + bi$ where $i = \sqrt{-1}$), goes from $-i\infty$ to $+i\infty$ along the b-axis in the complex λ-plane.

Nyquist's criterion of stability is widely used in the theory of electric circuits and of servo-mechanisms. It, however, uses data obtained from the response of the system to persistent harmonic disturbance. Such disturbance is of little use in the theory of adapting systems. and will not be discussed here.

20/9. Some examples will illustrate various facts relating to stability in linear systems.

Example 1: The diagonal terms a_{ii} represent the intrinsic stabilities of the variables; for if all variables other than x_i are held constant, the linear system's i-th equation becomes

$$dx_i/dt = a_{ii}x_i + c,$$

256

where c is a constant, showing that under these conditions x_i will converge to $-c/a_{ii}$ if a_{ii} be negative, and will diverge without limit if a_{ii} be positive.

If the diagonal terms a_{ii} are much larger in absolute magnitude than the others, the latent roots tend to the values of a_{ii}. It follows that if the diagonal terms take extreme values they determine the stability.

Example 2: If the terms a_{ij} in the first $n-1$ rows (or columns) are given, the remaining n terms can be adjusted to make the latent roots take any assigned values.

Example 3: The matrix of the Homeostat equations of S. 19/11 is

$$\begin{bmatrix} \cdot & \cdot & & \cdot & 1 & \cdot & \cdot & \cdot \\ \cdot & \cdot & \cdot & \cdot & \cdot & 1 & \cdot & \cdot \\ \cdot & \cdot & \cdot & \cdot & \cdot & \cdot & 1 & \cdot \\ \cdot & \cdot & \cdot & \cdot & \cdot & \cdot & \cdot & 1 \\ a_{11}h & a_{12}h & a_{13}h & a_{14}h & -j & \cdot & & \cdot \\ a_{21}h & a_{22}h & a_{23}h & a_{24}h & \cdot & -j & \cdot & \cdot \\ a_{31}h & a_{32}h & a_{33}h & a_{34}h & \cdot & \cdot & -j & \cdot \\ a_{41}h & a_{42}h & a_{43}h & a_{44}h & \cdot & \cdot & \cdot & -j \end{bmatrix}$$

If $j = 0$, the system must be unstable, for the eight latent roots are the four latent roots of $[a_{ij}]$, each taken with both positive and negative signs. If the matrix has latent roots $\mu_1, \ldots, \mu_8$, and if $\lambda_1, \ldots, \lambda_4$ are the latent roots of the matrix $[a_{ij}h]$, and if $j \neq 0$, then the λ's and μ's are related by $\lambda_p = \mu_q^2 + j\mu_q$. As $j \to \pm \infty$ the 8-variable and the 4-variable systems are stable or unstable together.

Example 4: In a stable system, fixing a variable may make the system of the remainder unstable. For instance, the system with matrix

$$\begin{bmatrix} 6 & 5 & -10 \\ -4 & -3 & -1 \\ 4 & 2 & -6 \end{bmatrix}$$

is stable. But if the third variable is fixed, the system of the first two variables has matrix

$$\begin{bmatrix} 6 & 5 \\ -4 & -3 \end{bmatrix}$$

and is unstable.

Example 5. Making one variable more stable intrinsically (Example 1 of this section) may make the whole unstable. For instance, the system with matrix

$$\begin{bmatrix} -4 & -3 \\ 3 & 2 \end{bmatrix}$$

is stable. But if a_{11} becomes more negative, the system becomes unstable when a_{11} becomes more negative than $-4\frac{1}{2}$.

Example 6: In the $n \times n$ matrix

$$\left[\begin{array}{c:c} a & b \\ \hdashline c & d \end{array} \right]$$

in partitioned form, let the order of $[a]$ be $k \times k$. If the k diagonal elements a_{ii} become much larger in absolute value than the rest, the latent roots of the matrix tend to the k values a_{ii} and the $n - k$ latent roots of $[d]$. Thus the matrix, corresponding to $[d]$,

$$\begin{bmatrix} 1 & -3 \\ 1 & 2 \end{bmatrix}$$

has latent roots $+1\cdot5 \pm 1\cdot658\iota$, and the matrix

$$\begin{bmatrix} -100 & -1 & 2 & 0 \\ -2 & -100 & -1 & 2 \\ 0 & -3 & 1 & -3 \\ 2 & -1 & 1 & 2 \end{bmatrix}$$

has latent roots $-101\cdot39$, $-98\cdot62$, and $+1\cdot506 \pm 1\cdot720\iota$.

Corollary· If system $[d]$ is unstable but the whole 4-variable system is stable, then making x_1 and x_2 more stable intrinsically will eventually make the whole unstable.

Example 7· The holistic nature of stability is well shown by the system with matrix

$$\begin{bmatrix} -3 & -2 & 2 \\ -6 & -5 & 6 \\ -5 & 2 & -4 \end{bmatrix}$$

in which each variable individually, and every pair, is stable; yet the whole is unstable.

The probability of stability

20/10. The probability that a system should be stable can be made precise only after the system has been defined, ' stability ' defined for it, and then a proper sample space defined. In general, the number of possible meanings of ' probability of stability ' is too large for extensive treatment here. Each case must be considered individually when such consideration is called for.

A case of some interest because of its central position in the theory is the probability that a *linear* system shall be stable, when its matrix is filled by random sampling from given distributions. The problem then becomes:

A matrix of order $n \times n$ *has elements which are real and are random samples from given distributions. Find the probability that all the latent roots have negative real parts.*

This problem seems to be still unsolved even in the special cases in which all the elements have the same distributions, selected to be simple, as the ' normal ' type e^{-x^2}, or the ' rectangular ' type, constant between $-a$ and $+a$. Nevertheless, as I required some indication of how the probability changed with increasing n, the rectangular distribution (integers evenly distributed between -9 and $+9$) was tested empirically. Matrices were formed from Fisher and Yates' Table of Random Numbers, and each matrix was then tested for stability by Hurwitz' rule (S. 20/7). Thus a typical 3×3 matrix was

$$\begin{bmatrix} -1 & -3 & -8 \\ -5 & 4 & -2 \\ -4 & -4 & -9 \end{bmatrix}$$

In this case the second determinant is -86; so it need not be tested further. The testing becomes very time-consuming when the matrices exceed 3×3, for the time taken increases approximately as n^5. The results are summarised in Table 20/10/1.

Order of matrix	Number tested	Number found stable	Per cent stable
2×2	320	77	24
3×3	100	12	12
4×4	100	1	1

TABLE 20/10/1.

The main feature is the rapidity with which the probability tends to zero. The figures given are compatible ($\chi^2 = 4.53$,

$P = 0\cdot 10$) with the hypothesis that the probability for a matrix of order $n \times n$ is $1/2^n$. That this may be the correct expression for this particular case is suggested partly by the fact that it may be proved so when $n = 1$ and $n = 2$, and partly by the fact that, for stability, the matrix has to pass all of n tests. And in fact about a half of the matrices failed at each test. If the signs of the determinants in Hurwitz' test are statistically independent, then $1/2^n$ would be the probability in this case.

In these tests, the intrinsic stabilities of the variables, as judged by the signs of the terms in the main diagonal, were equally likely to be stable or unstable. An interesting variation, therefore, is to consider the case where the variables are all intrinsically stable (all terms in the main diagonal distributed uniformly between 0 and -9).

The effect is to increase their probability of stability. Thus when n is 1 the probability is 1 (instead of $\frac{1}{2}$); and when n is 2 the probability is $\frac{3}{4}$ (instead of $\frac{1}{4}$). Some empirical tests gave the results of Table 20/10/2.

Order of matrix	Number tested	Number found stable	Per cent stable
2×2	120	87	72
3×3	100	55	55

TABLE 20/10/2.

The probability is higher, but it still falls as n is increased.

A similar series of tests was made with the Homeostat. Units were allowed to interact with settings determined by the uniselectors, which were set at one position for one test, the usual ultrastable feedback being severed. The percentage of stable combinations was found when the number of units was two. Then the percentage was found for the same general conditions except that three units interacted; and then four. The general conditions were then changed and a new triple of percentages found. And this was repeated six times altogether. As the general conditions sometimes encouraged, sometimes discouraged, stability, some of the triples were all high, some all low; but in every case the per cent stable fell as the number of interacting

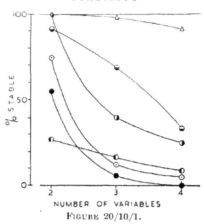

NUMBER OF VARIABLES

FIGURE 20/10/1.

units was increased. The results are given in Figure 20/10/1, in which each triple lies on one line.

These results prove little; but they suggest that the probability of stability is small in large systems assembled at random. It seems, therefore, that large linear systems should be assumed to be unstable unless evidence to the contrary is produced.

CHAPTER 21

Parameters

21/1. In the previous two chapters we have considered the state-determined system when it was isolated, with constant conditions around it, or when no change came to its input. We now turn to consider the state-determined system when it *is* affected by changes in the conditions around it, when it is no longer isolated, or when changes come to its input. We turn, in other words, to consider the 'machine with input' of *I. to C.*, Chapter 4.

Experience has shown that this change corresponds to the introduction of parameters into the canonical representations so that they become of the form

$$dx_i/dt = f_i(x_1, \ldots, x_n; a_1, a_2, \ldots) \qquad (i = 1, \ldots, n)$$

21/2. If the a's are fixed at *particular* values the result is to make the f's a particular set of functions of the x's and thus to specify a particular state-determined system. From this it follows that *each particular set of values at the a's specifies a particular field.* In other words, the two sets: (1) the values at the a's and (2) the fields that the system can show *can be set in correspondence* —perhaps the most fundamental fact in the whole of this book. (Figure 21/8/1 will illustrate it.)

It should be noticed that the correspondence is not one-one but

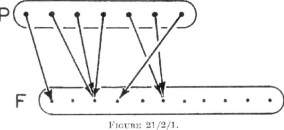

FIGURE 21/2/1.

may be many-one, for while one value of the vector $(a_1, a_2, \ldots)$ will indicate one and only one field, several such vectors may indicate the same field. Thus the relation is a mapping of Bourbaki's type. The possibilities are sufficiently indicated in Fig. 21/2/1; in the upper line P, each dot represents one value of the vector of parameter-values $(a_1, a_2, \ldots)$; in the lower line F, each dot represents one field. Notice that (1) every vector value indicates a field, (2) no vector value indicates more than one field; (3) a field may be indicated by more than one vector value; (4) some fields may be unindicated.

21/3. If the a's can take m combinations of values then m fields are possible. The m fields will often be distinct, but the possibility is not excluded that the m may include repetitions, and thus not be all different.

21/4. If a parameter changes continuously (i.e. by steps that may be as small as we please), then it will often happen that the corresponding changes in the field will be small; but nothing here excludes the possibility that an arbitrarily small change in a parameter may give an arbitrarily *large* change in the field. Thus the fields will often be, but need not necessarily be, a continuous function of the parameters.

21/5. If a parameter affects immediately only certain variables, it will appear only in the corresponding f's. Thus the canonical representation (of a machine with input a)

$$dx_1/dt = f_1(x_1, x_2; a)$$
$$dx_2/dt = f_2(x_1, x_2)$$

corresponds to a diagram of immediate effects

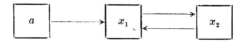

21/6. Change of parameters can represent *every* alteration which can be made on a state-determined system, and therefore on any physical or biological ' machine '. It includes every possibility of experimental interference. Thus if a set of variables that are joined to form the system $x = f(x)$ are changed in their relations so that they form the system $\dot{x} = \phi(x)$, then the change can equally well be represented as a change in the single system $x = \psi(x;\ \alpha)$ For if α can take two values, 1 and 2 say, and if

$$f(x) \equiv \psi(x;\ 1)$$
$$\phi(x) \equiv \psi(x;\ 2)$$

then the two representations are identical.

As example of its method, the action of S. 8/11, where the two front magnets of the Homeostat were joined by a light glass fibre and so forced to move from side to side together, will be shown so that the joining and releasing are equivalent in the canonical equations to a single parameter taking one of two values.

Suppose that units x_1, x_2 and x_3 were used, and that the magnets of 1 and 2 were joined. Before joining, the equations were (S. 19/11)

$$\begin{aligned}
dx_1/dt &= a_{11}x_1 + a_{12}x_2 + a_{13}x_3 \\
dx_2/dt &= a_{21}x_1 + a_{22}x_2 + a_{23}x_3 \\
dx_3/dt &= a_{31}x_1 + a_{32}x_2 + a_{33}x_3
\end{aligned}$$

After joining, x_2 can be ignored as a variable since x_1 and x_2 are effectively only a single variable. But x_2's output still affects the others, and its force still acts on the fibre. The equations therefore become

$$\begin{aligned}
dx_1/dt &= (a_{11} + a_{12} + a_{21} + a_{22})x_1 + (a_{13} + a_{23})x_3 \\
dx_3/dt &= \qquad\qquad (a_{31} + a_{32})x_1 + \qquad\quad a_{33}x_3
\end{aligned}$$

It is easy to verify that if the full equations, including the parameter b, were·

$$\begin{aligned}
dx_1/dt &= \{a_{11} + b(a_{12} + a_{21} + a_{22})\}x_1 + (1 - b)a_{12}x_2 \\
&\qquad\qquad\qquad\qquad\qquad\qquad + (a_{13} + ba_{23})x_3 \\
dx_2/dt &= \qquad\qquad a_{21}x_1 \qquad + a_{22}x_2 + \qquad a_{23}x_3 \\
dx_3/dt &= \qquad\quad (a_{31} + ba_{32})x_1 + (1 - b)a_{32}x_2 + \qquad a_{33}x_3
\end{aligned}$$

then the joining and releasing are identical in their effects with giving b the values 1 and 0 respectively. (These equations are sufficient but not, of course, necessary.)

21/7. A variable x_k behaves as a **null-function** if it has the following properties, which are easily shown to be necessary and sufficient for each other:

(1) As a function of the time, it remains at its initial value x_k^0.

(2) In the canonical equations, $f_k(x_1, \ldots, x_n)$ is identically zero

(3) In the equations of S. 19/7, $F_k(x_1^0, \ldots, x_n^0; t) \equiv x_k^0$.

(Some region of the phase-space is assumed given.)

In a state-determined system, the variables other than the step- and null-functions will be referred to as **main variables**.

Theorem: *In a state-determined system, the subsystem of the main-variables forms a state-determined system provided no step-function changes from its initial value.*

Suppose $x_1, \ldots x_k$ are null- and step-functions and the main-variables are $x_{k+1}, \ldots, x_n$. The canonical equations of the whole system are

$$
\left.
\begin{aligned}
&dx_1/dt = 0 \\
&\quad \cdot \ \cdot \ \cdot \ \cdot \ \cdot \ \cdot \\
&dx_k/dt = 0 \\
&dx_{k+1}/dt = f_{k+1}(x_1, \ \ldots, x_k, x_{k+1}, \ldots, x_n) \\
&\quad \cdot \ \cdot \ \cdot \ \ \cdot \ \cdot \ \cdot \ \cdot \\
&dx_n/dt = f_n(x_1, \quad \cdot \ x_k, x_{k+1}, \ldots, x_n)
\end{aligned}
\right\}
$$

The first k equations can be integrated at once to give $x_1 = x_1^0$, $\ldots, x_k = x_k^0$. Substituting these in the remaining equations we get:

$$
\left.
\begin{aligned}
&dx_{k+1}/dt = f_{k+1}(x_1^0, \ldots, x_k^0, x_{k+1}, \ldots, x_n) \\
&\quad \cdot \ \cdot \ \cdot \ \cdot \ \cdot \ \cdot \ \cdot \ \cdot \\
&dx_n/dt. = f_n(x_1^0, \ldots, x_k^0, x_{k+1}, \ldots, x_n)
\end{aligned}
\right\}
$$

The terms $x_1^0, \ldots, x_k^0$ are now constants, not effectively functions of t at all. The equations are therefore in canonical form; so the system is state-determined over any interval not containing a change in $x_1^0, \ldots, x_k^0$.

Usually the selection of variables to form a state-determined system is determined by the real, natural relationships existing in the real 'machine', and the observer has no power to alter them without making alterations in the 'machine' itself. The theorem, however, shows that without affecting whether it is state-determined the observer may take null-functions into the system or remove them from it as he pleases.

It also follows that the statements ' parameter a was held constant at a^0 '. and ' the system was re-defined to include a, which, as a null-function, remained at its initial value of a^0 ' are merely two ways of describing the same facts.

21/8. The fact that the field is changed by a change of parameter implies that the stabilities of the lines of behaviour may be changed   For instance, consider the system

$$dx_1/dt = -x_1 + ax_2, \qquad dx_2/dt = x_1 - x_2 + 1.$$

When $a = 0$, 1, and 2 respectively, the system has the three fields shown in Figure 21/8/1.

FIGURE 21/8/1 . Three fields of x_1 and x_2 when a has the values (left to right) 0, 1, and 2.

When $a = 0$ there is a stable state of equilibrium at $x_1 = 0$, $x_2 = 1$; when $a = 1$ there is no state of equilibrium; when $a = 2$ there is an unstable state of equilibrium at $x_1 = -2$, $x_2 = -1$ The system has as many fields as there are values to a.

Joining systems

21/9. (Again the basic concepts have been described in *I. to C.*, S 4/7; here we will describe the theory in continuous systems.)

The simple physical act of joining two machines has, of course, a counterpart in the equations, shown more simply in the canonical than in the equations of S 19/7

One could, of course, simply write down equations in all the variables and then simply let some parameter a have one value when the parts are joined and another when they are separated. This method, however, gives no insight into the real events in ' joining ' two systems.   A better method is to make the parameters of one system into defined functions of the variables of the other.   When this is done, the second dominates the first.   If parameters in each are made functions of variables in the other, then a two-way interaction occurs. For instance, suppose we start with the 2-variable system

$$\left.\begin{array}{l} dx/dt = f_1(x,\ y;\ a) \\ dy/dt = f_2(x,\ y) \end{array}\right\}\text{and the 1-variable system } dz/dt = \phi(z;\ b)$$

then the diagram of immediate effects is

If we make a some function of z, $a = z$ say for simplicity, the new system has the equations

$$\left.\begin{array}{l} dx/dt = f_1(x,\ y;\ z) \\ dy/dt = f_2(x,\ y) \\ dz/dt = \phi(z;\ b) \end{array}\right\}$$

and the diagram of immediate effects becomes

If a further join is made by putting $b = y$, the equations become

$$\begin{array}{l} dx/dt = f_1(x,\ y;\ z) \\ dy/dt = f_2(x,\ y) \\ dz/dt = \phi(z;\ y) \end{array}$$

and the diagram of immediate effects becomes

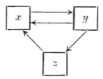

In this method each linkage uses up one parameter. This is reasonable; for the parameter used by the other system might have been used by the experimenter for arbitrary control. So the method simply exchanges the experimenter for another system.

This method of joining does no violence to each system's internal activities: these proceed as before except as modified by the actions coming in through the variables which were once parameters.

21/10. **Theorem:** *The whole made by joining parts is richer in ways of behaving than the system obtained by leaving the parts isolated.*

(The argument is simple and clear if it is supposed that each part has a finite number of states possible, and if the number of input states is also finite. The result for the infinite case, being the limit of the finite case, is the same as that stated, but would need a special technique for its discussion.)

Suppose the system consists of p parts, each capable of being in any one of s states, with p and s assumed finite. Then, whether joined or not, the set of all the parts has s^p states possible. (Put $s^p = k$, for convenience.)

If the whole is richly joined, each of these k states may go, in a transition, to any of the k states; for the transition of each part is not restricted (since it is allowed to be conditional on, and to vary with, the states of the other parts). The number of transformations is thus k^k.

If, however, the parts are not joined, the transformations of each part cannot vary with the states of the others; so the transformation of the whole must be built up by taking a single transformation from each part. Each part, with s states, has s^s transformations; so the whole will have $(s^s)^p$ transformations possible. This equals k^s.

As s is less than k, k^s is less than k^k; whence the theorem.

21/11. If $X_1, \ldots, X_n$ is a state of equilibrium in a system

$$dx_i/dt = f_i(x_1, \ldots, x_n; a_1, \ldots) \qquad (i = 1, \ldots, n)$$

for certain a-values, and the system is then joined to some y's by making the a's functions of the y's, then $X_1, \ldots, X_n$ will still be a state of equilibrium (of the x-system) when the y's make the a's take their original values. Thus the zeros of the f's, and the states of equilibrium of the x-system, are *not* altered by the operation of joining.

21/12. On the other hand, the stabilities may be altered grossly.

In the general case, when the f's are unrestricted, this proposition is not easily given a meaning. But in the linear case (to which all continuous systems approximate, S. 20/5) the meaning is clear. Three examples will be given.

Example 1: Two systems may give a stable whole if joined one way, but an unstable whole if joined another way. Consider the 1-variable systems $dx/dt = x + 2p_1 + p_2$ and $dy/dt = -2r - 3y$

268

If they are joined by putting $r = x$, $p_1 = y$, the system becomes

$$dx/dt = x + 2y + p_2 \atop dy/dt = -2x - 3y$$

The latent roots of its matrix are -1, -1, so it is stable. But if they are joined by $r = x$, $p_2 = y$, the roots become $+0.414$ and -2.414; and it is unstable.

Example 2 · Stable systems may form an unstable whole when joined. Join the three systems

$$dx/dt = -x - 2q - 2r$$
$$dy/dt = -2p - y + r$$
$$dz/dt = p + q - z$$

all of which are stable, by putting $p = x$, $q = y$, $r = z$. The resulting system has latent roots $+1$, -2, -2.

Example 3 : Unstable systems may form a stable whole when joined. Join the 2-variable system

$$dx/dt = 3x - 3y - 3p \atop dy/dt = 3x - 9y - 8p$$

which is unstable, to $dz/dt = 21q + 3r + 3z$, which is also unstable, by $q = x$, $r = y$, $p = z$. The whole is stable.

The state-determined system

21/13. It is now clear that there are, in general, two ways of getting to know a complex dynamic system (i.e. one made of many parts).

One way is to know the parts (ultimately the individual variables) in isolation, and how they are joined. ' Knowing ' each part, or variable, means being able to write down the corresponding lines of the canonical representation (if not in mathematical symbolism then in any other way that gives an unambiguous statement of the same facts). Knowing how they are joined means that certain parameters to the parts can be eliminated (for they are functions of the variables). In this way the canonical representation of the whole is obtained. Integration will then give the lines of behaviour of the whole. Thus we can work from an empirical knowledge of the parts and their joining to a *deduced* knowledge of the whole.

The other way is to observe the whole and its lines of behaviour.

These observations give the functions of S. 19/7. Differentiation of these (as in the Corollary of S. 19/9) will give the canonical representation, and thus those of the parts, to which the other variables now come as parameters. Thus we can also work from an empirical knowledge of the whole to a *deduced* knowledge of the parts and their joining.

21/14. It is now becoming clear why the state-determined system, and its associated canonical representation, is so central in the theory of mechanism. If a set of variables is state-determined, and we elicit its canonical representation by primary operations, then our knowledge of that system is *complete*. It is certainly not a complete knowledge of the real " machine ' that provides the system, for this is probably inexhaustible; but it *is* complete knowledge of the system abstracted—complete in the sense that as our predictions are now single-valued and verified, they have reached (a local) finality. If a tipster names a single horse for each race, and if his horses always win, then though he may be an ignorant man in other respects we would have to admit that his knowledge in this one respect was complete.

The state-determined system must therefore hold a key place in the theory of mechanism, by the strategy of S. 2/17. Because knowledge in this form is complete and maximal, all the other branches of the theory, which treat of what happens in other cases, must be obtainable from this central case as variations on the question. what if my knowledge is incomplete in the following way . . . ?

So we arrive at the systems that actually occur so commonly in the biological world—systems whose variables are not all accessible to direct observation, systems that must be observed in some way that cannot distinguish all states, systems that can be observed only at certain intervals of time, and so on.

21/15. Identical with the state-determined system is the ' noiseless transducer ' defined by Shannon. This he defines as one that, having states α and an input x, will, if in state α_n and given input x_n, change to a new state α_{n+1} that is a function only of x_n and α_n:

$$\alpha_{n+1} = g(x_n, \alpha_n).$$

Though expressed in a superficially different form, this equation is identical with a canonical representation; for it says simply that if the parameters x and the state of the system are given, then the system's next state is determined. Thus the communication engineer, if he were to observe the biologist and the psychologist for the first time, would say that they seem to prefer to work with noiseless systems. His remark would not be as trite as it seems, for from it flow the possibilities of rigorous deduction.

CHAPTER 22

The Effects of Constancy

22/1. A variable behaves as a **step-function** over some given period of observation if it changes value at only a finite number of discrete instants, at which it changes value instantaneously and by a finite jump.

22/2. An example of a step-function in a system will be given to establish the main properties.

Suppose a mass m hangs downwards suspended on a massless strand of elastic. If the elastic is stretched too far it will break and the mass will fall. Let the elastic pull with a force of k dynes for each centimeter increase from its unstretched length, and, for simplicity, assume that it exerts an opposite force when compressed. Let x, the position of the mass, be measured vertically downwards, taking as zero the position of the elastic when there is no mass.

If the mass is started from a position vertically above or below the point of rest, the movement will be given by the equation

$$\frac{d}{dt}\left(m\frac{dx}{dt} \right) = gm - kx \quad . \qquad . \qquad . \quad (1)$$

where g is the acceleration due to gravity. This equation is not in canonical form, but may be made so by writing $x = x_1$, $dx/dt = x_2$, when it becomes

$$\left.\begin{aligned} \frac{dx_1}{dt} &= x_2 \\ \frac{dx_2}{dt} &= g - \frac{k}{m}x_1 \end{aligned}\right\} \quad . \qquad . \qquad . \quad (2)$$

If the elastic breaks, k becomes 0, and the equations become

$$\left.\begin{aligned} \frac{dx_1}{dt} &= x_2 \\ \frac{dx_2}{dt} &= g \end{aligned}\right\} \qquad . \qquad . \qquad . \quad (3)$$

Assume that the elastic breaks if it is pulled longer than X.

The events may be viewed in two ways, which are equivalent.

We may treat the change of k as a change of parameter to the 2-variable system x_1, x_2, changing their equations from (2) above to (3) (S. 21/1). The field of the 2-variable system will change from A to B in Figure 22/2/1, where the dotted line at X

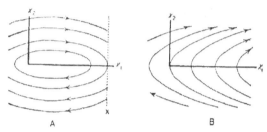

A   B

FIGURE 22/2/1 : Two fields of the system (x_1 and x_2) of S. 22/2. With unbroken elastic the system behaves as A, with broken as B. When the strand is stretched to position X it breaks.

shows that the field to its right may not be used (for at X the elastic will break).

Equivalent to this is the view which treats them as a 3-variable system: x_1, x_2, and k. This system is state-determined, and has one field, shown in Figure 22/2/2.

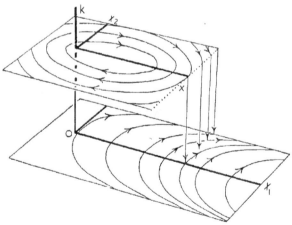

FIGURE 22/2/2 : Field of the 3-variable system.

In this form, the step-function must be brought into the canonical equations. A possible form is:

$$\frac{dk}{dt} = q\left(\frac{K}{2} + \frac{K}{2}\tanh\{q(X - x_1)\} - k\right) \qquad . \qquad (4)$$

where K is the initial value of the variable k, and q is large and positive As $q \to \infty$, the behaviour of k tends to the step-function form.

Another method is to use Dirac's δ-function, defined by $\delta(u) = 0$ if $u \neq 0$, while if $u = 0$, $\delta(u)$ tends to infinity in such a way that

$$\int_{-\infty}^{\infty} \delta(u)du = 1.$$

Then if $du/dt = \delta\{\phi(u, v, \ . \ . \ )\}$, du/dt will be usually zero; but if the changes of $u, v, \dots$ take ϕ through zero, then $\delta(u)$ becomes momentarily infinite and u will change by a finite jump. These representations are of little practical use, but they are important theoretically in showing that a step-function *can* occur in the canonical representation of a system.

22/3. In a state-determined system, a step-function will change value if, and only if, the system arrives at certain states: the **critical.** In Figure 22/2/2, for instance, all the points in the plane $k = K$ (the upper plane) and to the right of the line $x_1 = X$ are critical states for the step-function k when it has the initial value K.

The critical states may, of course, be distributed arbitrarily. More commonly, however, the distribution is continuous. In this case there will be a **critical surface**

$$\phi(k, x_1, \ . \quad ., x_n) = 0$$

which, given k, divides the critical from the non-critical states. In Figure 22/2/2, for instance, the surface intersects the plane $k = K$ at the line $x_1 = X$. (The plane $k = 0$ is not intersected by it, for there are no states in this system whose occurrence will result in k changing from 0)

Commonly ϕ is a function of only a few of the variables of the system. Thus, whether a Post Office type relay opens or shuts depends only on the two variables: the current in the coil, and whether the relay is already open or shut.

Such relays and critical states occur in the Homeostat. When

two, three or four units are in use, the critical surfaces will form
(to a first approximation) a square, cube, or tesseract respectively
in the phase-space around the origin   The critical states will fill
the space outside this surface. As there is some backlash in the
relays, the critical surfaces for opening are not identical with
those for closing.

Systems with multiple fields

22/4. If, in the previous example, someone unknown to us were
occasionally to break and sometimes to replace the elastic, and if
we were to test the behaviour of the system x_1, x_2 over a prolonged
time including many such actions, we would find that the system
was often state-determined with a field like A of Figure 22/2/1,
and often state-determined with a field like B; and that from time
to time the field changed suddenly from the one form to the other

Such a system could be said without ambiguity to have two
fields. Similarly, if parameters capable of taking r combinations
of values were subject to occasional change by some other,
unobserved system, a system might be found to have r fields.

22/5. The argument can be used to some degree in the converse
direction, for the correspondence of S. 21/2 may be used, with
caution, conversely; for though the number of fields does not
prescribe the number of parameter-values it does prescribe their
minimal number with precision. Thus fields that change like the
first row of letters in S. 9/13 demand a minimum of 4 parameter-
values, while those that change like the second row demand a
minimum of 15.

If the observer should find that one field persists, the minimal
number of parameter-values is, of course, one. If the field should
change suddenly to a new field, which persists, he may deduce
that the parameter-value *must* have changed (for no single value
could give two fields), and that the minimal number of values
over the new persistence is again one. Thus he may legitimately
deduce that the *minimal* variety attributable to the parameter-
values is, on the scale of S 7/13, that of the step-function—the
null-function provides too little, and the part-function an unnecessary excess   (Compare S. 9/10–13.)

The ultrastable system

22/6. The definition and description already given in S. 7/26 have established the elementary properties of the ultrastable system. A restatement in mathematical form, however, has the advantage of rendering a misunderstanding less likely, and of providing a base for quantitative studies.

If a system is ultrastable, it is composed of main variables x, and of step-functions a, so that the whole is state-determined·

$$dx_i/dt = f_i(x;\ a) \qquad (i = 1, \ . \ . \ , n)$$
$$da_i/dt = g_i(x;\ a) \qquad (i = 1, 2, \ . \ . \ .)$$

The functions g_i must be given some form like that of S. 22/2. The system is started with the representative point within the critical surface $\phi(x) = 0$, contact with which makes the step-functions change value. When they change, the new values of a_i are to be random samples from some distribution, assumed given.

Thus in the Homeostat, the equations of the main variables are (S. 19/11):

$$dx_i/dt = a_{i1}x_1 + a_{i2}x_2 + a_{i3}x_3 + a_{i4}x_4 \qquad (i = 1, 2, 3, 4)$$

The a's are step-functions, coming from a distribution of 'rectangular' form, lying evenly between -1 and $+1$. The critical surfaces of the a's are specified approximately by $|x| \pm \frac{\pi}{4} = 0$. Each individual step-function a_{jk} depends only on whether x_j crosses the critical surface.

As the a's change discontinuously, an analytic integration of the differential equations is not, so far as I am aware, possible. But the equations, the description, and the schedule of the uniselector-wirings (the random samples) define uniquely the behaviour of the x's and the a's. So the behaviour could be computed to any degree of accuracy by a numerical method.

22/7. How many trials will be necessary, on the average, for a terminal field to be found ? If an ultrastable system has a probability p that a new field of the main variables will be stable, and if the fields' probabilities are independent, then the number of fields occurring (including the terminal) will be, on the average, $1/p$.

For at the first field, a proportion p will be terminal, and $q\ (= 1 - p)$ will not. Of the latter, at the second field, the proportion p will be terminal and q not; so the total proportion stable at the second field will be pq, and the number still unstable q^2. Similarly the proportion becoming terminal at the u-th field will be pq^{u-1}. So the average number of trials made will be

$$\frac{p + 2pq + 3pq^2 + \ldots + upq^{u-1} + \ldots}{p + pq + pq^2 + \ldots + pq^{u-1} + \ldots} = \frac{1}{p}.$$

Temporary independence

22/8. The relation of variable to variable has been treated by observing the behaviour of the whole system   But what of their effects on one another ?   Thus, if a variable changes in value, can we distribute the cause of this change among the other variables ?

In general it is not possible to divide the effect into parts, with so much caused by this variable and so much caused by that. Only when there are special simplicities is such a division possible. **In general, the change of a variable results from the activity of the whole system, and cannot be subdivided quantitatively.** Thus, if $dx/dt = \sin x + xe^y$, and $x = \frac{1}{2}$ and $y = 2$, then in the next 0 01 unit of time x will increase by $0\cdot042$, but this quantity cannot be divided into two parts, one due to x and one to y. Only when some special simplicity exists can the whole effect be represented meaningfully as the *sum* of two effects, one from each. Though not uncommon in theoretical physics, such simplicities are rare in biological systems.

22/9. Given a state-determined system, its field, a line of behaviour in it, and a particular portion P of the line; given also that x_p is a part-function, then the following are equivalent, in that the truth (or falsity) of any one implies the truth (or falsity) of all the others:

(1) x_p is constant (inactive);

(2) $dx_p/dt \equiv 0$;

(3) $f_p(\ldots, x_p, \ldots) \equiv 0$;

(4) $x_p = x_p^0$ independently of t;

(5) $F_p(x^0; t) \equiv x_p^0$, with such values of t as do not take the line out of P;

277

all being understood to refer only to the region P. (The equivalences follow readily from the properties of the equations of S. 19/9 and their integrals.)

22/10. Given a state-determined system and two transitions from two initial states which differ only in their values of x_j^0 (the difference being Δx_j^0), the variable x_k is **independent** of x_j if x_k's transition is identical in the two cases. Analytically, x_k is independent of x_j in the conditions given if

$$F_k(x_1^0, \ldots, x_j^0, \ldots; dt) = F_k(x_1^0, \ldots, x_j^0 + \Delta x_j^0, \ldots; dt) \quad (1)$$

In other words, x_k is independent of x_j if x_k's behaviour is invariant when the initial state is changed by Δx_j^0. (This ' change ' by Δx_j^0 must not be confused with the change dt.)

This narrow definition provides the basis for further development. In practical application, the identity (1) may hold over all values of Δx_j^0 (within some finite range, perhaps); and may also hold for all initial states of x_k (within some finite range, perhaps). In such cases the test whether x_k is independent of x_j is whether

$$\frac{\partial}{\partial x_j^0} F_k(x^0, \ t) \equiv 0.$$

The range over which the relation or equation holds must always be specified (either explicitly or by implication).

Diagrams of effects

22/11. The diagram of immediate effects and the canonical representation have a simple relation   Starting with the pragmatic and empirical point of view of S. 2/7, we assume that the observer gets his basic knowledge of the system by primary operations. These operations will give him the functions F, of S. 19/7 and also (by S. 4/12) the diagram of immediate effects. Now the test for whether to draw an arrow from x_j to x_k is essentially the same as the test applied algebraically to see whether x_j^0 occurs effectively in F_k, and the outcomes must correspond. But (by the Corollary, S. 19/9) whether F_k does or does not contain x^0 effectively over a single step dt must correspond with whether f_k does or does not contain x_j effectively. Thus, in the diagram of *immediate* effects an arrow will run from x_j to x_k if and only if, in the canonical representation, x_j occurs effectively in f_k. (The range of f's arguments is assumed to be specified.)

22/12. The diagram of *ultimate* effects can also be shown to have the property that an arrow goes from x_i to x_k if and only if, in the equations of S. 19/7, x_j^0 occurs effectively in F_k (over some specified range).

(These matters were discussed more fully in the First Edition, but need not be repeated at length.)

22/13. It is worth noticing that, given n arbitrary points, a diagram of immediate effects can be drawn by the arbitrary placing of any number of arrows. That of the ultimate effects cannot, however, be so drawn; for an arrow from p to q and one from q to r imply an arrow from p to r. Thus, while diagrams of immediate effects are, in general, unrestricted, those of ultimate effects must be transitive.

22/14. The thesis of S 12/10 can now be treated rigorously. Figure 12/10/1 is given to be the diagram of immediate effects, and the whole is assumed to be isolated and state-determined. (For compactness below, the *sub*script A will be used to mean 'any variable in the A-set'; and similarly for B and C) Then the canonical representation of the whole must be of the form

$$\left.\begin{aligned} \dot{x}_A &= f_A(x_A,\ x_B) \\ \dot{x}_B &= f_B(x_A,\ x_B.\ x_C) \\ \dot{x}_C &= f_C(x_B,\ x_C) \end{aligned}\right\} \qquad . \qquad . \qquad . \quad (1)$$

with x_C not in f_A, and x_A not in f_C. The two parts of the theorem can now be proved.

(1) Suppose the B's are null-functions (over some specified range). They are therefore constant. Write their values collectively as β. The topmost line of (1) then becomes

$$\dot{x}_A = f_A(x_A,\ \beta)$$

which shows that the system composed of the variables x_A is state-determined (so long as β is constant) Further, the integrals F_A of these equations cannot contain x_C^0, so the system A is independent of the system C.

A similar proof will show that C is state-determined and

independent of A. Thus a wall of constancies (the B's null-functions) between the systems A and C is sufficient to leave them each state-determined and independent of the other.

(2) Suppose the systems A and C are each found to be state-determined and independent of one another, the whole is given to be state-determined, and there is known to be no immediate connexion from A to C or from C to A, but there *is* effective connexion between A and B, and between C and B—what can be deduced about the variables in B?

The lack of connexion between A and C shows that the canonical representation must have the form of (1) above. With

$$x_A = f_A(x_A,\ x_B)$$

the A's can be state-determined only if all the B's are constant (not effectively functions of the time). So the B's must be null-functions.

References

ASHBY, W Ross. Adaptiveness and equilibrium. *Journal of Mental Science*, **86**, 478 ; 1940.

Idem The physical origin of adaptation by trial and error. *Journal of general Psychology*, **32**, 13 ; 1945.

Idem. Effect of controls on stability. *Nature*, **155**, 242 , 1945.

Idem. Interrelations between stabilities of parts within a whole dynamic system *Journal of comparative and physiological Psychology*, **40**, 1 ; 1947.

Idem The nervous system as physical machine with special reference to the origin of adaptive behaviour *Mind*, **56**, 1 ; 1947

Idem. Design for a brain *Electronic Engineering*, **20**, 379 ; 1948.

Idem. The stability of a randomly assembled nerve-network. *Electroencephalography and clinical Neuro-physiology*, **2**, 471 ; 1950

Idem. Can a mechanical chess-player outplay its designer ? *British Journal for the Philosophy of Science*, **3**, 44 , 1952.

Idem. An introduction to cybernetics London, 3rd imp., 1958.

BOURBAKI, N. *Théorie des ensembles;* facsicule de résultats. A.S.E.I. No. 1141 ; Paris : 1951.

Idem. Algèbre. A S E I No. 1144

Idem. Topologie. A.S E I. No 1142.

BOYD, D. A., and NIE, L. W. Congenital universal indifference to pain. *Archives of Neurology and Psychiatry*, **61**, 402 ; 1949.

CANNON, W. B. *The wisdom of the body.* London, 1932.

CAREY, E J , MASSOPUST, L. C., ZEIT, W., HAUSHALTER, E., and SCHMITZ, J. Experimental pathologic effects of traumatic shock on motor end plates in skeletal muscle. *Journal of Neuropathology and experimental Neurology*, **4**, 134 ; 1945.

COWLES, J. T. Food-tokens as incentives for learning by chimpanzees. *Comparative Psychology Monographs*, **14**, No. 71 , 1937–8.

DANCOFF, S. M., and QUASTLER, H. Information content and error rate of living things. In *Information theory in biology*, edited H. Quastler. Urbana, 1953.

GIRDEN, E., and CULLER, E. Conditioned responses in curarised striate muscle in dogs. *Journal of comparative Psychology*, **23**, 261 ; 1937.

GRANT, W. T. Graphic methods in the neurological examination : wavy tracings to record motor control. *Bulletin of the Los Angeles Neurological Society*, **12**, 104 ; 1947.

GRINDLEY, G. C. The formation of a simple habit in guinea-pigs. *British Journal of Psychology*, **23**, 127 ; 1932–3.

HARRISON, R. G Observations on the living developing nerve fiber. *Proceedings of the Society for experimental Biology and Medicine*, **4**, 140 , 1906–7.

HILGARD, E. R., and MARQUIS, D. G. *Conditioning and learning* New York, 1940.

HOLMES, S. J. A tentative classification of the forms of animal behavior. *Journal of comparative Psychology*, **2**, 173 , 1922.

HUMPHREY, G. *The nature of learning.* London, 1933.

HURWITZ, A. Über die Bedingungen, unter welchen eine Gleichung nur Wurzeln mit negativen reelen Teilen besitzt. *Mathematische Annalen*, **46**, 273 ; 1895

JENNINGS, H. S. *Behavior of the lower organisms.* New York, 1906.

LASHLEY, K S Nervous mechanisms in learning. In *The foundations of experimental psychology*, edited C Murchison Worcester, 1929.

LEVI, G Ricerche sperimentali sovra elementi nervosi sviluppati ' in vitro '. *Archiv fur experimentelle Zellforschung*, 2, 244 ; 1925–6.

LORENTE DE NÓ, R Vestibulo-ocular reflex arc. *Archives of Neurology and Psychiatry*, 30, 245 ; 1933.

McDOUGALL, W *Psychology* New York, 1912.

MARINA, A. Die Relationen des Palae-encephalons (Edinger) sind nicht fix. *Neurologisches Centralblatt*, 34, 338 , 1915.

MORGAN, C. LLOYD *Habit and instinct*. London, 1896

MOWRER, O. H. An experimental analogue of ' regression ' with incidental observations on ' reaction-formation '. *Journal of abnormal and social Psychology*, 35, 56 , 1940.

MULLER, G. E., and PILZECKER, A. Experimentelle Beitrage zur Lehre vom Gedachtnis *Zeitschrift fur Psychologie und Physiologie der Sinnesorgane*. Erganzungsband No. 1 ; 1900

NYQUIST, H. Regeneration theory *Bell System technical Journal*, 11, 126 ; 1932.

PARKER, G. *The evolution of man*. New Haven, 1922.

PAULING, L. In *Cerebral mechanisms in behavior*, edited Lloyd A Jeffress. New York, 1951.

PAVLOV, I. P. *Conditioned reflexes*. Oxford, 1927.

RIGUET, J Sur les rapports entre les concepts de machine de multipole et de structure algébrique *Comptes rendues de l'Académie des Sciences*, 237, 425 ; 1953

ROBINSON, E S. Some factors determining the degree of retroactive inhibition *Psychological Monographs*, 28, No. 128 , 1920.

ROSENBLUETH, A., WIENER, N, and BIGELOW, J. Behavior, purpose and teleology. *Philosophy of Science*, 10, 18 , 1943.

SHANNON, C. E , and WEAVER, W. *The mathematical theory of communication* Urbana, 1949

SHERRINGTON, C. S. *The integrative action of the nervous system*. New Haven, 1906.

SKAGGS, E. B. Further studies in retroactive inhibition. *Psychological Monographs*, 34, No 161 , 1925

SOMMERHOFF, G. *Analytical biology* Oxford, 1950.

SPEIDEL, C. C. Activities of amoeboid growth cones, sheath cells, and myelin segments as revealed by prolonged observation of individual nerve fibers in frog tadpoles *American Journal of Anatomy*, 52, 1 ; 1933.

Idem. Effects of metrazol on tissues of frog tadpoles with special reference to the injury and recovery of individual nerve fibers. *Proceedings of the American Philosophical Society*, 83, 349 , 1940.

SPERRY, R. W. Effect of crossing nerves to antagonistic limb muscles in the monkey *Archives of Neurology and Psychiatry*, 58, 452 , 1947.

TEMPLE, G. *General principles of quantum theory*. London, 2nd ed , 1942.

WIENER, N. *Cybernetics*. New York, 1948.

WOLFE, J. B. Effectiveness of token-rewards for chimpanzees. *Comparative Psychology Monographs*, 12, No. 60 , 1935–6.

YOUNG, J. Z. In *Evolution*, edited G R. de Beer. Oxford, 1938.

Index

The reference is to the page. A number in **bold-faced** type indicates a definition.

283

CPSIA information can be obtained
at www.ICGtesting.com
Printed in the USA
BVHW040918211019
561643BV00011B/139/P